Frontiers in Physical Sciences

Editors

RAKESH KUMAR TIWARI
AMBRISH KUMAR SRIVASTAVA

NOTION PRESS

NOTION PRESS

India. Singapore. Malaysia.

ISBN: 979-8897241972

Dedicated to

(Late) Prof. Laxmi Narayan Tripathi

Contents

Prof. L. N. Tripathi ix

Legacy of Wisdom and Advocacy xi

Preface xiii

1. DFT Studies on Some Bioactive Molecules and Superhalogen Clusters 19

    Introduction.. 19

    Methodology 21

    Results and Discussion 21

    Conclusions and Remarks............................. 39

2. Photonic Spin Hall Effect: Numerical Analysis for Plexcitonic System... 41

    Introduction.. 41

    Photonic Spin Hall Effect: Review.............. 42

    Plexcitonic Structure 44

    Mathematical Analysis 45

    Results and Discussions................................ 46

    Conclusions... 48

3. Barium Strontium Titanate (BST) Glass Ceramics49

    Introduction.. 49

    Synthesis Techniques 54

    Characterizations and Dielectric Properties............ 58

    Challenges and Future Directions 66

    Conclusion 66

4. A Journey of Measurement of Linear Attenuation Coefficient 67

Introduction 67

Linear/Mass attenuation coefficient (μ)/ (μ_m) 68

Literature of Attenuation Coefficient....................... 69

Two Media Method.. 71

Measurement Procedure of μ............................... 74

Conclusions 74

5. Analysis of various parameters for Polyaniline-Metal Oxide Composite Langmuir-Blodgett Thin Films and their Electrical and Optical Properties.. 77

Introduction 77

Materials and Methods.. 78

Characterization Techniques................................. 83

Results and Discussion 84

Applications... 85

Future Scope 87

6. DFT Study for the Substantial Properties of the Small ZnS and ZnSe Nanoclusters 88

Nanoscience and Nanotechnology......................... 88

Nanomaterials and Nanostructures....................... 89

II–VI Semconducting Compounds 90

Theoretical Work.. 91

Theoretical Techniques 91

Zinc Sulfide And Zinc Selenide Nanoclusters............ 93

7. Unveiling Stellar Patterns: Photometric Insights into Galactic open cluster 97

Introduction 97

Observations & Data Reduction............................ 100

Data Analysis & Results 105

Discussion... 112

Summary and Conclusion 115

8. Quantum Chemical Investigation on Vibrational Dynamics and Ground State Electronic Properties of a Non-Linear Optical Material 117

Introduction.. 117

Methodology 120

Results & Discussion 121

Conclusion 134

9. Study of atmospheric molecule of environmental importance: CO_2 136

Introduction.. 136

Atmospheric Trace Gases: Carbon dioxide............. 141

Research Methodology 144

Result and Discussion 147

10. Study of Intermolecular Interaction of Pyridine and HO-(CH2)n-O-C6H4-C6H4-CN (HnCBP) Liquid Crystal Molecules by using AIM Calculations 151

Introduction.. 151

Method of calculation 155

Results and Discussion 157

Conclusion 175

11. Electrical Transport Study of Potassium Metaborate: KBO_2 176

Introduction.. 176

Material Preparation and Experimental technique 177

Result and Discussion 178

Conclusion 189

12. Japanese Encephalitis Virus (JEV): A Review ... 190

Introduction.. 190

Methodology 194

Results and Discussion 196

Conclusion 208

viii

Prof. L. N. Tripathi

I take immense pride in offering my most sincere felicitations to my teacher and research guide, the late Professor L.N. Tripathi. Born in 1940 in the small village of Medha, Jaunpur, Uttar Pradesh, he received his early education in his village. He completed his intermediate studies at Raja Harpal Singh Intermediate College, Singra Mau, Jaunpur. He joined T.D. College, Jaunpur, in 1957, where he earned his B.Sc. He then joined the Department of Physics at Gorakhpur University in 1959 and completed his M.Sc. in 1961, being part of the second batch of the physics department.

Professor Tripathi's academic brilliance was evident as he consistently topped his class, from junior high school (district topper) to high school and intermediate (UP board topper), and as the college topper in B.Sc. He also led his batch in M.Sc. He completed his Ph.D. in 1967 under the supervision of Professor Devendra Sharma, focusing on 'Infrared and Electronic Absorption Spectra of Some Di-Derivatives of Benzene'. Professor Devendra Sharma was the founding head of the department and had worked previously in the laboratories of Dr. G. Herzberg, a Canadian Nobel laureate and Professor K. S. Krishnan (FRS, and co-worker of Raman Effect).

Beginning his career in 1962 as an assistant professor at Gorakhpur University, Professor Tripathi emerged as a pioneering figure in luminescence research. When the new field of solid-state physics was introduced in 1964, he spearheaded research in allied areas, notably luminescence. He established one of the finest labs in India dedicated to electroluminescence, photoluminescence, phosphorescence, and thermoluminescence research. His groundbreaking work laid the foundation for luminescence studies at Gorakhpur, earning him recognition both nationally and internationally.

Under his exemplary guidance, more than ten students completed their Ph.D. degrees and published numerous research papers in prestigious journals. Professor Tripathi also authored two graduate-level books, 'An Introduction to Modern Physics' and 'Snatak Prayogik Bhautiki', as well as an intermediate-level book, 'Prayogatmak Bhautiki'.

Undoubtedly, he was an exceptional teacher and mentor. Professor Tripathi had a profound love for teaching, which kept him devoted to this noble profession until his passing. Beyond being a distinguished physicist, he was a person of great human qualities—humble and always willing to help others with kindness. His teaching techniques were outstanding, and he was the go-to person for all our physics queries.

Throughout his career, he progressed through all academic ranks, from assistant professor to professor. In 1998, the UP government appointed him as a member of the Uttar Pradesh Higher Education Commission (UPHEC), and he became its chairman in 2001. He also served as an advisor to many societies, including IAPT, LSI, SREIT, and SAST. He retired as a professor in 2003.

This remarkable physicist, who laid the groundwork for luminescence research in Gorakhpur, departed from us on Diwali in 2021, leaving a legacy of academic excellence and human warmth.

Sanjay Kumar Mishra

02-02-2025

Legacy of Wisdom and Advocacy

As a daughter, it is a great honor to write a few words for the book "Frontiers in Physical Sciences," edited by Dr. Rakesh Kumar Tiwari and Dr. Ambrish Kumar Srivastava of Deen Dayal Upadhyaya Gorakhpur University. This book is dedicated to my father, the late Prof. Laxmi Narayan Tripathi, an eminent scholar in the field of Physical Sciences.

Born on April 2, 1940, in Merha, a small village in Jaunpur, Uttar Pradesh, my father faced challenges early in life, losing his father at a young age. As the eldest among three sisters and three brothers, he took on the responsibility of caring for his family while pursuing his education. He completed his schooling in the village, intermediate studies at Raja Harpal Singh Intermediate College in Singramau, and received his B.Sc. from TD College, Jaunpur, in 1959. He earned his M.Sc. from Gorakhpur University in 1961. A brilliant scholar, he completed his Ph.D. in 1967 under Professor Devendra Sharma, focusing on the "Infrared and Electronic Absorption Spectra of Some Di-Derivatives of Benzene."

He began his career as an assistant professor in the Physics Department at Gorakhpur University in 1962 and rose to the rank of professor. In 1999, he was appointed as a member of the Uttar Pradesh Higher Education Service Commission and later served as its Chairman.

Admired by his students as "LNT sir," he was known for his ability to simplify complex topics and for his dedication to teaching. He published numerous research papers in national and international journals in spectroscopy and luminescence, and he established a state-of-the-art laboratory for students. He guided many research scholars who have since achieved prominence in academia and politics. His books include "An Introduction to Modern Physics," "Snatak Prayogik Bhautiki," and "Prayogatmak Bhautiki."

Beyond academia, my father was a gentle and kind-hearted individual. He married my mother, Smt. Amrita Tripathi, at a young age, and after securing his position at the university, he brought his siblings to Gorakhpur for further education. My uncle, Dr. Jaiprakash Tripathi, and aunt, Professor Kalawati Shukla, both excelled in their studies and had successful careers.

My siblings and I were fortunate to have him as our father. My elder brother, Dr. Lokesh Tripathi, is a professor in the B.Ed. department at BRD Degree College, Deoria. My elder sister, Dr. Rachna Tripathi, is a professor in sociology at VMLG Degree College, Ghaziabad. My younger sister, Mrs. Kalpana Tripathi, is an entrepreneur in Gorakhpur. As for me, I am serving as an IAS officer in the state government of Uttar Pradesh.

A social reformer, my father passionately advocated for women's education and self-reliance. He upheld these values in his life, ensuring my aunt received higher education despite societal pressures to marry her off at a young age.

Vandana Tripathi, IAS

02-02-2025

Preface

It is my great pleasure to introduce this collection of articles, which stems from the "6th Refresher Course on the Frontiers of Physics", held from December 11 to December 24, 2024, at the Department of Physics, Deen Dayal Upadhyaya Gorakhpur University, Gorakhpur with collaboration with UGC-Malviya Mission Teachers Training Centre, Gorakhpur. Deen Dayal Upadhyaya Gorakhpur University is one of the leading teaching and research institutions in India, accredited as A++ by NAAC. This online course brought together an exceptional group of participants, including renowned scientists from across India, creating a collaborative platform for advancing the frontiers of physics.

This book is presented in loving memory of our teacher Professor L. N. Tripathi, whose profound contributions to the field of physics and his tireless dedication to fostering scientific excellence continue to inspire us all. Prof. Tripathi's legacy as a mentor, educator, and researcher is woven into the very fabric of this work. His passion for physics and commitment to the development of young scientists were the guiding forces behind this course, and it is only fitting that this book serves as a tribute to his enduring impact on the academic community.

The journey of compiling a book within a given short time frame was no small feat, but with the support of specialists in various fields, we have been able to bring this work to fruition. The chapters presented here reflect cutting-edge research and discoveries in key areas such as solid-state physics, nanotechnology, astrophysics, soft materials, nonlinear materials, and quantum mechanics. Additionally, topics like the treatment of single photons through entanglement and the latest developments in advanced quantum mechanics are explored in detail, offering fresh perspectives on some of the most pressing questions in the field.

The rapid development of new technologies, coupled with powerful experimental tools and the growing influence of artificial intelligence, has drastically transformed the landscape of scientific research. Today, the traditional boundaries between disciplines—chemistry, biology, and mathematics—are increasingly converging. This interdisciplinary approach is providing new insights into the deep concepts of nature and is helping to shape the extension and future of physical sciences.

Moreover, the application of quantum mechanics is shedding new light on complex biological phenomena. For example, reaction mechanisms and the role of catalysts are now being understood through the eyes of quantum theory. The creation of advanced software has enabled researchers to tackle intricate biological problems, such as those related to the central dogma of molecular biology. These developments signal a remarkable acceleration in scientific advancements in the boundary of physical sciences.

In parallel, progress in spectroscopy has ushered in a new era of understanding at the atomic and molecular levels. With the advent of electron microscopy, we are now able to explore natural phenomena at the atomic scale, leading to unprecedented clarity in our understanding. Single-photon spectroscopy, in particular, marks a significant advancement in the field of molecular spectroscopy, further enhancing our ability to investigate and understand the behavior of matter on a fundamental level.

This book is a testament to the wide range of innovative research presented during the Refresher Course in the Department of Physics. The chapters cover diverse topics in contemporary physics and interdisciplinary studies, offering a comprehensive exploration of the latest advancements in various subfields.

Chapter 1 delves into the use of Density Functional Theory (DFT) to explore the properties of bioactive molecules and superhalogen clusters, providing valuable insights for future molecular design. Based on the numerical analysis of the photonic spin Hall effect within plexcitonic systems, **Chapter 2** offers new perspectives on light-matter interactions and the potential for advanced photonic devices. **Chapter 3** investigates the synthesis, characterization, and dielectric properties of BST glass ceramics, highlighting their potential for future technological applications in electronics and energy storage. Exploring the linear attenuation coefficient through various methods, **Chapter 4** provides a comprehensive approach to measuring material properties and their implications for radiology and material science. **Chapter 5** examines the fabrication and properties of polyaniline-metal oxide composite thin films, focusing on their electrical and optical characteristics, and the potential for use in advanced sensors and electronics. By utilizing DFT calculations, **Chapter 6** explores the electronic properties of ZnS and ZnSe nanoclusters, contributing to the understanding of their behavior in nanotechnology and optoelectronics. With a focus on photometric analysis, **Chapter 7** provides insights into the structure and evolution of galactic open clusters, advancing our understanding of stellar dynamics and the Milky Way. **Chapter 8** offers a quantum chemical analysis of the vibrational and electronic properties of non-linear optical materials, shedding light on their potential for use in advanced photonic applications. **Chapter 9** highlights the environmental significance of carbon dioxide, providing a comprehensive study of its atmospheric presence and implications for climate science and policy. Focusing on the intermolecular interactions in liquid crystal molecules, **Chapter 10** explores their properties using AIM calculations, with implications for advanced materials in display technology and molecular engineering. **Chapter 11** focuses on the electronic transport properties of potassium metaborate and its transition from normal to superionic solid phase. **Chapter 12** deals with the Japanese Encephalitis Virus (JEV) and its inhibition by certain bioactive molecules.

These chapters summarize and complement the overall theme of the book, each offering a unique contribution to the advancing frontiers of physical sciences. The work is enriched not only by the groundbreaking research presented but also by the lasting influence of Prof. L. N. Tripathi, whose legacy continues to inspire and guide these explorations. We are very much thankful to Prof. Poonam Tandon, Hon'ble Vice-Chancellor and Prof. Shantanu Rastogi, Pro Vice-Chancellor of Gorakhpur University. Our heartfelt thanks go to Prof. Sugriva Nath Tiwari, Former Head of the Physics Department and Dean of Science Faculty at Gorakhpur University and Former President of the physics Chapter of the Indian Science Congress Association as well as Prof. Sunita Murmu, Director of UGC-Malviya Mission Teachers Training Centre, Gorakhpur. Deen Dayal Upadhyaya Gorakhpur University. Their insightful discussions and invaluable support have been instrumental in shaping the present form of this book. It is worthwhile to mention that D.D.U. Gorakhpur University is celebrating its Heerak Jayanti (Diamond Jubilee) this year, 2025.

Rakesh Kumar Tiwari

Ambrish Kumar Srivastava

03-02-2025 (Basant Panchami)

1. DFT Studies on Some Bioactive Molecules and Superhalogen Clusters

- *Ambrish Kumar Srivastava*

Department of Physics, Deen Dayal Upadhyaya Gorakhpur University, Gorakhpur

Introduction

The computational exploration of biologically active molecules and small clusters, highlights their structural, spectral, and electronic properties. By biologically active molecules, we mean that the molecules show some biological activity. In contrast, A *cluster* is an ensemble of bound units (atoms or molecules) that is intermediate in size between a molecule and a bulk solid. Generally, any system comprising somewhere between 3 and 3×10^7 units is considered a cluster. Using advanced methods, the studies cover a diverse range of systems, from synthetic compounds to natural products and novel clusters with unique chemical properties. The study begins with a synthetic compound, 4-Amino-3-(4-hydroxybenzyl)-1H-1,2,4-triazole-5(4H)-thione (4AHT) and its tautomer using combined experimental and theoretical methods. 4AHT has been synthesized by fusing[1] a well-titurated mixture of 4-hydroxyphenylacetic acid and thiocarbohydrazide. The derivatives of 1,2,4-triazole are known to

---

[1] B. K. Sarojini, P. S. Manjula, Manpreet Kaur, Brian J. Anderson and Jerry P. Jasinski, *Acta Cryst. E70 (2014) o48–o49.*

exhibit anti-inflammatory[2], antiviral[3], antimicrobia[4] and antidepressant activities[5]. Following this, the focus shifts to natural products, such as triclisine and rufescine, extracted from Amazonian wines, *Abuta rufescens* and *Triclisia gilletii*, respectively. These azafluoranthene-class compounds demonstrate significant biological activities, including anti-HIV, antifungal, and cytotoxic effects[6,7]. Detailed studies reveal the structural and vibrational properties that underpin their bioactivity. This exploration further examines the intriguing domain of superhalogen clusters[8], including gold chloride $(AuCl_n)$ and gold oxide (AuO_n) species, which exhibit remarkable oxidizing properties. We have introduced the superhalogen behaviour of gold oxyfluoride, $Au(OF)_n$, for the first time using OF ligands. In addition, we have included AuO_xF_y clusters in which both O and F act as individual ligands. Applications of superhalogens in energy storage are also discussed, including their role in hydrogen storage materials[9] and lithium-ion battery electrolytes[10,11]. These findings emphasize the transformative potential of superhalogen clusters in sustainable technologies. This work integrates these diverse yet interconnected studies, providing a cohesive narrative on the power of computational methods to unravel the complexities of biologically active molecules and small clusters.

---

[2] *M. D. Mullican, M. W. Wilson, D. T. Connor, C. R. Kostlan, D. J. Schrier, R. D. Dyer, J. Med. Chem. 36 (1993) 1090–1099.*

[3] *D. H. Jones, R. Slack, S. Squires, K. R. H. Wooldridge, J. Med. Chem. 8 (1965) 676–680.*

[4] *S. A. Shams El-Dine, A. A. B. Hazzaa, Pharmazie 29 (1974) 761–768.*

[5] *J. M. Kane, M. W. Dudley, S. M. Sorensen, F. P. Miller, J. Med. Chem. 31 (1988) 1253–1258.*

[6] *H. Morita, K. Matsumoto, K. Takeya and H. Itokawa, Chem. Pharm. Bull. 41 (1993) 1307–1308.*

[7] *D. S. Swaffar, C. J. Holley, R. W. Fitch, K. R. Elkin, C. Zhang, J. P. Sturgill and M. D. Menachery, Planta Med. 78 (2012) 230–232.*

[8] *G. L. Gutsev, A. I. Boldyrev, Chem. Phys. 56 (1981) 277-283.*

[9] *S. Orimo, Y. Nakamori, J. R. Eliseo, A. Zuttel, Craig M. Jensen, Chem. Rev. 107 (2007) 4111-4132.*

[10] *L. A. Dominey, Lithium Batteries; Elsevier Science B. V.: Netherlands (1994).*

[11] *G. A. Nazri, G. Pistoia, Lithium Batteries: Science and Technology; Kluwer Academic Publishers: Boston (2004).*

Methodology

Computational studies were carried out using density functional theory (DFT) implemented in Gaussian 09[12]. Geometry optimizations and spectral simulations utilized hybrid functionals like B3LYP and ωB97xD with basis sets such as 6-31+G(d,p) and 6-311+G(d). Time-dependent DFT (TD-DFT) was used to simulate UV-visible spectra, while 1H-NMR chemical shifts were calculated using the GIAO method.

For systems involving gold clusters, the B3PW91 functional and Stuttgart/Dresden pseudopotential (SDD) accounted for relativistic effects, with 6-311+G* applied to ligands. Lithium-based systems were optimized with ωB97xD, considering long-range interactions. Molecular visualizations were created using Chemcraft software. This streamlined methodology enabled precise predictions of molecular properties, providing valuable insights into the studied systems' bioactivity and potential applications.

Results and Discussion

Bioactive Molecules

Figure 1 illustrates the optimized structure of 4AHT, where the phenyl ring is nearly perpendicular to the triazole ring. The bond angle C3-C21-C13 is calculated to be 113.5°, closely matching the crystallographic value of 113°. Other computed parameters also show strong agreement with crystallographic data (R^2 > 0.9). While 4AHT exists predominantly in its thione form in the solid state, it exhibits NH-SH tautomerism in the liquid state. The geometry of its thiol tautomer is also analyzed and shown in Figure 1.

---

[12] M. J. Frisch, G. W. Trucks, H. B. Schlegel, et al. Gaussian 09, Revision B.01, Gaussian Inc., Wallingford CT, 2010

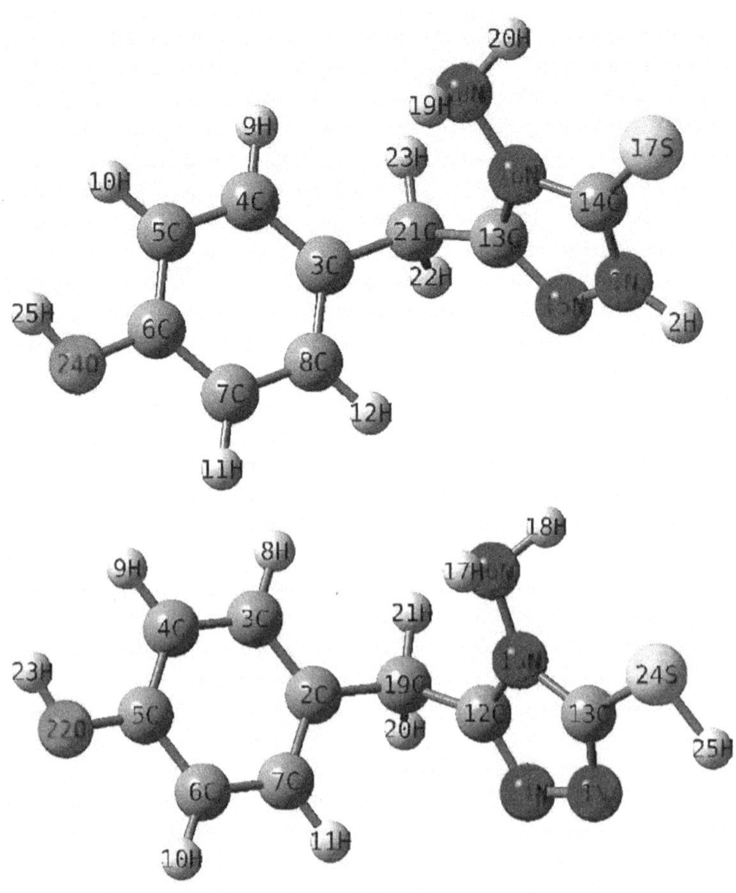

Fig. 1. Equilibrium structures of 4AHT computed at B3LYP/6-31+G(d,p) level in thiol (upper) and thiol (lower) forms.

The calculated wavenumbers of 4AHT using B3LYP/6-31+G(d,p) were scaled using a scale factor $(\nu_{scaled} = 0.9648\nu_{calculated})$[13] and a scaling equation $(\nu_{scaled} = 22.1 + 0.9543\nu_{calculated})$[14]. The scaling equation proved more effective for higher wavenumbers (above 1800 cm^{-1}), while the scale factor worked better for lower wavenumbers. The FT-IR spectrum of 4AHT, shown in Figure 2, includes C-H stretching vibrations (3088–2949 cm^{-1}) and C-C modes in the lower

---

[13] J. P. Merrick, D. Moran, L. Radom, J. Phys. Chem. A 111 (2007) 11683-11700.
[14] M. Alcolea Palafox, Int. J. Quantum Chem. 77 (2000) 661-684A.

region, both aligning well with experimental data. Peaks corresponding to CH_2 stretching and NH_2 antisymmetric stretching are also accurately reproduced.

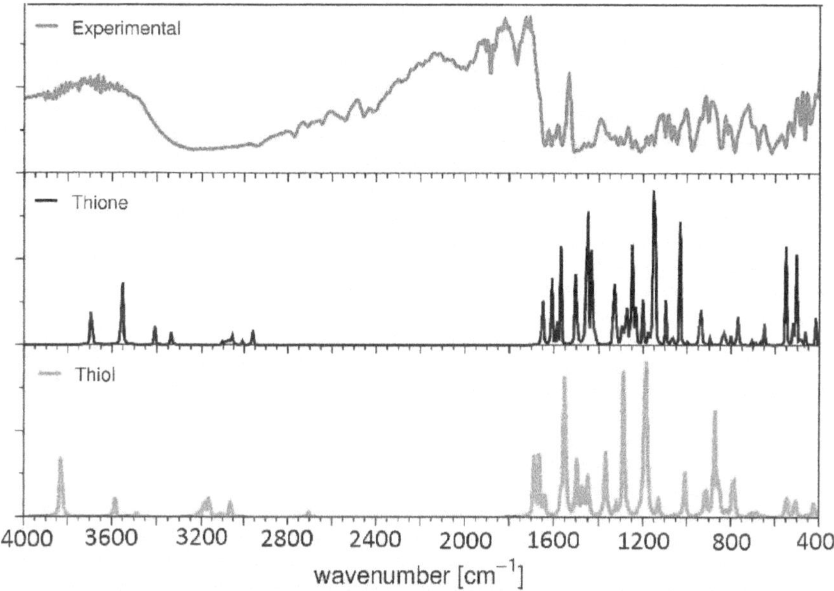

Fig. 2. FT-IR spectrum of 4AHT recorded by KBr disc method (upper) and calculated IR spectrum at B3LYP/6-31+G(d,p) level (lower).

The UV-vis spectra simulated using TD-DFT in ethanol solvent (Figure 3) reveal excited states consistent with experimental bands. The first excited state involves transitions HOMO-2 to LUMO+1 and LUMO+2, matching the 270 nm band. The second and third excited states are dominated by HOMO+1 to LUMO and HOMO to LUMO transitions, accurately reproducing the experimental peak at 252 nm. The fourth and fifth excited states correspond to transitions HOMO to LUMO+1 and LUMO+2, aligning with the 242 nm band. TD-DFT results for the thiol form also reproduce experimental peaks, suggesting its dominance in solution.

NMR spectra indicate that 4AHT predominantly exists in its thione form in DMSO solvent. The singlet peak of hydrogen (=NH) in the thione form is calculated at 9.2 ppm, closely matching the experimental 9.3 ppm, while the corresponding -SH peak in the thiol form appears at 4.8 ppm. A strong correlation (R^2 = 0.9453) between calculated and experimental ^{1}H-NMR shifts further validates the results.

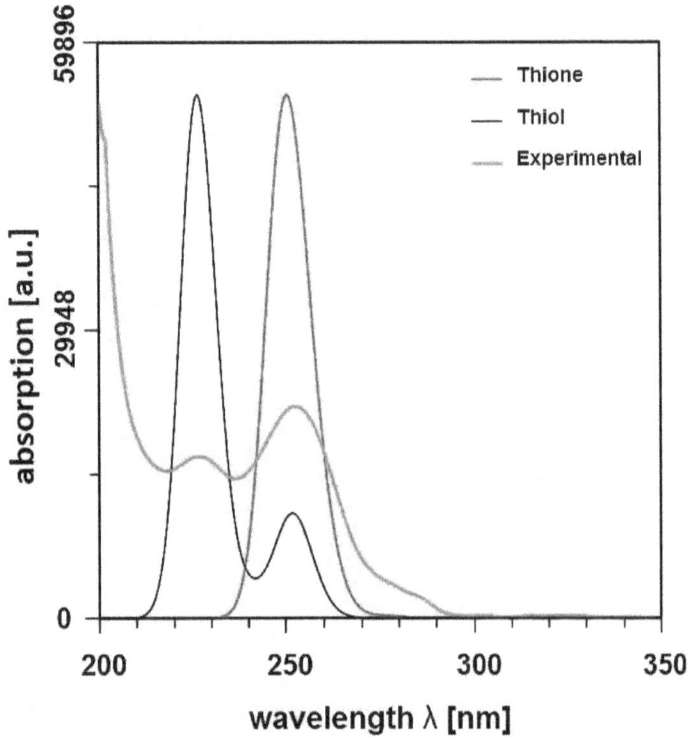

Fig. 3. UV-visible spectrum of 4AHT recorded in ethanol (upper) and calculated UV-visible spectrum at TD-DFT//B3LYP/6-31+G(d,p) level (lower).

To investigate the biological and pharmacological potential of 4AHT, we employed the PASS program. It has been used to predict the biological activity of a variety of molecules[15], which analyzes structure-activity relationships (SAR) from a database of over 46,000 drugs and drug candidates. The predictions highlight that 4AHT exhibits significant inhibition properties, especially as a cyclin-dependent kinase 5 (CDK5) inhibitor. CDK5 is crucial in neuronal

---

[15]*A. K. Srivastava, A. K. Pandey, S. Jain, N. Misra, Spectrochim. Acta A 136 (2015) 682-689.*

maturation, migration, and cancer cell proliferation, and its inhibition can be beneficial in cancer treatment[16]. Further molecular docking studies, with a total e-value of -185.21, suggest that 4AHT fits well with the CDK5 receptor, confirming its potential as an effective CDK5 inhibitor.

Further, the optimized geometries of triclisine and rufescine, calculated at the B3PW91/6-311+G(d,p) level of theory, are shown in Figure 4. Both molecules feature four planar ring systems, with the upper ring (R1) containing a nitrogen substitution and the lower ring (R4) attached to two $-OCH_3$ groups at consecutive positions C1 and C6. Rufescine has two additional $-OCH_3$ groups, located at C2 of R4 and C16 of R3.

QTAIM calculations reveal two intramolecular hydrogen bonds in triclisine and three in rufescine. In rufescine, the additional $-OCH_3$ group enables O21 to act as an acceptor in two hydrogen bonds: O21...H29 and O21...H33. The total interaction energies are calculated to be 4.12 kcal/mol for triclisine and 6.7 kcal/mol for rufescine. The enhanced hydrogen bonding in rufescine suggests greater chemical reactivity compared to triclisine.

Vibrational frequencies of both molecules, calculated at the same level of theory, align well with observed experimental values. CH stretching modes in triclisine are found between 3094 and 3051 cm^{-1}, while in rufescine, these occur at slightly higher wavenumbers (3111–3065 cm^{-1}), consistent with the electron-withdrawing effect of additional $-OCH_3$ groups in rufescine. In both molecules, the highest frequencies correspond to CH stretching of R3. Below 1500 cm^{-1}, bending modes associated with the ring systems and $-OCH_3$ groups exhibit mixing with torsional modes. For example, a highly intense mode at 1469 cm^{-1} in rufescine, polarized along R4, involves CCC stretching, CH_3

---

[16] M. Malumbres, P. Pevarello, M. Barbacid, J. R. Bischoff, *Trends Pharm. Sci.* 29 (2008) 16-21.

rocking, and CH bending. A similar mode appears at 1473 cm⁻¹ in triclisine.

The CN stretching mode in triclisine occurs at 1588 cm⁻¹, lower than in rufescine (1599 cm⁻¹), reflecting the impact of additional functional groups. Similarly, CH_3 scissoring modes adjacent to oxygen atoms appear at lower wavenumbers in triclisine (1433 cm⁻¹) compared to rufescine (1446 cm⁻¹). Intense out-of-plane bending and torsional modes dominate the lower frequency region (<800 cm⁻¹), with experimental agreement generally excellent, though deviations may arise from intermolecular interactions and anharmonic effects.

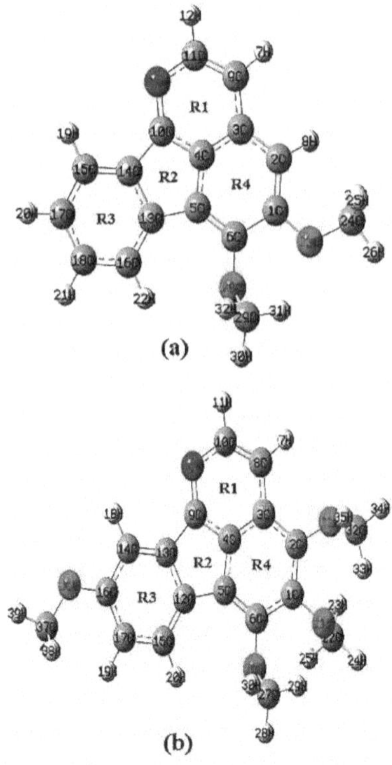

Fig. 4. Optimized molecular geometries of triclisine (a) and rufescine (b) at B3PW91/6-311+G(d,p) level of theory.

Frontier molecular orbitals provide insight into chemical reactivity[17]. HOMO-LUMO plots (Figure 5) reveal delocalized HOMOs across the ring systems and LUMOs extending across the molecules, excluding nitrogen in rufescine. The energy gap is higher in triclisine (4.01 eV) than in rufescine (3.56 eV), suggesting greater reactivity for rufescine, consistent with its stronger hydrogen bonding.

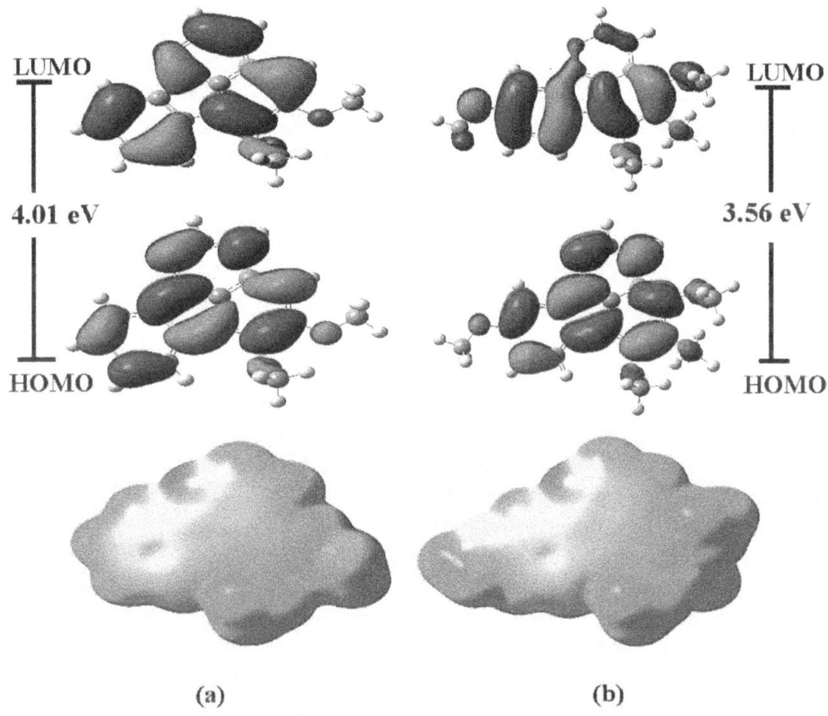

Fig. 5. HOMO, LUMO and MESP surfaces of triclisine (a) and rufescine (b).

Molecular electrostatic potential (MESP)[18] maps, also shown in Figure 5, highlight the nitrogen atom in R1 as the most electronegative region in both molecules, acting as an electron donor. Red regions denote electron-rich areas, while blue regions represent electron-poor zones, providing insight into potential binding sites.

---

[17] *H. Sklenar and J. Jager, Int. J. Quantum Chem. 16 (1979) 467.*
[18] *J. S. Murray and K. Sen, Molecular Electrostatic Potentials: Concepts and Applications (Elsevier, Amsterdam, Netherlands) (1996)*

Gold-Based Superhalogens and Mixed Complexes

$AuCl_n$ Clusters (n = 1–6)

Gold (Au) is the most popular example of transition metal series. Optimized geometries of neutral $AuCl_n$ clusters and their corresponding anions ($n = 1$ to 6) are shown in Figure 6. These species favor lower spin states regardless of their charges. The geometries of neutral $AuCl_n$ closely resemble those of their anionic counterparts for n ≤ 5. However, for $AuCl_3^-$ and $AuCl_5^-$, one of the Au-Cl bond lengths increases, weakening the bond due to the addition of an extra electron. In the $AuCl_6^-$ anion, unlike its neutral counterpart, all six chlorine atoms bind atomically to the gold atom, forming an octahedral structure. This results in the maximum of five chlorine atoms binding to gold in neutral $AuCl_5$, while six chlorine atoms bind in the $AuCl_6^-$ anion. The existence of $AuCl_5$ (but not $AuCl_6$) and $AuCl_6^-$ confirms that the maximum oxidation state of gold is +5. Thus, oxidation states of gold higher than +5 should be cautiously approached.

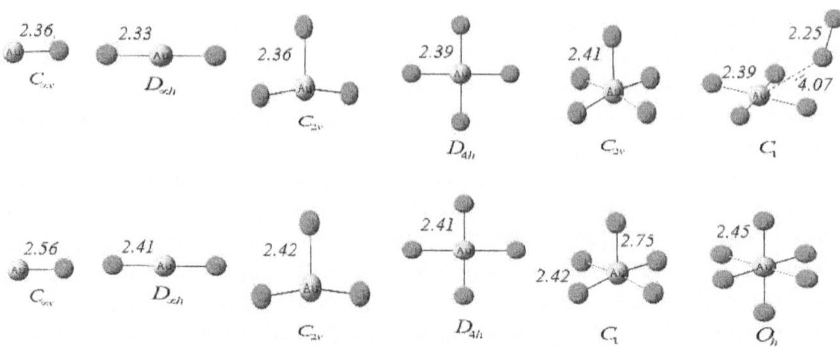

Fig. 6. Equilibrium geometries of neutral (left) and anionic (right) $AuCl_n$ species (n = 1 - 6). Bond lengths (in Å) are also shown.

To assess the stability of $AuCl_n$ anions, we examined their dissociation into chlorine atoms or Cl_2 molecules. All anionic species are stable against dissociation into Cl atoms, as indicated by positive dissociation energies (D_e). However, the dissociation energies exhibit dips at $n = 3$ and $n = 5$, corresponding to an increase in one of the Au-

Cl bond lengths in $AuCl_3$ and $AuCl_5$ anions, which reduces their stabilities. The stability of $AuCl_n^-$ decreases as more chlorine atoms are added. The high oxidation state of Au is achieved through the involvement of inner shell d electrons in bonding, which increases as the number of chlorine atoms increases up to $n = 5$. This supports the notion that the maximum possible oxidation state of gold is +5.

The superhalogen properties of $AuCl_n$ species were evaluated through their adiabatic electron affinities (EA). The EA increases with the number of chlorine atoms, reaching a peak value of 6.36 eV for $n = 5$, before decreasing. For $n \geq 2$, the EA values suggest these species exhibit superhalogen behavior. This high EA is attributed to the increasing positive charge on the Au atom, which rises with the number of chlorine atoms but saturates at 0.53 e in $AuCl_3$. In $AuCl^-$, over 75% of the extra electron resides on gold. As more chlorine atoms are added, the extra electron delocalizes across the chlorine atoms. In $AuCl_4$ and $AuCl_5$, the positive charge on gold nearly matches that in their anions, explaining the increase in EA up to $n = 5$. For $n = 6$, the decrease in EA is due to a 30% increase in the localization of the extra electron on gold in $AuCl_6^-$, as well as a more stable structure with chlorine atoms forming a Cl_2 moiety in the neutral form.

$Au(OF)_n$ Clusters (n = 1−6)

The equilibrium geometries of neutral $Au(OF)_n$ complexes and their anions are depicted in Figure 7. All species prefer the lowest spin multiplicities, with singlet states for odd n in $Au(OF)_n$ and doublet states for even n in both neutral and anionic species. This trend is similar to those observed in case of AuF_n[19] as well as $Au(CN)_n$[20] species. The calculated $< S^2 >$ values for doublet $Au(OF)_2$, $Au(OF)_4$ and $Au(OF)_6$ structures are 0.757, 0.754, and 0.833, respectively, which

[19] P. Koirala, M. Willis, B. Kiran, A. K. Kandalam, P. Jena, J. Phys. Chem. C 114 (2010) 16018-16024.

[20] D. Samanta, M. M. Wu, P. Jena, Inorg. Chem. 50 (2011) 8918-8925.

are close to the expected value of 0.750, confirming that the calculated states are pure and not spin-contaminated.

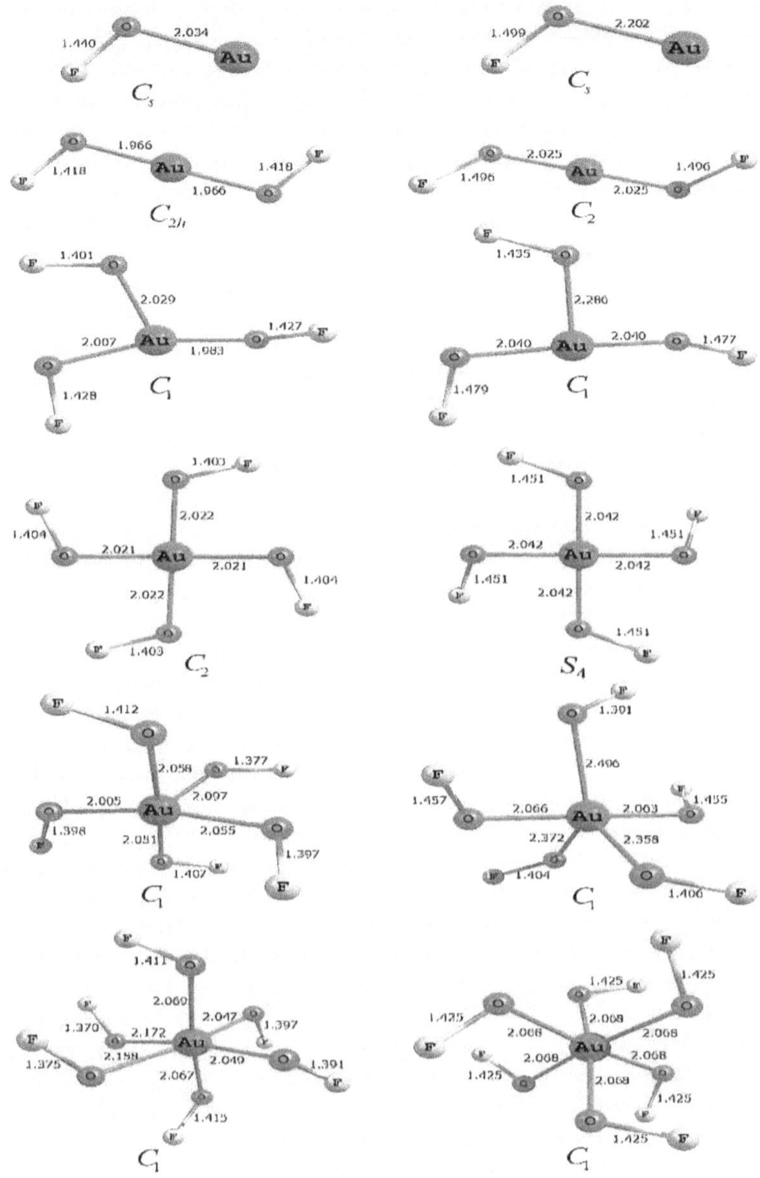

Fig. 7. Equilibrium structures of neutral Au(OF)$_n$ species (left) and their anions (right) for n = 1−6. The bond-lengths (in Å) are also displayed.

The Au-O bond lengths in $Au(OF)_n$ range from 1.97 Å to 2.10 Å, while those in the anions range from 2.03 Å to 2.20 Å. A similar trend is observed for O-F bond lengths. The bond angles Au-O-F in $Au(OF)_n^-$ differ only marginally from their neutral counterparts, with angles of 108.1° and 111.7° in AuOF and $Au(OF)_2$, respectively, changing to 114.4° in $AuOF^-$ and 109.4° in $Au(OF)_2^-$.

The adiabatic electron affinity (AEA) and vertical detachment energy (VDE) values for $Au(OF)_n$ are larger than the electron affinities of halogens (3.40 eV for F and 3.61 eV for Cl) for $n \geq 2$, classifying $Au(OF)_n$ as superhalogens for $n \geq 2$. This behavior can be explained by the delocalization of extra electrons over the OF moieties. The AEAs of AuF_n, $AuCl_n$, $Au(CN)_n$, and $Au(OF)_n$ species were compared, revealing that the EA of $Au(OF)_n$ increases progressively, reaching a peak value of 6.43 eV at $n = 5$, after which it stabilizes. The AEAs of $Au(OF)_n$ are smaller than those of AuF_n or $Au(CN)_n$ species, but comparable to those of $AuCl_n$ species. This indicates that all these complexes behave as superhalogens for $n \geq 2$.

The AEA of the OF moiety (2.38 eV) is capable of forming complexes with Au that yield AEAs comparable to $AuCl_n$ species. Despite CN ligands having a larger EA (3.93 eV), $Au(CN)_n$ complexes exhibit larger AEAs than AuF_n species, though CN tends to dimerize due to its large binding energy. The binding energy of the $(CN)_2$ dimer is 8.08 eV, significantly larger than that of F_2 (1.38 eV). On the other hand, the binding energy of the $(OF)_2$ dimer is 1.80 eV, suggesting that OF better stabilizes Au complexes than CN.

$AuO_xF_y^-$ clusters (x, y = 1–4; x + y = 2–5)

The optimized geometries of $AuO_xF_y^-$ ($x + y$ = 3-5) species are displayed in Figure 8. The ground-state structures of $AuOF_2^-$ and AuO_2F^- are nearly identical, favouring higher spin states. $AuOF_3^-$ and $AuO_2F_2^-$ adopt the lowest spin states, with $AuOF_3^-$ forming a planar rhombic structure with two opposite Au-F bonds of 1.99 Å. The $AuO_2F_2^-$ species exist in two isomers for each spin state: a rhombic planar singlet D_{2h} structure and a scissors-shaped structure, the latter having an energy 2.79 eV higher. AuO_3F^- closely resembles $AuOF_3^-$ but prefers a quartet spin state. The $AuO_2F_3^-$ species adopt a planar rhombic structure, while $AuO_3F_2^-$ features a triplet ground state.

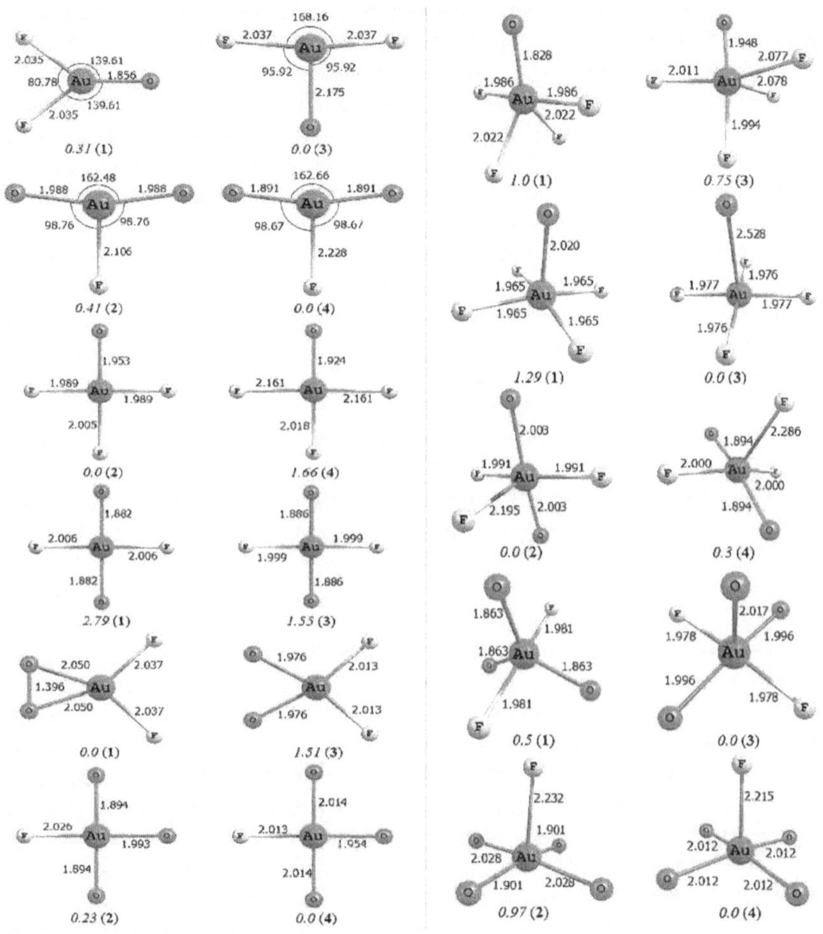

Fig. 8. Equilibrium structures of $AuO_xF_y^-$ (x + y = 2 −5) complex along with possible isomers. The bond lengths (in Å), bond angles (in °), relative energy (in eV, italicized) and spin multiplicity (in brackets, bold) are also given.

The VDEs of all $AuO_xF_y^-$ species exceed the electron affinity of halogen atoms, indicating that all belong to the superhalogen class. The highest VDE (9.38 eV) occurs for $AuO_2F_3^-$, about three times the electron affinity of F. The lowest VDE (3.88 eV) is observed for $AuOF^-$. These results suggest that $AuO_xF_y^-$ species represent a new class of superhalogen anions, with varying oxidation states of Au from +2 to +8.

$AuO_n{}^{q-}$ clusters (q = 0 −3; n = 1−4)

The optimized geometries of $AuO_n{}^{q-}$ species for $q = 0$ to 3 and $n = 1$ to 4 are shown in Figure 9. For $n = 1$, the lowest spin state is favored. As the number of O atoms increases, the ground state shifts to higher spin states. For $n = 2$, higher-spin states (quartet or triplet) are favored for all molecular charges. The preferred spin multiplicity depends on the charge for $n > 2$, with $AuO_3{}^-$ favoring a quartet state for $q = 0$ and a quintet state for $q = 1$.

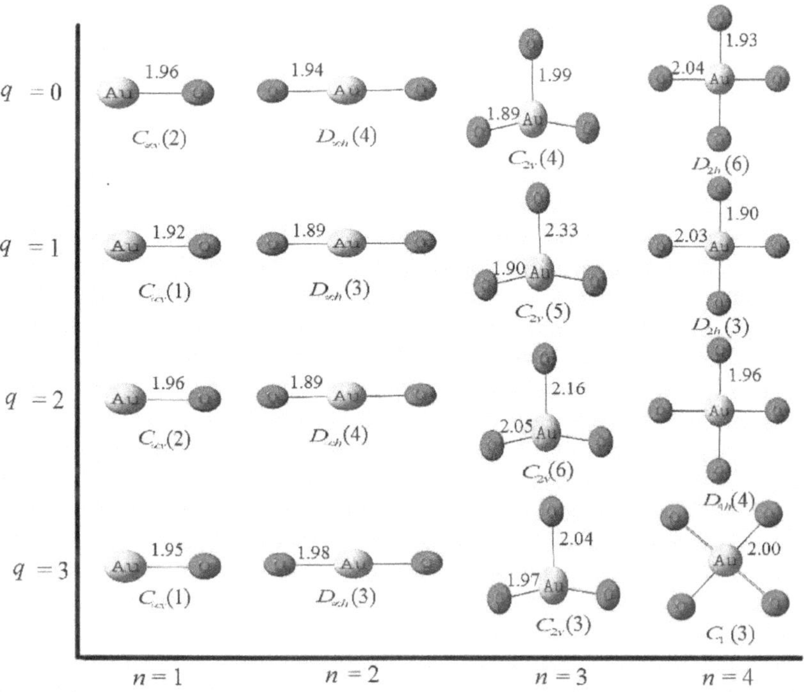

Fig. 9. Ground state geometries of $AuO_n{}^{q-}$ species. Symmetry (spin multiplicity) and bond-lengths (in Å) are also shown.

For $n = 2$, AuO_n becomes a linear structure. The geometry of AuO_3 takes a triangular planar structure in which two bond lengths are equal but the third becomes longer. Similarly, AuO_4 favors a rectangular planar geometry in which two opposite bond lengths become equal. It is also interesting to note that geometries of AuO_n^{q-} are almost independent of molecular charge q and essentially similar for $q = 0$ and 1.

We find that AuO_n^{q-} species possess the lowest possible energy concerning $q = 1$ for all values of n. Thus (mono) anionic species are relatively more stable than their neutral counterparts. Furthermore, for $n = 1$, AuO_n is 1.03 eV lower in energy than AuO_n^{2-} but 0.36 eV higher in energy for $n = 2$. This difference becomes more significant with the increasing values of n. For example, AuO_4 is 3.23 eV higher in energy than AuO_4^{2-}. Unlike $q = 0$ to 2, AuO_n^{q-} species are relatively higher in energies for $q = 3$. All AuO_n and AuO_n^{-} species are found to be stable against fragmentation to O atom. The higher dissociation energy value of 6.66 eV of AuO_2^{-} and lower value of 2.93 eV of AuO_3 are consistent with corresponding bond-lengths in these species. The stability of AuO_n^{q-} species suggests that Au can bind successively up to four O atoms in their neutral as well as anionic forms. Furthermore, these species are relatively more stable for $q = 1$. Thus, the maximum oxidation state of Au can be +7, at least in the case of bonding with O atoms.

The adiabatic EA is calculated as the energy difference between AuO_n^{q-} species for $q = 0$ and $q = 1$, both in their ground state geometries. The adiabatic EA of AuO_n increases with the increase in peripheral O atoms up to $n = 3$ and reaches a peak value of 4.3 eV for AuO_3. The EA of AuO_2, 3.76 eV reveals s superhalogen behaviour of AuO_n species for $n \geq 2$. These large EAs result due to delocalization of extra electron over several O atoms.

Complex Hydrides for Hydrogen Storage

Developing complex hydrides as practical hydrogen storage materials requires a comprehensive understanding of their electronic structures and the energetics associated with their dehydrogenation and rehydrogenation processes. We begin by discussing $LiBH_4$. In its crystal form, each Li^+ ion is coordinated to four BH_4^- ions arranged in a tetrahedral configuration, resulting in significant deformation of the BH_4^- ion. This structural feature is mirrored in the optimized structures of BH_4^- and $LiBH_4$, suggesting that the bulk phase characteristics are retained in the cluster. The BH_4^- ion adopts a tetrahedral geometry with a bond length of 1.243 Å, whereas in $LiBH_4$, the B–H bond lengths vary from 1.210 Å to 1.264 Å. The VDE of BH_4^- is calculated to be 4.50 eV. To design $BH_{4-x}(BH_4)_x^-$ hyperhalogens (where $x = 1$–4), we progressively replace hydrogen atoms in the BH_4^- superhalogen with BH_4 moieties. The optimized structures of these hyperhalogens, displayed in Fig. 10, show that their VDEs increase compared to that of BH_4^-, reaching a maximum of 7.28 eV for $B_5H_{16}^-$, where BH_4 replaces all hydrogen atoms. This increase in VDE is attributed to the large electron affinity (EA) of BH_4, which facilitates the delocalization of the extra electron over the peripheral BH_4 groups. The delocalization becomes more pronounced with an increasing number of BH_4 moieties, thereby raising the VDE of the corresponding anions.

Additionally, we examine the equilibrium structures of Li-complexes with these hyperhalogens in Figure 10. As shown, the Li atom interacts with four, three, two, and one hydrogen atoms from the $BH_{4-x}(BH_4)_x^-$ hyperhalogens for $x = 1, 2, 3$, and 4, respectively. Notably, the hydrogen content of $LiBH_4$ (18.51 wt%) is higher than that of $LiAlH_4$ (10.62 wt%), making $LiBH_4$ a favorable candidate for hydrogen storage. The hydrogen content of $LiBH_{4-x}(BH_4)_x$ complexes exceeds that of $LiBH_4$ and increases monotonically from 19.81 wt% ($x = 1$) to 20.91 wt% ($x = 4$). Thus, the $LiBH_{4-x}(BH_4)_x$ complexes are preferable to $LiBH_4$ due to their higher hydrogen storage capacity. The dehydrogenation reaction of $LiBH_4$ follows the process: $LiBH_4 \rightarrow LiH$

+ B + 3/2 H_2, with $LiBH_4$ releasing three of its four hydrogen atoms upon melting at 280°C, decomposing into LiH and boron[21]. Similarly, we considered the dehydrogenation of $LiBH_{4-x}(BH_4)_x$ complexes into LiH, boron, and hydrogen, calculating the dehydrogenation energy (ΔE). For these complexes, ΔE correlates linearly with the VDE of the $BH_{4-x}(BH_4)_x^-$ anions, with a high correlation coefficient (R^2 = 0.98).

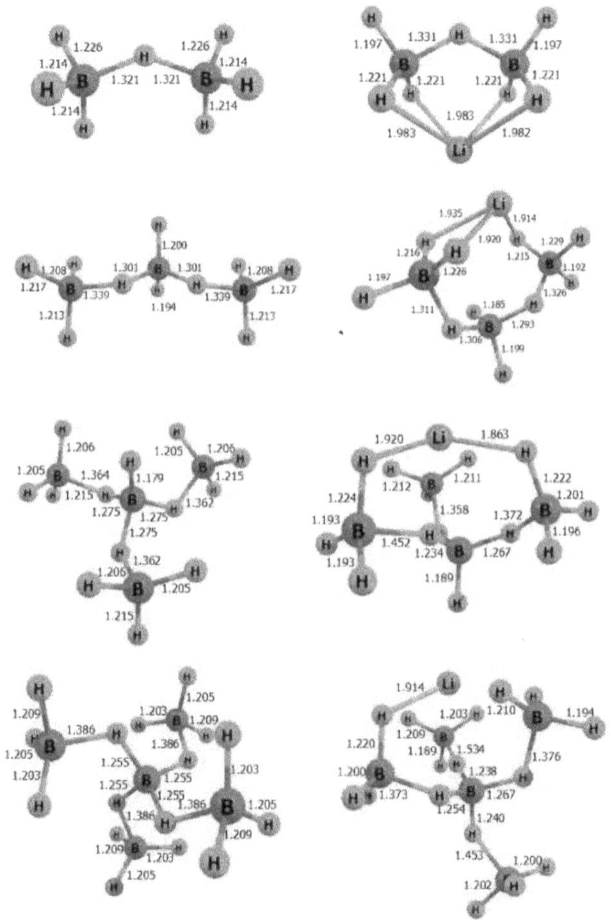

Fig. 10. Equilibrium structures of $BH_{4-x}(BH_4)_x^-$ hyperhalogen anions (left) and $LiBH_{4-x}(BH_4)_x$ complexes (right) obtained at ωB97xD/6-311+G(d) level for x = 1–4. Bond lengths (in Å) are also given.

---

[21] D. S. Stasinevich, G. A. Egorenko, Russ. J. Inorg. Chem. 13 (1968) 341.

Although $LiBH_{4-x}(BH_4)_x$ complexes demonstrate high hydrogen storage capacity, it is crucial to assess their kinetic and thermodynamic stability against dissociation into $LiBH_4$ and borane (BH_3). Our analysis indicates that these complexes are both kinetically and thermodynamically stable, with stability increasing as the VDE of the hyperhalogen anions rises. This suggests that $LiBH_{4-x}(BH_4)_x$ complexes could potentially be synthesized from $LiBH_4$ and borane, at least via a gas-phase reaction.

Superhalogens in Electrolytic Salts for Lithium-Ion Batteries (LIBs)

Next, we examine the role of superhalogens in typical electrolytic salts used in LIBs, including $LiBF_4$, $LiPF_6$, $LiClO_4$, $LiFePO_4$ and $LiAsF_6$ etc. The VDEs of the anions in these salts exceed that of the halogen atoms, classifying them as superhalogens. These species offer the advantage of being halogen-free and non-toxic. The equilibrium structures of Li-salts with these anions are shown in Figure 11. Since most of these anions consist of halogen atoms, which are toxic and therefore environmental safety remains a grave issue. As an attempt to overcome this issue, Li-salts of BeF_3^-, AuF_6^-, NO_3^-, BH_4^-, $B_3H_8^-$ and $CB_{11}H_{12}^-$ have been considered[22]. Additionally, we consider the Li-complexes of $BH_{4-y}(BH_4)_y^-$ ($y = 1\text{–}4$) hyperhalogen anions and their corresponding Li-salts, also displayed in Figure 10.

To function as efficient electrolytes, Li-salts must enhance the conductivity of the electrolytic medium by dissociating into lithium ions. We evaluated the dissociation of Li–X complexes into Li^+ and X^-, calculating the dissociation energy ($\Delta E[Li^+]$) or binding energy (E_b), as listed in Table 3. For an effective electrolyte, the $\Delta E[Li^+]$ should be comparable to or smaller than that of commercial electrolytes. For instance, $\Delta E[Li^+]$ for $LiPF_6$ (5.73 eV) is smaller than that of $LiBF_4$ (6.08 eV), making $LiPF_6$ more conductive.

---

[22] *S. Giri, S. Bahera, P. Jena, Angew. Chem. Int. Ed. 53 (2014) 13916-13919.*

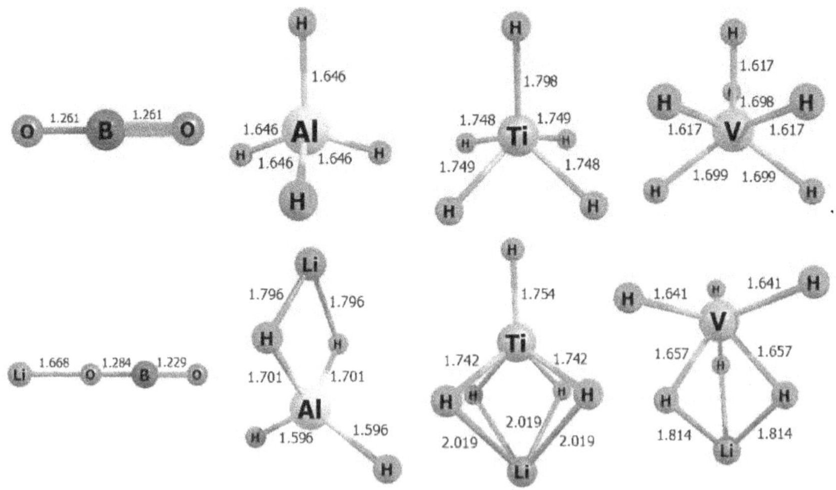

Fig. 11. Equilibrium structures of BO_2^-, AlH_4^-, TiH_5^- and VH_6^- superhalogen anions along with their Li-salts. The bond lengths in Å are calculated at ωB97xD/6-311+G(d) level.

Previously proposed electrolytic salts, such as $LiCB_{11}H_{12}$ and $LiAuF_6$, have $\Delta E[Li^+]$ values of 5.08 eV and 5.50 eV, respectively. For our proposed salts, $\Delta E[Li^+]$ ranges from 6.00 eV ($LiAlH_4$) to 6.36 eV ($LiBO_2$), values comparable to commercial electrolytes. Notably, $LiBH_4$ has already been studied as a potential electrolytic salt[23]. $LiAlH_4$ is an even better candidate due to its smaller $\Delta E[Li^+]$ value, resulting in higher conductivity. Among the $LiBH_{4-y}(BH_4)_y$ (y = 1–4) complex salts, LiB_2H_7 shows a smaller $\Delta E[Li^+]$ than $LiBH_4$, which decreases further for LiB_3H_{10}. Furthermore, $\Delta E[Li^+]$ values for LiB_4H_{13} and LiB_5H_{16} are smaller than those of $LiBF_6$ and $LiPF_6$, respectively. Based on the $\Delta E[Li^+]$ values, LiB_4H_{13} and LiB_5H_{16} stand out as promising candidates for use as electrolytic salts in LIBs. Their larger anions also offer greater mobility for Li^+ ions, improving the performance of LIBs.

Additionally, for an electrolytic salt to be practical, it must be stable, particularly against complexation with water (H_2O). We calculated the complexation energy ($\Delta E[H_2O]$) to assess the stability of Li-salts in the presence of water. Ideally, the water affinity of these salts should be comparable to or smaller than that of traditional electrolytic salts like

---

[23] M. Matsuo, Y. Nakamori, K. Yamada, S. Orimo, Appl. Phys. Lett. 91 (2007) 224103.\

LiBF$_4$ and LiPF$_6$. The ΔE[H$_2$O] values of the LiBH$_{4-y}$(BH$_4$)$_y$ (y = 1–4) salts are comparable to those of LiBH$_4$ and LiB$_3$H$_8$ previously proposed. LiB$_3$H$_8$, indicating that these Li-borohydride complexes have favorable characteristics for use as electrolytic salts in LIBs. Note that many efforts have already been made to stabilize LiPF$_6$ by choosing appropriate additives to electrolytic solvents [24].

Conclusions and Remarks

In summary, we conducted various theoretical studies on different molecular systems using density functional theory (DFT) and related methods. A comprehensive study on the thione and thiol tautomers of 4AHT was carried out, with bond lengths found to be in good agreement with corresponding crystallographic values. The FT-IR spectrum of 4AHT, recorded using the KBr disc method, was analyzed by assigning vibrational modes and calculating their potential energy distributions. The UV-visible spectrum of 4AHT was studied using time-dependent DFT (TD-DFT), where electronic transitions for various excited states were calculated, reproducing the experimental peaks accurately. The 1H-NMR spectrum was analyzed using the Gauge-Independent Atomic Orbital (GIAO) method, and the calculated chemical shifts showed excellent correlation with experimental values (linear correlation coefficient of 0.9453). Spectral analyses suggest that 4AHT predominantly exists in the thione form in the solid state and undergoes NH-SH tautomerism in the liquid phase. Additionally, the biological activity of 4AHT was predicted and discussed.

Further studies were conducted on the molecular interactions of triclisine and rufescine using both DFT and the Quantum Theory of Atoms in Molecules (QTAIM) approach. QTAIM analysis revealed weak intra-molecular C−H⋯O interactions in both molecules, with triclisine showing two interactions and rufescine three. Normal mode analyses were performed to assign significant vibrational modes, and

---

[24] S. S. Zhang, J. Power Sources 162 (2006) 1379–1394.

the calculated vibrational spectra were compared to experimental FT-IR spectra, showing excellent agreement. The electronic properties of these molecules were evaluated using the highest occupied molecular orbital (HOMO), lowest unoccupied molecular orbital (LUMO), and molecular electrostatic potential (MESP) surfaces.

A systematic study of the $AuCl_n$ (n = 1 to 6) species revealed that the +5-oxidation state is the highest and most favorable for gold. The adiabatic electron affinities (AEAs) indicated that these species exhibit superhalogen behavior for $n \geq 2$, peaking at 6.36 eV for $n = 5$. Additionally, we investigated $Au(OF)_n$ complexes (n = 1−6) in neutral and monoanionic states, where OF groups bind dissociatively to the central gold core. The AEAs of these complexes were found to be comparable to AuCln, with $n \geq 2$ showing superhalogen behavior. We also studied the stabilization of higher oxidation states in these complexes, finding that they are stable only up to the +5-oxidation state, after which they dissociate into molecular oxygen.

Moving forward, the concept of superhalogens was utilized to design hyperhalogen anions, $BH_{4-x}(BH_4)_x^-$ (x = 1−4), and their lithium complexes, $LiBH_{4-x}(BH_4)_x$. These complexes were found to have higher hydrogen storage capacity than $LiBH_4$. A linear relationship between the dehydrogenation energy of $LiBH_{4-x}(BH_4)_x$ and the vertical detachment energies (VDE) of $BH_{4-x}(BH_4)_x^-$ was observed. Additionally, the thermodynamic stability of these complexes was analyzed in terms of dissociation into $LiBH_4$ and borane. We explored the design of new electrolytic salts for lithium-ion batteries (LIBs) based on superhalogen anions, including Li-salts of BO_2^-, AlH_4^-, TiH_5^- and VH_6^-. These halogen-free salts were found to have comparable ionization energies to conventional electrolytes like $LiBF_4$, making them suitable for LIBs. Their water affinity was also comparable to traditional electrolytic salts, suggesting that their use would not negatively impact the lifespan of LIBs.

2. Photonic Spin Hall Effect: Numerical Analysis for Plexcitonic System

- *Triranjita Srivastava*

Department of Physics, University of Allahabad, Prayagraj

Introduction

The unprecedented development in science and technology has made a significant advancement in the field of photonics, transforming both the idea and the applications of electromagnetic waves, beyond the classical optics. It is well known that the reflection/refraction of light from an optical interface follows a well-defined trajectory predicted by the laws of geometrical optics. However, for an incident beam having finite width, the beam centroid gets shifted ($\sim$ few nm) in longitudinal and transverse directions with respect to the plane of incidence, known as Goos Hänchen (GH) and Imbert–Fedorov (IF) shifts, respectively[25,26]. In 1947, the first experimental discovery of the longitudinal shift was made by Goos and Hänchen. Later in 1948, the GH shift was theoretically explained by Artmann[1,2]. Further, the IF shift, was initially postulated by Fedorov in 1955, and experimentally confirmed by Imbert in 1972. It is known that IF shift involves the

---

[25] *Aiello A. (2012). Goos–Hänchen and Imbert–Fedorov shifts: a novel perspective. New J. Phys. 14, 013058.*

[26] *Bliokh K. Y. and Aiello A. (2013). Goos–Hänchen and Imbert–Fedorov beam shifts: an overview. J. Opt. 15 014001.*

spin-orbit interaction of light and hence widely known as photonic spin Hall effect (PSHE)[1,2]. This effect is an optical counterpart of the spin Hall effect in an electrical system, where the refractive index gradient plays the role of electric potential gradient and the spin photons corresponds to the spin electrons[27].

In this chapter, the detailed description of PSHE, numerical analysis followed by results and discussions are presented.

Photonic Spin Hall Effect: Review

Over the past decade, PSHE has earned a lot of interest in the fields of biochemical sensing, precision metrology, image edge detection and spin-optics, nanophotonics[28,29]. When the light propagates through inhomogeneous medium/refractive index gradients, the PSHE is observed. This effect is the manifestation of the splitting of the linearly polarized (LP) light into opposite spin states (i.e. Right Circularly Polarized (RCP) and Left Circularly Polarized (LCP) components), due to spin–orbit coupling and thereby conservation of angular momentum[4,5]. As the light has a small photon momentum, so, it exhibits weak spin–orbit coupling resulting into subwavelength transverse shift which limits its applications. Also, the literature survey reveals that the transverse IF shift is polarization dependent and highly influenced by several structural and beam parameters, such as; beam waist and phase of incident beam, angle of incidence.

Therefore, with the aim to attain enhanced transverse shift (~ few tens of μm), and to explore its wide applications, the investigations on the PSHE has been carried out in various photonic structures. Pillon et al., in 2005, experimentally investigated PSHE for leaky guided

---

[27] Srivastava T., Chitriv S., Sahu S., Gorai P., Jha R. (2022) *Photonic spin Hall effect using hybrid Tamm plasmon polariton. J. Appl. Phys. 132 (20): 203103.*

[28] Liu S., Chen S., Wen S. and Luo H. (2022). *Photonic spin Hall effect: fundamentals and emergent applications. Opto-Electron Sci. 1, 220007.*

[29] Sheng L., Chen Y., Yuan S., Liu X., Zhang Z., Jing H., Kuang L., Zhou X. (2023). *Photonic spin Hall effect: Physics, manipulations, and applications. Progress in Quantum Electronics. 91–92, 100484.*

mode[30]. Later, in 2011, H. Luo et. al., experimentally studied the PSHE near the Brewster angle with IF shift up to 3200 nm[31]. In 2013, Liu et. al., investigated these shifts at dielectric/topological insulator interface[32]. In 2014, Goswami et. al., theoretically studied PSHE ~ 100 μm in an electro-optically tunable liquid crystal and ZnSe prism, exhibiting long range surface plasmons[33]. Later, in 2015, Grosche et. al. proposed graphene coated surfaces, by tuning the conductivity of the graphene[34]. Ye et. al., in 2019, theoretically explored PSHE at Weyl semimetal interface and demonstrated the sensitivity of the shift to Weyl points separation[35]. Recently, Yang et. al., in 2021, theoretically attained giant GH and IF shifts ~ 120 times the wavelength of light in the Dirac metamaterials[36]. Thereafter, many other advanced photonic structures, such as, Tamm plasmon polariton waveguide[37], metallo-dielectric/plasmonic structures[38,39], surface exciton polariton based

[30] *Pillon F., Gilles H., Girard S., Laroche M., Kaiser R., and Gazibegovic A. (2005). Goos-Hänchen and Imbert-Fedorov shifts for leaky guided modes. J. Opt. Soc. Am. B 22, 1290-1299.*

[31] *Luo H., Zhou X., Shu W., Wen S., and Fan D. (2011). Enhanced and switchable spin Hall effect of light near the Brewster angle on reflection. Phys. Rev. A 84, 043806.*

[32] *Liu F., Xu J., Song G., and Yang Y. (2013). Goos–Hänchen and Imbert–Fedorov shifts at the interface of ordinary dielectric and topological insulator. J. Opt. Soc. Am. B 30, 1167-1172.*

[33] *Goswami N., Kar A., Saha A. (2014). Long range surface plasmon resonance enhanced electro-optically tunable Goos–Hänchen shift and Imbert–Fedorov shift in ZnSe prism. Optics Communications 330, 169-174.*

[34] *Grosche S., Ornigotti M., and Szameit A. (2015). Goos-Hänchen and Imbert-Fedorov shifts for Gaussian beams impinging on graphene-coated surfaces. Opt. Express 23, 30195-30203.*

[35] *Ye G., Zhang W., Wu W., Chen S., Shu W., Luo H., and Wen S. (2019). Goos-Hänchen and Imbert-Fedorov effects in Weyl semimetals. Phys. Rev. A 99, 023807.*

[36] *Yang Q., Xu W., Chen S., Wen S., and Luo H. (2021). Nonspecular effects in the vicinity of a photonic Dirac point. Phys. Rev. A, 103, 023522.*

[37] *Srivastava T., Chitriv S., Sahu S., Gorai P., Jha R. (2022) Photonic spin Hall effect using hybrid Tamm plasmon polariton. J. Appl. Phys. 132 (20): 203103.*

[38] *Yu, X., Wang, X., Li, Z., Zhao, L., Zhou, F., Qu, J. & Song, J. (2021). Spin Hall effect of light based on a surface plasmonic platform. Nanophotonics, 10, 3031-3048.*

[39] *Hedhly, M.; Wang, Y., Zeng, S.; Ouerghi, F.; Zhou, J.; Humbert, G. (2022). Highly Sensitive Plasmonic Waveguide Biosensor Based on Phase Singularity-Enhanced Goos–Hänchen Shift. Biosensors, 12, 457.*

refractive index sensor[40], plexcitonic systems[41] have also been investigated.

Here, for illustration and simulation, plexcitonic structure[17,42] has been considered to present the numerical analysis of the PSHE, discussed later in Section 4.

Plexcitonic Structure

A plexcitonic system, as shown in Fig. 1, comprises of 4 layers of high refractive index-momentum matching element (say, SF11), plasmonic active metal (Gold; Au), organic semiconductor (J-aggregates dye, *i.e.*, 5,50,6,60-tetra-chloro-1,10-diethyl-3,30-di(4-sulfobutyl) benzimidazolo carbocyanine; TDBC) and air as analyte. The thickness of Ag and TDBC layers is depicted by 'd_m' and 't' respectively. Here the Gaussian beam from laser source (wavelength; λ) is incident on one face of the prism and the reflected light is collected from its other face.

It is to emphasize that TDBC possess strong dipole moment owing to the linear chain-like structure of J-aggregate molecules, thereby exhibiting sharp absorption and emission spectra. Also, the TDBC molecules can be deposited on any substrate using a spin-coating/dip-coating technique from its aqueous solution in ambient conditions. In the present configuration, the coupling of the surface plasmon polariton and surface exciton polariton, excited at the metal and TDBC interface respectively, results into a hybrid plasmonic mode, known as surface plasmon exciton polariton. It is commonly termed as "*plexciton*".

---

[40]*Dong P., Xiang Y., Li R., Wang C., Cheng C., Cheng J. (2023). A Promising Mechanism for Photonic Spin Hall Effect and Refractive Index Sensing: Surface Exciton Polaritons. Annalen Der Physik,* **535,** *2300309.*

[41]*Sahu S., Srivastava T., Jha R. (2023). Plexcitonic system for high photonic spin Hall effect. Appl. Phys. Lett.* **123,** *203302.*

[42]*Srivastava T., Jha R. (2020). Plexcitonic nose based on an organic semiconductor. Appl. Phys. Lett.* **117,** *093301.*

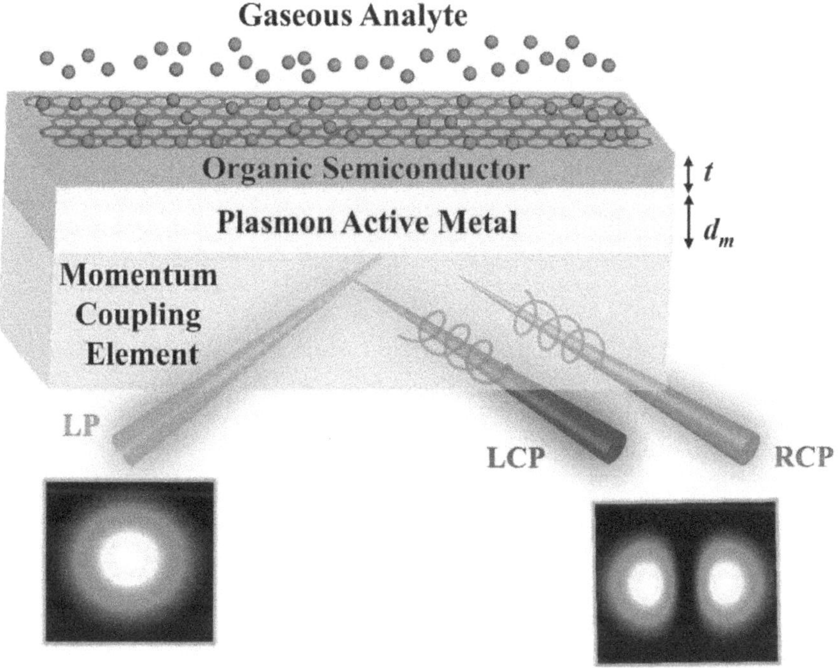

Fig. 1 Schematic of plexcitonic structure, showing PSHE; splitting of LP light into LCP and RCP components

Mathematical Analysis

In this work, we employed standard transfer matrix method using N-layer model to obtain the Fresnel's reflection coefficients for s and p-polarized light. The corresponding transfer matrix in any (say kth) medium is given by,

$$(T_k)_{s(p)} = \left[Cos(\beta_k) - \left(\frac{i}{q_k}\right) Sin(\beta_k) - iq_k Sin(\beta_k) Cos(\beta_k) \right]$$

Where

$$\beta_k = k_0 d_k \sqrt{(n_k^2 - (n_1 sin\theta_i)^2)}, \quad q_k = \frac{\sqrt{(n_k^2 - (n_1 sin\theta_i)^2)}}{m}$$

k_0 is the wave vector in a vacuum, θ_i is the angle of incidence in 1st medium, m = n_k^2 (1) for p (s) polarized light, n_k and d_k are the refractive index and thickness of the kth medium, respectively.

Assuming the structure to have N-layers, and the 1st and Nth layers are semi-infinite, the total transfer matrix (T) is given by,

$$T_{s(p)} = \prod_{k=2}^{N-1}(T_k)_{s\,(p)} = [X_{11}\ X_{12}\ X_{21}\ X_{22}\,]$$

The Fresnel's reflection coefficient for s- and p- polarized light is

$$r_{s\,(p)} = \frac{(X_{11}+X_{12}q_N)q_1-(X_{21}+X_{22}q_N)}{(X_{11}+X_{12}q_N)q_1+(X_{21}+X_{22}q_N)},$$

and the reflectivity is defined as $R_{s\,(p)} = \left| r_{s(p)} \right|^2$.

It is to be noted that the Fresnel's reflection coefficients are complex; $r_{s(p)} = \left| r_{s(p)} \right| e^{i\phi_{s(p)}}$; φ_s (φ_p) is phase of the reflected s (p-pol) light. The transverse shift $\delta_s^\pm$ and $\delta_p^\pm$ for s- and p-polarized Gaussian beam, respectively is given by:

$$\delta_p^\pm = \mp \frac{k_1 w_0^2\left\{1+\frac{|r_s|}{|r_p|}\cos\cos(\phi_s-\phi_p)\right\}\cot\cot\theta_i}{k_1^2 w_0^2+\left|\frac{\partial\ln\ln r_p}{\partial\theta_i}\right|^2+\left|\left(1+\frac{r_s}{r_p}\right)\cot\cot\theta_i\right|^2}$$

$$\delta_s^\pm = \mp \frac{k_1 w_0^2\left\{1+\frac{|r_p|}{|r_s|}\cos\cos(\phi_p-\phi_s)\right\}\cot\cot\theta_i}{k_1^2 w_0^2+\left|\frac{\partial\ln\ln r_s}{\partial\theta_i}\right|^2+\left|\left(1+\frac{r_p}{r_s}\right)\cot\cot\theta_i\right|^2}$$

Here (+) and (-) corresponds to the *LCP* and *RCP* components respectively, corresponding to the splitted light beam, k_1 is the propagation wave vector in the 1st layer and w_0 is the beam waist radius of the incident beam, and θ_i is the angle of incidence for the central wave vector. It to be noted that the high value of $\delta_p^\pm$ can only be attained for high $\left(\frac{|r_s|}{|r_p|}\right)$. In this chapter, the simulations have been done at an operating wavelength λ=532 nm, and the refractive index of different layers is considered at the same.

Results and Discussions

Figure 2 shows the variation of the reflectivity for s- and p-polarized incident light with respect to the angle of incidence for d_m = 36 nm and t = 26 nm. A dip corresponding to p-polarized light is observed at the resonance angle, thereby depicting excitation of plexcitonic mode.

Also, a very high $\left(\frac{|r_s|}{|r_p|}\right) \sim 700$ is obtained for p-polarized mode at the resonance angle.

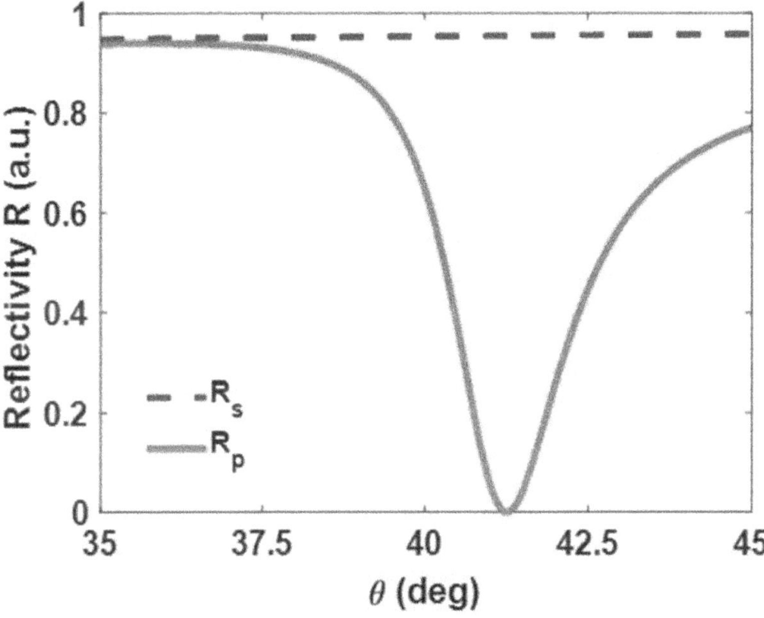

Fig. 2 Variation of reflectivity with respect to the incidence angle θ_i

Further, Fig. 3 illustrates the variation of the transverse shift corresponding to the LCP (δ_p^+) and RCP (δ_p^-). As expected, due to the high $\left(\frac{|r_s|}{|r_p|}\right)$ at the resonance angle an extremely high transverse shift $\sim$ 60 µm has been achieved. Such value of transverse shift is high as compared to the existing state-of-the-art.

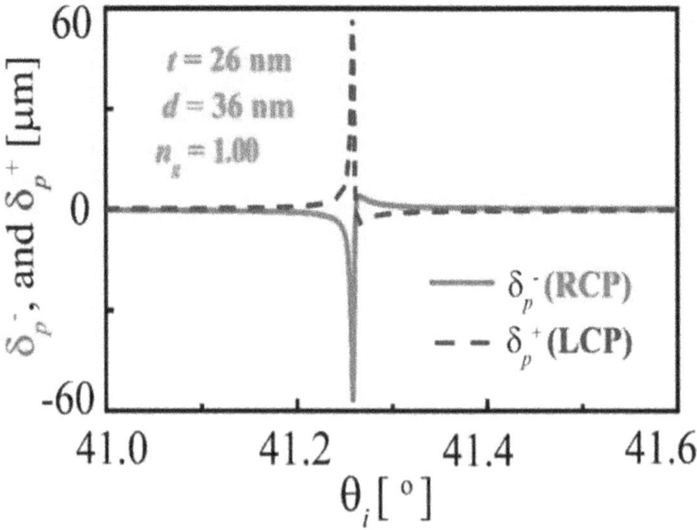

Fig. 3 Variation of transverse shift corresponding to the LCP (δ_p^{+}) and RCP (δ_p^{-}) components with respect to the incidence angle θ_i

Conclusions

In conclusion, a short review on photonic spin Hall effect has been presented in this chapter. The numerical analysis of the PSHE for plexcitonic system has been carried out in detail. It is believed that the high transverse shift obtained in the plexcitonic structure will be beneficial for advanced photonic applications, such as precision metrology, spin -optics and biochemical sensing.

3. Barium Strontium Titanate (BST) Glass Ceramics

- *Avadhesh Kumar Yadav*

Department of Physics, F.A.A. Govt. PG College Mahmudabad, Sitapur

Introduction

Barium Strontium Titanate (BST) glass ceramics are a fascinating class of materials with a unique combination of dielectric, ferroelectric, and structural properties. These materials have garnered significant attention due to their potential applications in electronics, telecommunications, and energy storage devices. This chapter explores the synthesis, structural characteristics, and applications of BST glass ceramics, offering insights into their potential for advancing material science and technology.

Properties of Barium Strontium Titanate Glass Ceramics

Barium Strontium Titanate (BST) glass ceramics exhibit an impressive suite of properties that make them a material of choice for a variety of advanced applications. Their unique combination of structural, dielectric, ferroelectric, piezoelectric, and electro-optic properties is a direct consequence of their perovskite-based crystal structure and their ability to form nanocrystalline phases within an amorphous matrix.[43],[44] This diagram represents the phase transitions

---

[43] A.K. Yadav, C. Gautam, *Journal of Materials Science: Materials in Electronics*, 25 (2014) 5165–5187.
[44] A.K. Yadav, C.R. Gautam, *Advances in Applied Ceramics*, 113 (2014) 193-207.

of Barium Titanate ($BaTiO_3$) as a function of temperature and their corresponding effects on unit cell parameters, spontaneous polarization, and dielectric constant. The phase transitions of $BaTiO_3$ are clearly depicted with temperature on the x-axis as indicated in Figure 1. The key structural phases are **Rhombohedral** (below ~-90°C), **Orthorhombic** (between ~-90°C and ~0°C), **Tetragonal** (between ~0°C and ~120°C), and **Cubic** (above ~120°C). These transitions indicate a ferroelectric to paraelectric behavior. At low temperatures, the material remains in distorted ferroelectric phases (rhombohedral, orthorhombic, tetragonal) and at higher temperatures (~120°C), the structure transitions into the cubic paraelectric phase, where spontaneous polarization disappears. The spontaneous polarization (y-axis left) decreases sharply at each phase transition. **Rhombohedral → Orthorhombic**: Slight decrease, **Orthorhombic → Tetragonal**: Noticeable drop, **Tetragonal → Cubic**: Polarization vanishes completely, indicating the paraelectric nature of the cubic phase. The behavior reflects the reduction in ferroelectricity as symmetry increases with rising temperature. The dielectric constant increases significantly near the phase transitions, particularly at the **Tetragonal → Cubic transition** (~120°C). The peak dielectric constant occurs at this transition due to the high permittivity in the paraelectric phase. The dielectric constants behave differently in the tetragonal phase, emphasizing the anisotropy of the material. This behavior is critical for applications in capacitors and other electronic devices, where $BaTiO_3$'s high dielectric constant is utilized. These tunable behaviors of barium titanate make it very attractive for research with some substitutions like strontium in place of barium.[45,46]

---

[45] A. Karvounis, F. Timpu, V. V. Vogler-Neuling, R. Savo, R. Grange, Adv. Optical Mater. 8, (2020) 2001249.
[46] E. Aksel, J. L. Jones, Sensors, 10 (2010) 1935-1954.

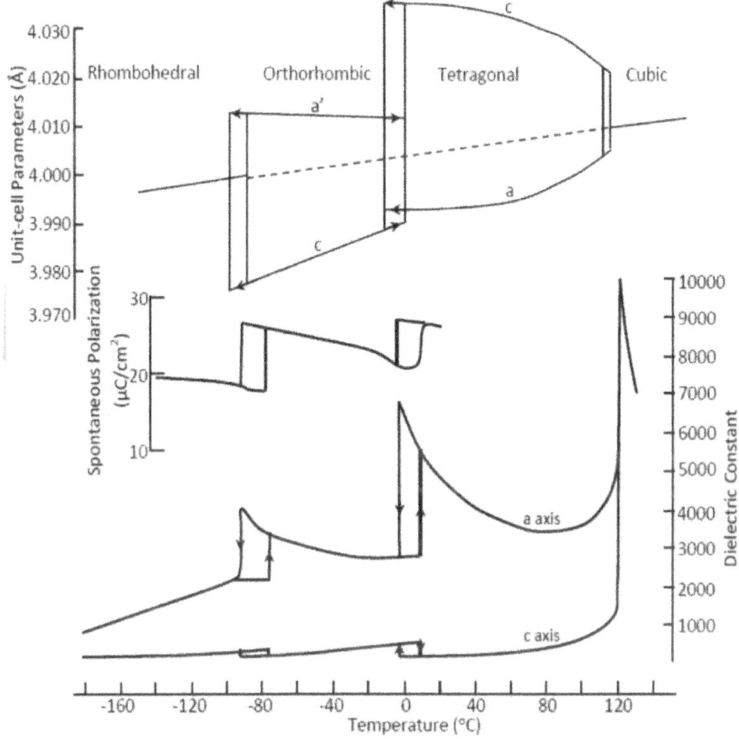

Figure 1: Tunable crystal structure and dielectric behavior of BaTiO3 [Adapted under the terms of a Creative Commons Attribution CC-BY license.4 Copyright 2010, The Authors, published by MDPI.]

Structural Properties

The perovskite structure of BST, with its characteristic ABO_3 configuration, contributes to its exceptional stability and flexibility in composition tuning. By altering the ratio of barium to strontium, the lattice parameters can be adjusted to optimize the material's functional characteristics. When embedded in a glassy matrix, BST forms uniformly dispersed nanocrystals, enhancing mechanical strength, reducing grain boundary effects, and improving the overall homogeneity of the material. The glass ceramic matrix also provides resistance to environmental degradation, making BST suitable for long-term use in harsh conditions.

Dielectric Properties

One of the hallmark features of BST glass ceramics is their high dielectric constant, which is a critical parameter for capacitive applications. The dielectric constant of BST can be precisely tuned by varying the barium-to-strontium ratio, enabling the optimization of materials for specific frequency ranges and temperature conditions. Additionally, the low dielectric loss exhibited by BST ensures efficient energy storage and minimal energy dissipation, making it ideal for use in advanced capacitors and tunable microwave devices. The dielectric properties are also highly stable across a broad temperature range, further enhancing their applicability in dynamic environments.

Ferroelectric Properties

BST glass ceramics exhibit ferroelectric behavior due to the displacement of titanium ions in their perovskite lattice. This property manifests as spontaneous polarization, which can be reversed by the application of an external electric field. The Curie temperature of BST, which marks the transition between ferroelectric and paraelectric phases, can be controlled by composition tuning. This tunability allows for the design of materials that retain ferroelectric properties over a wide operational temperature range. These characteristics are particularly advantageous for memory storage devices, where ferroelectricity enables non-volatile data retention.[47]

Piezoelectric and Pyroelectric Properties

The ability of BST to convert mechanical stress into electrical energy (piezoelectricity) and to generate an electrical charge in response to temperature changes (pyroelectricity) expands its range of applications. These properties are particularly valuable in the development of sensors, actuators, and infrared detectors. For example, BST-based piezoelectric sensors can detect minute pressure

---

47 A.K. Yadav, C.R. Gautam, J Mater Sci: Mater Electron 25 (2014) 3532–3536.

changes with high sensitivity, while pyroelectric infrared detectors are critical components in thermal imaging systems.

Electro-Optic Properties

BST glass ceramics exhibit a significant electro-optic coefficient, making them suitable for applications in modulating and switching light in photonic devices. The transparency of the glassy matrix combined with the electro-optic response of the BST phase allows for efficient manipulation of light signals, which is essential for telecommunications and laser technologies. The ability to operate at high speeds and low power consumption further underscores the utility of BST in advanced optical systems.

Thermal and Mechanical Properties

The incorporation of BST into a glass ceramic matrix enhances its thermal and mechanical stability. BST glass ceramics typically exhibit high thermal conductivity, low thermal expansion, and excellent resistance to thermal shock, making them suitable for use in high-temperature environments. Additionally, their mechanical robustness ensures durability and longevity, even under cyclic loading and extreme operational conditions.

Energy Storage Capability

BST glass ceramics are recognized for their high energy density and dielectric breakdown strength, making them exceptional candidates for energy storage applications. Their ability to store and release electrical energy efficiently is critical for the development of next-generation supercapacitors and dielectric capacitors. By optimizing the microstructure and composition, researchers have achieved materials with enhanced energy storage capacity and improved charge-discharge efficiency.[48]

Environmental Stability

BST glass ceramics are inherently resistant to environmental factors such as moisture, oxidation, and chemical corrosion. This resistance ensures the reliability of devices utilizing BST materials, even in challenging operational settings such as aerospace and marine environments.

In summary, the properties of BST glass ceramics make them a versatile and indispensable material for modern technology. From their high dielectric constant and ferroelectric behavior to their piezoelectric, pyroelectric, and electro-optic capabilities, BST glass ceramics represent a confluence of advanced material characteristics. Their structural stability, combined with exceptional thermal and mechanical properties, further broadens their range of applications. Continued advancements in synthesis techniques and compositional tuning are expected to unlock new possibilities for BST glass ceramics, paving the way for innovations in electronics, energy, and photonics.

Synthesis Techniques

Conventional Melt-Quenching Method

The synthesis of barium strontium titanate (BST)-borosilicate glass ceramics involves the preparation of a homogenous mixture of the starting materials, followed by melting, quenching, and subsequent heat treatment to form the desired crystalline phases. The melt quench method is a widely used technique for the synthesis of glass ceramics due to its simplicity and the ability to produce materials with tailored properties. In this method, the precursor materials are first melted at high temperatures, then rapidly cooled to obtain a glassy structure. Upon further heat treatment, crystalline phases form

---

[48] A.K., Yadav, C.R. Gautam, P. Singh, RSC Adv., 5 (2015) 2819-2826

within the glass matrix, leading to the formation of glass ceramics with specific dielectric and structural properties. Below is a detailed procedure for synthesizing BST-borosilicate glass ceramics by the melt quench method as indicated in flow chart, see Figure 2.

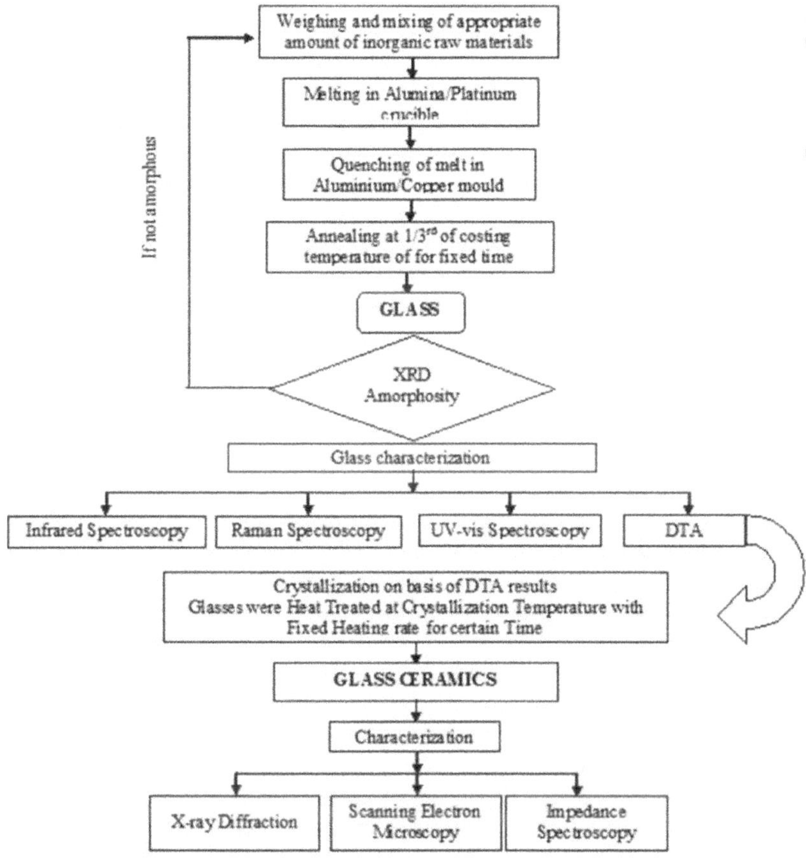

Figure 2: Flow Chart for Synthesis method and characterization of BST glass and glass ceramics [adopted from our published article[49] with permission from Taylor & Francis]

[49]A.K. Yadav, C.R. Gautam, Advances in Applied Ceramics, 113 (2014) 193-207.

Materials

Barium carbonate ($BaCO_3$), Strontium carbonate ($SrCO_3$), Titanium dioxide (TiO_2), Silicon dioxide (SiO_2), Boron oxide (B_2O_3), and Lanthanum oxide (La_2O_3) (optional, to enhance nucleation and growth).

Methodology

1. Preparation of Raw Materials:

- Accurately weigh the starting materials barium carbonate ($BaCO_3$), strontium carbonate ($SrCO_3$), titanium dioxide (TiO_2), silicon dioxide (SiO_2), and boron oxide (B_2O_3). The molar ratio of Ba:Sr: Titanium in the final mixture is typically (1-x):x:1, where x represents the proportion of strontium (usually between 0 and 1).
- A small amount of lanthanum oxide (La_2O_3) may be added to enhance nucleation and growth.

2. Melting:

- The raw materials are mixed thoroughly in a ball mill or mortar to achieve a uniform blend.
- Transfer the mixture into a platinum crucible or a similar high-temperature container.
- Heat the mixture in a furnace to a temperature between 1100°C and 1300°C for 3 to 4 hours to form a homogeneous melt.
- The temperature is selected to ensure complete melting of the raw materials and the formation of a liquid phase.

3. Quenching:

- After the melting process is complete, the molten material is rapidly cooled or quenched by pouring it onto a metal plate or using a water bath. This rapid cooling prevents the crystallization of the components and results in the formation of a glassy structure.

- The resulting glass is typically in the form of a thin, flat sheet or a lump, depending on the pouring method.

4. Heat Treatment (Crystallization):

- To convert the glass into a glass ceramic, the quenched glass is subjected to a heat treatment process. The heat treatment temperature and duration depend on the desired crystalline phases and properties.
- Typically, the glass is heated to a temperature range between **800°C to 1100°C** for 1 to 4 hours. This step allows for the nucleation and growth of the **barium strontium titanate (BST)** phase within the glass matrix.
- The heat treatment temperature must be optimized to encourage the crystallization of **BST** while maintaining the integrity of the glass matrix.

5. Cooling and Final Characterization:

- After the heat treatment, the glass ceramic is allowed to cool slowly at room temperature.
- The final product is a BST-borosilicate glass ceramic, which exhibits the combined properties of both the crystalline and glassy phases, such as enhanced dielectric properties, mechanical strength, and thermal stability.

6. Characterization:

- The synthesized glass ceramics can be characterized using several techniques to evaluate their structure and properties:
- **X-ray Diffraction (XRD)**: To identify the crystalline phases and determine the degree of crystallinity.

- ○ **Scanning Electron Microscopy (SEM)**: To observe the microstructure, including the size and distribution of the crystalline phases.
- ○ **Dielectric and electrical characterization**: To evaluate the electrical properties, such as dielectric constant and loss, as a function of frequency.

The synthesis of barium strontium titanate-borosilicate glass ceramics by the melt quench method allows for the formation of a material that combines the desirable properties of both glasses and ceramics. The BST phase, which is responsible for the dielectric properties, is embedded within the borosilicate glass matrix, resulting in materials with high dielectric constants and low dielectric losses. The borosilicate glass matrix provides good thermal stability and structural integrity.

The key advantages of the melt quench method include its simplicity, the ability to produce materials with controlled composition, and the flexibility to modify the material properties by adjusting the composition and heat treatment conditions. However, challenges include controlling the crystallization process to obtain the desired phase and avoiding the formation of undesirable phases.

Characterizations and Dielectric Properties

X-Ray Diffraction

Figure 3 shows the X-ray diffraction pattern of BST glass (Figure 3a) and BST glass ceramics (Figure 3b-d). The first image indicates the amorphous nature BST glass sample. This glass samples are heat treated then sample become glass ceramics. The XRD patterns at three different temperatures show the different crystal structure of BST glass ceramics. At 0°C temperature, XRD pattern shows the Orthorhombic $Ba_{1.91}Sr_{0.09}TiO_4$ as major crystalline phase and at 50°C, major crystalline phase is tetragonal structure $BaSrTiO_3$ whereas the cubic crystal structure BaSrTiO$_3$ was found at 150°C. The secondary phase of Ba$_2$TiSi$_2$O$_8$ was for each temperature.

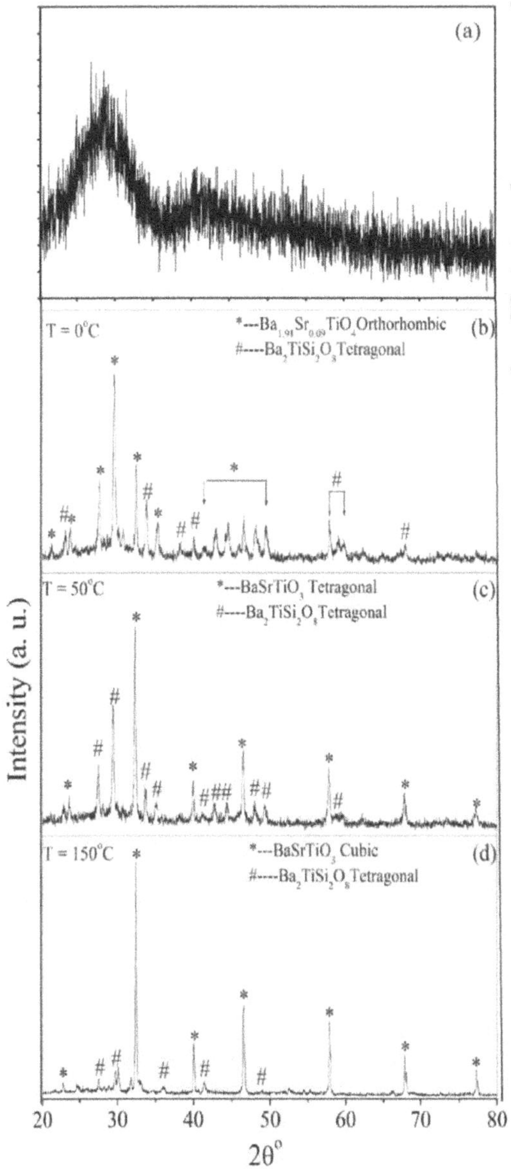

Figure 3: a) X-ray diffraction pattern BST5K1F0.4, and (b-d) BST5K1L0.3S831 at temperatures 0, 50 and 150 °C [adopted with permission from published paper[8,9] in Springer]

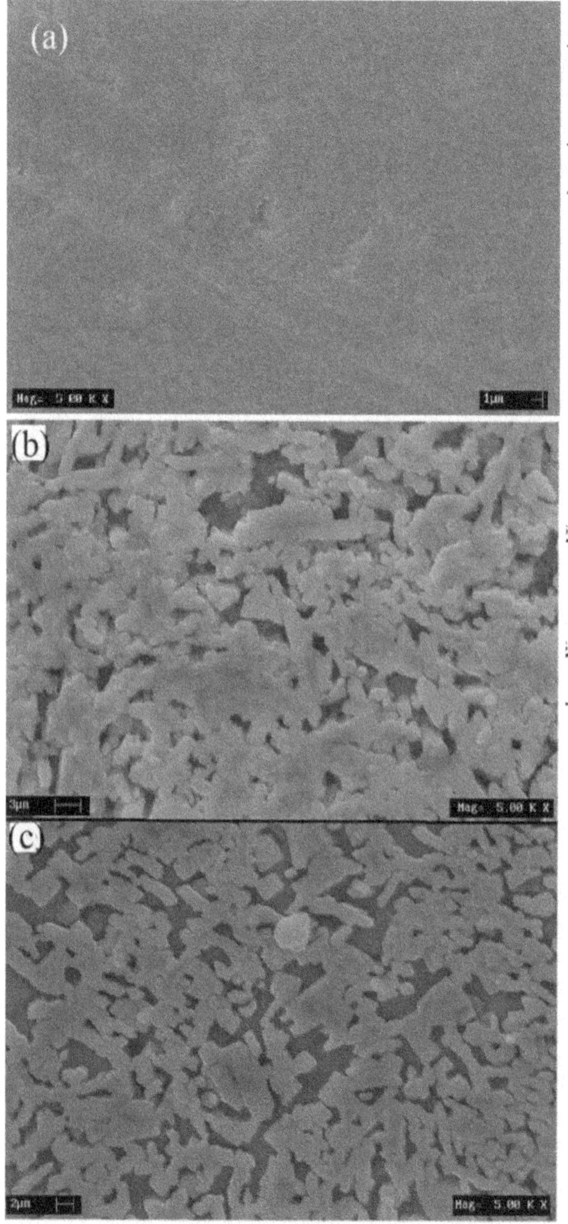

Figure 4: SEM image of glass sample (a) BST5K1F0.4 & glass ceramic samples (b) BST5K1F0.4T844 & (c) BST5K1F0.4S844 [adopted with permission from published paper[9] in RSC].

The presence of $Ba_2TiSi_2O_8$ in all temperatures indicates a secondary, stable crystalline phase. This figure demonstrates the temperature-induced crystallization behavior of BST glass into glass-ceramics. The gradual formation of crystalline phases and phase transitions are clearly visible in the XRD patterns.[50,51]

Microstructural Analysis

Figure 4 (a-c) shows the scanning electron micrographs of BST glass and glass ceramics. First image (a) indicate micrograph of BST Glass. The surface in image (a) appears smooth and uniform with no visible crystalline grains. This indicates the amorphous nature of the BST glass. The absence of grain boundaries or crystalline structures confirms a glassy phase. Image (b) depicts BST Glass-Ceramic sample (BST5K1F0.4T844) heat treated for three hours. This shows the emergence of crystalline grains within the glass matrix. The grains are irregularly shaped and dispersed, suggesting partial crystallization of the amorphous phase. Voids and gaps between grains indicate that crystallites are still growing. The micrograph in image (c) shows BST Glass-Ceramic sample (BST5K1F0.4S844) for heat treated for six hours. This reveals a more developed crystalline structure with larger and well-defined grains. The grains appear more interconnected, showing the progression of crystallization. The overall surface morphology is rougher, with distinct grain boundaries and fewer voids compared to (b). This morphological evolution aligns with the earlier XRD patterns, where increased crystallization with temperature was observed.

Dielectric Behaviour

Figure 5 presents the **dielectric properties** of BST glass-ceramics as a function of temperature and frequency. Specifically, it includes: **(a): Relative permittivity** εr vs. Temperature and **(b): Dielectric loss, Tanδ** vs. Temperature. The relative permittivity increases with

---

[50]*A.K. Yadav, C.R. Gautam, J Mater Sci: Mater Electron 25 (2014) 3532–3536.*
[51] *A.K., Yadav, C.R. Gautam, P. Singh, RSC Adv., 5 (2015) 2819-2826*

increasing temperature across all frequencies (20 Hz to 100 kHz). At lower frequencies (20 Hz, 100 Hz), Relative permittivity is significantly higher compared to higher frequencies (1 kHz, 10 kHz, 100 kHz). Its value shows a steep increase at higher temperatures (above ~100°C), particularly at lower frequencies. At higher frequencies (e.g., 100 kHz), the increase in εr is smaller and more gradual. The higher relative permitivity at low frequencies is due to the presence of space charge polarization and other low-frequency relaxation processes. As temperature increases, the ions in the glass-ceramic matrix become more mobile, enhancing the polarization and resulting in higher permittivity. At higher frequencies, the dipoles cannot align quickly enough with the alternating electric field, leading to lower relative permittivity. The dielectric loss (Tanδ) is plotted as a function of temperature for different frequencies. At low frequencies (20 Hz, 100 Hz), the dielectric loss is higher and increases slightly with temperature. At higher frequencies (10 kHz, 100 kHz), the dielectric loss is relatively low and shows minimal variation with temperature. A slight increase in Tanδ is observed at higher temperatures, especially at low frequencies. Dielectric loss originates from energy dissipation due to ionic migration and dipolar relaxation. At low frequencies, significant losses occur due to the movement of charge carriers and space charge polarization. At high frequencies, the losses are minimal because the charge carriers and dipoles cannot respond to the fast-changing electric field. The dielectric behavior of BST glass-ceramics is highly frequency-dependent and temperature-sensitive. At low frequencies, both relative permittivity and dielectric loss increase significantly with temperature due to the dominance of space charge polarization and ionic conduction. At high frequencies, the dielectric response is more stable with temperature because the polarization mechanisms become limited.

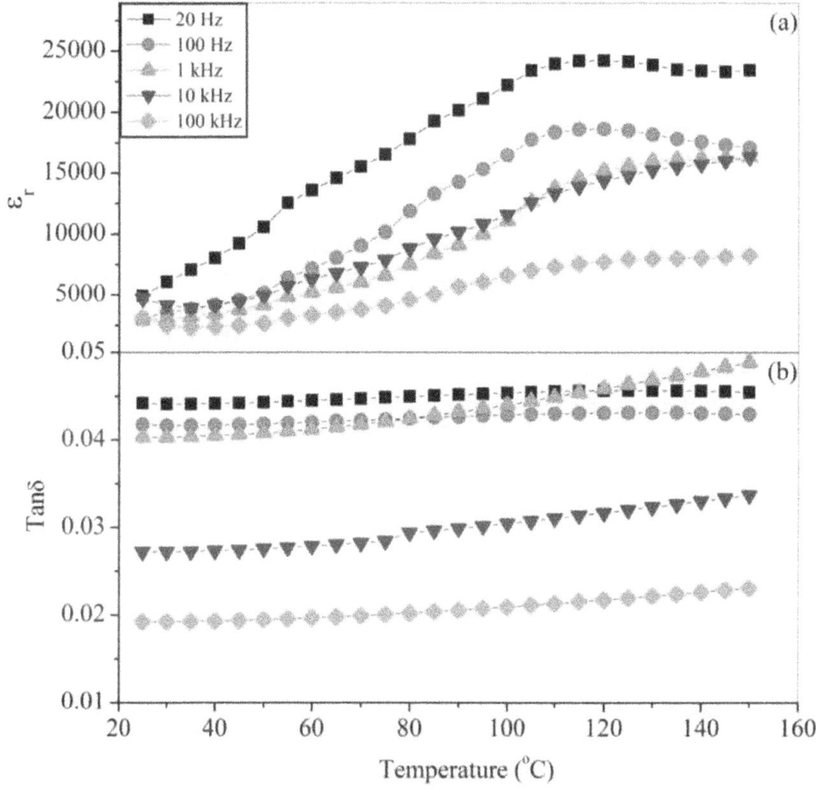

Figure 5: Variation of (a) relative permittivity, ε_r vs temperature and (b) Dielectric loss, tanδ vs temperature [adopted with permission from published paper[52] in RSC].

BST glass ceramics exhibit a high dielectric constant, which is tunable by adjusting the barium-to-strontium ratio. This tunability arises from the structural and compositional characteristics of the perovskite lattice, where the substitution of larger barium ions with smaller strontium ions alters the polarizability of the lattice. The high dielectric constant is primarily due to the displacement of titanium ions within the oxygen octahedra, which creates a strong local polarization. Additionally, the nanocrystalline nature of BST within the glass ceramic matrix enhances dielectric performance by reducing grain boundary scattering and improving charge mobility. These

[52] *A.K., Yadav, C.R. Gautam, P. Singh, RSC Adv., 5 (2015) 2819-2826*

properties make BST glass ceramics ideal for applications in capacitors and tunable microwave devices, where high dielectric responses are critical for efficiency and functionality. In capacitors, dielectric loss refers to the energy dissipation that occurs when the dielectric material inside the capacitor is subjected to an alternating electric field. This dissipation manifests as heat and leads to reduced efficiency. A low dielectric loss material ensures that less energy is lost during each charge/discharge cycle, which is particularly important in applications where high performance and efficiency are required.[53,54,55]

- **Energy Efficiency**: Low dielectric loss results in lower energy waste, making the capacitor more efficient, especially for applications like power supplies and signal processing.
- **High-Frequency Performance**: In high-frequency circuits (e.g., RF or microwave applications), the loss of energy in the dielectric material can significantly affect the signal integrity and overall performance of the system. Materials with low dielectric loss help maintain signal strength and reduce noise or distortion.
- **Longer Lifespan and Reliability**: Capacitors with low dielectric loss have better thermal stability, which prevents excessive heating and premature degradation of the capacitor, enhancing its longevity and reliability.

Microwave devices such as antennas, filters, and transmission lines are often designed to operate at high frequencies. In these devices, low dielectric loss plays a crucial role in maintaining signal quality and ensuring minimal loss of power.

---

[53] A.K. Yadav, C.R. Gautam, P. Singh, J Mater Sci: Mater Electron 26 (2015) 5001–5008.
[54] C.R., Gautam, A.K. Yadav, P. Singh, Materials Research Innovations, 17 (2013) 148–153.
[55] A.K. Yadav, C.R. Gautam, P. Singh, Journal of Alloys and Compounds, 672 (2016) 52-58.

- **Signal Integrity**: For high-frequency microwave signals, any dielectric loss translates to power attenuation, resulting in reduced signal strength. Materials with low dielectric loss preserve the integrity of the microwave signal as it travels through waveguides, resonators, and transmission lines.
- **Higher Quality Factor (Q-factor)**: A low dielectric loss contributes to a higher Q-factor in microwave components. The Q-factor measures the sharpness of the resonance and the efficiency of energy storage in resonators and filters. A higher Q-factor is essential for devices such as filters in communication systems, where the goal is to have precise frequency response without significant energy loss.
- **Reduced Heating**: In microwave circuits, dielectric loss results in heat generation, which can impact the performance of the device. A low loss material reduces this heat buildup, maintaining thermal stability and preventing performance degradation over time.

- **Telecommunications**: In communication systems, especially in microwave frequencies, low dielectric loss ensures high-quality signal transmission with minimal interference, making it vital for the integrity of the signals in cell towers, satellite communications, and Wi-Fi systems.
- **Aerospace and Defence**: In aerospace applications, where reliable and efficient performance at high frequencies is required for radar systems, sensors, and communication devices, low dielectric loss materials ensure the devices perform optimally without significant signal degradation.
- **Medical Equipment**: For medical applications, such as MRI machines, low dielectric loss ensures that electromagnetic waves used in imaging are transmitted efficiently, which directly affects the quality of the diagnostic images produced.

Challenges and Future Directions

Despite their excellent properties, BST glass ceramics face challenges such as:

- High processing temperatures, which may limit their compatibility with certain substrates.
- Fragility of the glass ceramic matrix, which can affect device longevity.
- Optimization of doping and crystallization techniques to balance ferroelectric and dielectric properties.

Future research is likely to focus on:

- Nanostructuring: Enhancing the dielectric and ferroelectric properties through controlled nanostructuring.
- Doping: Exploring new dopants to further tailor properties for specific applications.
- Eco-friendly Synthesis: Developing greener synthesis methods to minimize environmental impact.
- Device Integration: Improving compatibility with flexible and integrated electronic devices.

Conclusion

Barium Strontium Titanate glass ceramics are versatile materials with immense potential in advanced technologies. Through innovative synthesis methods and compositional tuning, researchers continue to push the boundaries of their applications in telecommunications, energy storage, and sensing. Continued advancements in this field promise to unlock even greater possibilities for BST glass ceramics in the years to come.

4. A Journey of Measurement of Linear Attenuation Coefficient

- *Manoj Kumar Gupta*

Department of Physics, S. D. College Barnala, Punjab

Introduction

As the radiation interacts with matter, its intensity will decrease. It is important to know how radiation intensity decreases as it passes through a substance. The degree of attenuation is dependent on the absorber material and the energy of the radiation. For all the absorbing materials, the attenuation of gamma radiations is exponential in character. So many important physical spectroscopic parameters used for measuring the extent of attenuation of gamma ray as it passes through a given absorber are linear attenuation coefficient, mass attenuation coefficient, effective atomic number, intensity ratio, fluorescence yields, jump factor, jump ratio etc.

This chapter contains the literature, related to some commonly used atomic parameters such as, absorption coefficient, linear attenuation coefficient and its dependence of various factors. A review study and brief survey of literature helps to describe the problem formulation for any field of work. So, this chapter includes the maximum literature of related work in the text format in the next section. This chapter also provides the detail information about the importance as well as requirement of preset work.

Theoretical or experimental study of absorption coefficients (or linear/mass attenuation) of various particles like alpha particles, beta particles, X-rays, Gamma rays are used for different types of material medium by various workers from last ten decades, have been discussed here in this chapter. Therefore, the knowledge of some commonly used atomic parameters is the basic need of researchers which plays an imperative role in the measurements of atomic interactions of incident photon with matter.

Linear/Mass attenuation coefficient (μ)/ (μ_m)

Linear attenuation coefficient (μ) values indicate the rate at which photons interact as they move through material and are inversely related to the average distance of photons travel before interacting. The rate at which photons interact (attenuation coefficient value) is determined by the energy of the individual photons and the atomic number and density of the material. The mass attenuation coefficient, μ_m (cm^2/g) of the material can be calculated with a simple relation $\mu_m = \dfrac{\mu}{\rho}$, where ρ is the density of the material in g/cm^3. Mass attenuation coefficient values are actually normalized with respect to material density, and do not change with changes in density but the material density have a direct effect on linear attenuation coefficient values. The total attenuation rate associated with photoelectric and Compton interactions and given as:

μ(total) = μ(photoelectric) + μ(Compton).

Photoelectric interactions occur most commonly when the electron binding energy is slightly less than the photon energy and Compton interactions occur with electrons with relatively low binding energies.

Literature of Attenuation Coefficient

At first, measurements of mass attenuation coefficients were studied by Barka and Sadler (1909)[56], and its related parameters were compiled by Allen (1935)[57]. A major compilation of semi-empirical set of mass attenuation coefficients was provided by Victoreen (1949)[58]. Davisson and Evans (1951)[59] measured the linear attenuation coefficient for elements of Sn, Al, Pb, Ta, and Cu at 0.367-2.76 MeV gamma ray energies using narrow beam transmission geometry. Further, data tables of mass attenuation coefficient, for 24 elements at different photon energies in the region of 102.2 keV to 6.13 MeV were published by Davisson and Evans (1952)[60]. The mass attenuation coefficients for various elements from hydrogen to uranium between given incident photon energy range 0.411-2.62 MeV gamma rays were measured by Colgate (1952)[61]. Further, the mass attenuation coefficients for elements of 4≤Z≤84 at nine edge energies from of 88 keV to 2.75 MeV measured by Conner et al. (1970)[62]. After that, Millar (1975)[63] measured the X-ray attenuation coefficients for the elements in the range 6≤Z≤18 and along with substances of medical importance at incident photon energy range

---

[56] *Barka, C.G. and Sadler, C.A. 1909. The absorption of Rontgen rays. Philos. Mag. 17: 739-760.*

[57] *Allen, S.J.M. 1935. Mean values of the mass attenuation coefficients of the elements. Appendix IX. In: Compton, A. H., Allison, S. K. (Eds.), X-rays in Theory and Experiment. Van Nostrand, New York, p- 799.*

[58] *Victoreen, J.A. 1949. The calculation of X-ray mass absorption coefficients. J. Appl. Phys., 19 : 1141-1147.*

[59] *Davison, C.M. and Evans, R.D. 1951. Measurement of Gamma-ray absorption coefficients. Phys. Rev.81 : 404-411.*

[60] *Davison, C.M. and Evans, R.D. 1952. Gamma-ray absorption coefficients. Rev. Mod. Phys. 24: 79-107.*

[61] *Colgate, S.A. 1952. Gamma ray absorption measurements. Phys. Rev. 87 : 592-601.*

[62] *Conner, A.L., Atwater, H.F., Plassmann, E.H. 1970. Gamma-ray attenuation-coefficient measurements. Phys. Rev. A 1 : 539-544.*

[63] *Millar, R.H. 1975. Experimental X-ray attenuation coefficients at low photons energies for substances of medical importance. Phys. Med. Biol. 20 : 974-979.*

from 4 to 25 keV. Further, Rao et al. (1985)[64] measured experimentally the total attenuation coefficients in some alloys and compounds in the low incident photon energy region of 6.4-22.1 keV. After that, DOS based computer program XCOM was also developed by Berger and Hubbell (1987)[65] for calculating atomic cross sections and attenuation coefficients for any element, compound and mixture. Berger and Hubbell (1995)[66] has been published a compilation for the elements having atomic numbers from 1-92 and for forty-eight additional substances of dosimetry interest from energy range 1 keV to 100 GeV. Khanna et al. (1996)[67] measured the linear and mass attenuation coefficient of some heavy metal (Pb, Bi) oxide borate glasses at 662 keV. Later on, this well-known XCOM program was transformed to the Windows based software by Gerward et al. (2001)[68] and known as WinXCOM. On the other end, Chantler et. al. (2005)[69] also developed a window-based computer program FFAST to determine X-ray Form Factor, Attenuation and Scattering Tables on a window-based computer system.

---

[64] *Rao, K.J., Rao, G.N., Premchand K., Rao, B.V.T., Raju, M.L.N., Parthasaradhi, K. 1985. Total photon attenuation coefficient in alloys and compounds in the energy region 6.4 - 22.1 keV. Int. J. Pure Appl. Phys. 23 : 160-162.*

[65] *Berger M.J. and Hubbell J.H. 1987. XCOM: Photon Cross Sections on a Personal Computer, "NBSIR 87-3597, National Bureau of Standards (former name of NIST), Gaithersburg, MD.*

[66] *Berger M.J. and Hubbell, J.H. (1995) XCOM: photon cross-sections on a personnel computer (version 1.2), NBSIR85-3597, National Bureau of Standarts, Gaithersburg, MD, USA, Available from: <http://physics.nist.gov/>.*

[67] *Khanna A., Bhatti S.S., Singh K.J., Thind K.S. 1996. Gamma ray attenuation coefficients in some heavy metal oxide borate glasses at 662 keV. Nucl. Instr. Meth. B 114 : 217-220.*

[68] *Gerward L., Guilbert, N., Jensen, K.B., Levring, H. 2001. X-ray absorption in matter, reengineering XCom. Radiat. Phys. Chem. 60 : 23-24.*

[69] *Chantler, C.T., Olsen, K., Dragoset, R.A., Chang, J., Kishore, A.R., Kotochigova, S.A., Zucker, D.S. 2005. X-ray Form Factor, Attenuation and Scattering Tables, (version 2.1). [Online] Available:http://physics.nist.gov/ffast, National Institute of Standards and Technology.*

Two Media Method

All measurements relevant to linear and mass attenuation have been performed employing Standard narrow beam transmission geometry, where the target samples were regular shaped having definite thickness. Thus, from the literature it reveals that the measurement of linear/mass attenuation coefficient and its related parameters for various kind sample materials were studied by various researchers. For accurate measurements thickness of the material is required. But some of materials under study are ir-regular (i.e. non uniform) in thickness likely rock, sands, stone, ceramics, building materials, human body organs etc.

Thus, for these types of irregular shaped samples of unknown thickness, this method fails to deliver accurate results. To resolve this discrepancy for the knowledge of thickness, Silva and Appoloni (2000)[70] proposed "Two media Method" for the measurements of linear attenuation coefficient without knowledge of thickness of material and measured gamma ray attenuation coefficient of archaeological ceramic samples using this 'Two Media' method. Further, Elias (2003)[71] proposed theoretical modifications in this 'Two media' method and named as "Simplified Two Media" method by considering air as one of the media. He tries to resolve the concept of limited media combination and reduce the error up to some extent. The "Two Media Method" proposed by Silva and Appoloni (2000)[72]

---

[70] *Silva, R.M.C. and Appoloni, C.R. 2000. Two media method for gamma ray attenuation coefficient measurement of archaeological ceramic samples. Appl. Radiat. Isot. 53 : 1011–1016.*

[71] *Elias, E.A. 2003. Improvements in the two media method for measurements of gamma-ray linear attenuation coefficients. Appl. Radiat. Isot. 59 : 59–61.*

[72] *Silva, R.M.C. and Appoloni, C.R. 2000. Two media method for gamma ray attenuation coefficient measurement of archaeological ceramic samples. Appl. Radiat. Isot. 53 : 1011–1016.*

has been verified experimentally by Singh et al. (2007[73], 2008[74]) for irregular shaped samples by using fly-ash material as five different media in powder form. Further Sidhu et al. (2011)[75] had verified "Simplified Two Media" method experimentally for archaeological samples using air as medium 1 and liquid as a medium 2 in multiple combinations.

From literature, it is clear that the method gives better accuracy with requirement that medium should be homogeneous. Time to time researcher works to improve the accuracy of the method by choosing powder or liquid for better homogeneity of the medium. That's why Sidhu et al. (2011)[76] used liquid as medium instead of powder, to achieve better homogeneity of medium. But, as we know that solid metallic foils with regular shape, uniform thickness can provide much better homogeneity in medium than powder or liquid materials. Thus, 'Two Media Method' get improved by replacing the powder or liquid media with metallic foils and named as "Advanced Two Media" (ATM) Method by Gupta et. al. (2013)[77]. Linear attenuation coefficient of irregular targets having unknown thickness (La, Pr, Nd, Gd, Tb, Ho and Er) and regular targets of known thickness (Mo, Ag, Sn, W and Pb) at 59.54 keV have been measured by using a new technique named Advanced Two Media (ATM) method. Experimental setup of this

---

[73] Singh, S., Kumar, A., Thind, K. S., Mudahar, G. S. 2007. Two media method: An alternative methodology for the measurement of attenuation coefficients of irregular shaped samples. Nucl. Sci. Eng. 159 : 1-8.

[74] Singh, S., Kumar, A., Thind, K.S., Mudahar, G.S., 2008. Measurements of linear attenuation coefficients of irregular shaped samples by two media method. Nucl. Instr. Meth. B 266 : 1116-1121.

[75] Sidhu, B.S., Dhaliwal, A.S., Mann, K.S., Kahlon, K.S., 2011. Simplified two media method: A modified approach for measuring linear attenuation coefficient of odd shaped archaeological samples of unknown thickness. Applied Radiation and Isotopes. 69, 1516–1520.

[76] Sidhu, B.S., Dhaliwal, A.S., Mann, K.S., Kahlon, K.S., 2011. Simplified two media method: A modified approach for measuring linear attenuation coefficient of odd shaped archaeological samples of unknown thickness. Applied Radiation and Isotopes. 69, 1516–1520.

[77] Gupta, M.K., Sidhu, B.S., Dhaliwal, A.S., Kahlon, K.S., Mann, K.S., 2013. Advanced Two Media (ATM) method for measurement of Linear Attenuation Coefficient. Ann. of Nucl. Energy. 56, 251-254.

modified Advanced Two Media method with use of pure metallic foils as a medium 1 and 2 is shown in figure 1.

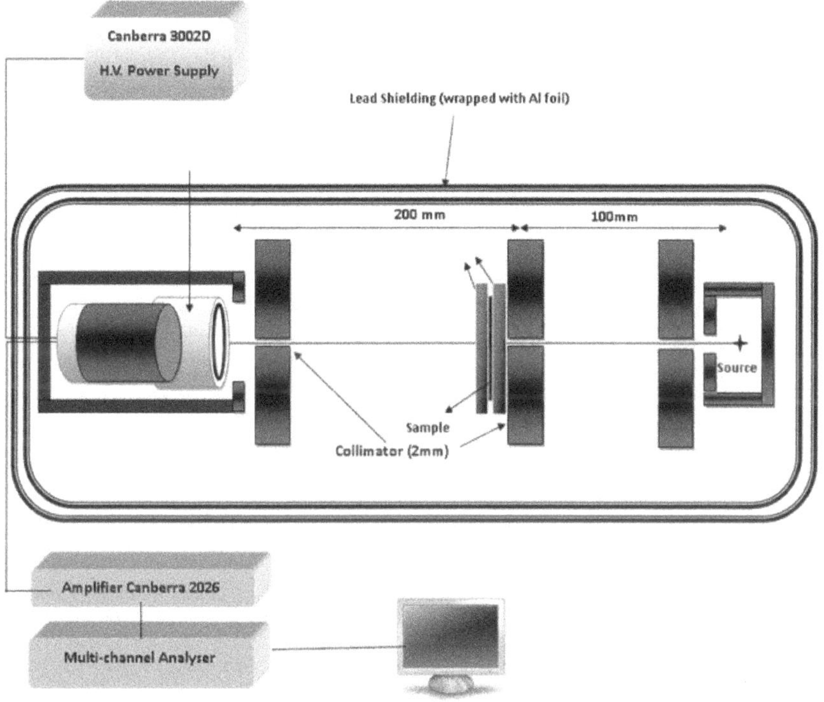

Figure 1: Experimental setup for the measurement of μ with ATM method

Further that, linear and mass attenuation coefficients of irregular shaped oxides of lanthanide (Pr6O11, Nd2O3, Gd2O3, Tb4O7, Ho2O3 and Er2O3) are measured by Singh et al. (2015)[78] using ATM method with gamma ray photons of incident energy 59.54 keV obtained from 241Am 100 mCi source.

---

[78] *Singh, G., Gupta, M.K., Dhaliwal, A.S., Kahlon, K.S., 2015. Measurement of Attenuation coefficient, effective atomic number and electron density of oxides of lanthanides by simplified ATM-method. Journal of Alloys and Compounds. 619, 356-360.*

Measurement Procedure of μ

Experimentally measurement procedure of linear attenuation coefficient of any kind of element or compound has been divided in two segments. At first, the authenticity of advanced two media method has been verified by measuring the linear attenuation coefficients of regular shaped targets (Mo, Ag, Sn, W, Pb). Secondly, the linear attenuation coefficients of irregular shaped targets of elements La, Pr, Nd, Gd, Tb Ho and Er has been measured using the same method.

The procedure adopted for Advanced Two Media (ATM) measurement is described as follows; first by the sample under study has been placed between two Al foils used as medium 1 and transmission beam intensity (I_{ms1}) of gamma rays has been measured through the whole assembly (sample and medium). After that transmission beam intensity (I_{m1}) without sample has been measured. Same procedure has been adopted for measurements of transmission beam intensities (I_{ms2}) and (I_{m2}) for same sample, using Ti foils as medium 2. Linear attenuation coefficient has been obtained for the sample by substituting (I_{ms1}), (I_{m1}), (I_{ms2}), (I_{m2}) in equation

$$\mu = \frac{\mu_2 - \mu_1 \left(Z_2 / Z_1 \right)}{1 - \left(Z_2 / Z_1 \right)} \quad \text{(Where } Z_1 = \ln \frac{I_{ms1}}{I_{m1}} \text{ and } Z_2 = \ln \frac{I_{ms2}}{I_{m2}} \text{)} \qquad (1)$$

To reduce the statistical error and achieve accuracy in results, the experiment was repeated five times for a given sample under study and measured mean of all values can be taken.

Conclusions

From the literature, we found that, there are some of commonly used parameters that play an important role in daily life of human beings. These parameters are used in terms of applications in radiation, nuclear physics with study of interaction of radiation with matter.

Periodically updates in these fields is major subject to work. The concept of requirement of thickness for the sample under study is completely eliminated.

Thus, the equation 1, provides an alternative platform for researchers, with different measurement technique of linear attenuation coefficient. The present measurement fulfils the objective of the measurement of attenuation coefficient by simplified ATM-method adopting a non-destructive technique. As ATM method involves the measurement of linear attenuation coefficient in more accurate way, so obtained values of effective atomic number, electron density and interaction cross-section also show the same level of accuracy. Hence, ATM method act as a tool for various research workers in the same field to work on linear attenuation coefficient of regular and irregular materials.

5. Analysis of various parameters for Polyaniline-Metal Oxide Composite Langmuir-Blodgett Thin Films and their Electrical and Optical Properties

- *Gurpreet Kaur Bhullar*

Physics Department, Mata Gujri College, Fatehgarh Sahib

Introduction

Polyaniline (PANI), a widely researched conducting polymer, exhibits excellent electrical and optical properties, making it a suitable candidate for advanced functional materials. Metal oxides such as zinc oxide (ZnO) and titanium dioxide (TiO_2) are well-known for their wide bandgap, high electron mobility, and optical transparency. Combining PANI with ZnO and TiO_2 yields nanocomposites with enhanced properties due to the synergistic interaction between the polymer matrix and metal oxide nanoparticles.

The Langmuir-Blodgett (LB) technique offers precise control over the molecular arrangement, enabling the formation of uniform and ultrathin films. This chapter discusses the synthesis of PANI-metal oxide nanocomposites using a chemical route, followed by LB deposition for thin film formation. Comprehensive structural, electrical, and optical characterizations are presented to establish the potential of these materials for various applications.

Materials and Methods

Materials and Synthesis of PANI-Metal Oxide Nanocomposites

Polyaniline (PANI) was synthesized by chemical oxidative polymerization of aniline in the presence of ammonium persulfate (APS) as the oxidant and its nano composites were prepared with Metal Oxides: Zinc oxide (ZnO) and titanium dioxide (TiO_2) nanoparticles prepared through chemical route. Solvents used were N-methyl-2-pyrrolidone (NMP), and deionized water. Substrates used for film deposition were quartz, silicon wafers, and indium tin oxide (ITO)-coated glass.

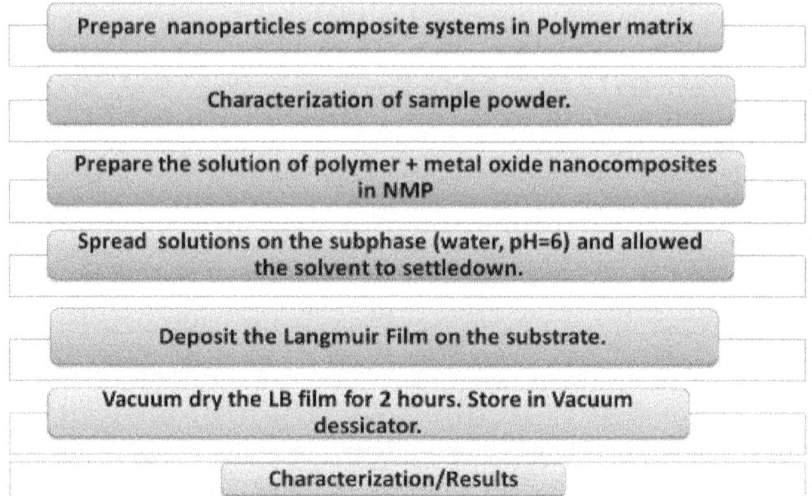

Figure 1. Methodology for preparing polyaniline -metal oxide nanocomposites and their Langmuir films.

Langmuir-Blodgett (LB) Film Formation

The LB technique was used for the deposition of nanocomposite thin films:

1. A dispersion of the PANI-metal oxide nanocomposite was prepared in chloroform.

2. The solution was spread on the water surface in a Langmuir trough to form a monolayer.

3. The monolayer was compressed to a desired surface pressure.

4. The monolayer was transferred onto solid substrates by vertical dipping.

5. The process was repeated to achieve multilayered films.

Parameter Affecting Langmuir Blodgett Films

The formation of Langmuir-Blodgett (LB) thin films is influenced by several key parameters, including the nature of the spread film, subphase composition and temperature, surface pressure during deposition, deposition speed, the type and nature of the solid substrate, and the time the solid substrate is stored in air or in the subphase between deposition cycles. The composition of the subphase, typically water, can be modified with salts, surfactants, or solvents, which affect the molecular interactions and packing density of the monolayer, thereby influencing the final film quality. The temperature of the subphase also plays a significant role; slight elevation promotes better molecular mobility and alignment, while excessive heat may disrupt the monolayer. Surface pressure, which controls the molecular packing density during deposition, is crucial for achieving uniformity and stability in the film. Deposition speed must be carefully controlled to ensure that the monolayer is transferred smoothly and uniformly onto the substrate. The type and nature of the solid substrate, including its material and surface roughness, significantly affect the adhesion and uniformity of the monolayer, requiring appropriate surface treatments for effective molecular adsorption. Additionally, the time the substrate is exposed to air or submerged in the subphase between deposition cycles can influence film quality. Prolonged exposure to air may lead to contamination, while extended submersion in the subphase can impact the molecular organization and transfer efficiency. By carefully optimizing these parameters, high-quality Langmuir-

Blodgett films with consistent and desirable properties can be reliably produced for various applications.[79]

Optimization of Parameters for growing Langmuir-Blodgett Films

Optimizing physical parameters for growing Langmuir-Blodgett (LB) films is crucial for obtaining high-quality, reproducible films with desirable properties. The Langmuir-Blodgett technique involves the deposition of a monolayer (or multilayer) of molecules at an air-water interface, followed by transfer onto a solid substrate, usually under controlled conditions. The optimization of these parameters requires careful consideration of various factors, including the chemical composition of the molecules, surface pressure, temperature, deposition speed, and substrate characteristics. Overview of the key physical parameters involved in optimizing Langmuir-Blodgett film growth:

Substrate Characteristics

The choice of substrate material, such as glass, gold, silicon wafers, or mica, affects the film's properties. Substrates should have a clean, smooth surface to ensure uniform deposition. Proper surface treatment, such as cleaning with organic solvents or oxygen plasma, is necessary to remove contaminants and improve molecular adsorption. Substrate temperature also plays a role, with lower temperatures helping prevent molecular desorption during deposition. However, excessive cooling can hinder film formation.

Surface Pressure (π)

Surface pressure, measured in dynes/cm, is crucial for optimal monolayer formation. The surface pressure is controlled via a Langmuir trough and must be optimized to balance molecular packing and stability. Compression of the monolayer at a constant or stepwise rate adjusts the packing density of molecules. Too high a pressure can lead to molecular deformation, while too low results in loosely packed

---

[79] R. Kaur, G.K. Bhullar, N.V.S. Rao, K.K. Raina, *Effect of pH on the control of molecular orientation in monolayer of bent-core liquid crystal materials by Langmuir Blodgett method, Liq. Cryst. 42 (1) (2014) 8–17.*

films. Surface pressure vs. molecular area isotherms provide insight into phase transitions, helping to identify the ideal pressure for deposition.

Deposition Parameters

The deposition speed, typically measured in mm/min, affects the homogeneity and smoothness of the LB film. A controlled, uniform speed is essential for high-quality films. Langmuir-Blodgett films can be deposited as a single monolayer or multiple layers, with the number of layers controlled to achieve the desired film thickness. The transfer ratio, which measures the efficiency of transferring the monolayer from the water surface to the substrate, is also crucial. A high transfer ratio ensures effective monolayer transfer with minimal distortion.

Temperature and Humidity

The water temperature of the subphase influences surface tension and molecular packing behavior. Slightly elevated temperatures can promote better molecular mobility and alignment at the interface, though excessive heat can disrupt the monolayer or lead to evaporation. Environmental conditions, such as humidity, also affect the film structure, particularly for hydrophilic molecules. Maintaining controlled humidity ensures stable deposition conditions and prevents the film from being affected by changes in moisture.

Molecular Properties

The molecular structure is vital in monolayer formation, with amphiphilic molecules having both hydrophilic (polar) and hydrophobic (non-polar) regions that self-assemble at the air-water interface. Commonly used molecules include fatty acids, phospholipids, and surfactants. Molecular size, shape, and rigidity also influence packing density and film quality, with compact, tightly packed structures leading to better films. Surface-active agents (surfactants) are selected based on their ability to lower the surface tension of water, and surfactants with low critical micelle concentration (CMC) are ideal for stable monolayers.

Subphase Composition

The subphase, usually water, can be modified with salts, surfactants, or solvents to enhance molecular interactions and improve film formation. The ionic strength of the subphase influences electrostatic interactions between molecules, affecting pacing densities and film characteristics. Additionally, the pH of the subphase can influence the ionization state of molecules, especially for acidic or basic surfactants, making pH adjustments important for optimizing molecular interactions at the interface.

Surface pressure-area isotherms of Langmuir-Blodgett (LB) films

Surface pressure-area isotherms of Langmuir-Blodgett (LB) films provide critical insights into the molecular organization of monolayers at the air-water interface. These isotherms are obtained by compressing the monolayer using barriers at a fixed temperature, revealing several distinct phases of molecular behavior. Initially, in the gaseous 2D phase, the molecules are sparsely distributed with minimal intermolecular interactions, resulting in low surface pressure. As compression increases, the monolayer enters the expanded 2D phase, where the molecules are more closely packed, but still maintain some disorder, and surface pressure rises accordingly. With further compression, the monolayer reaches the condensed 2D phase, where the molecules are tightly packed, highly ordered, and exhibit increased surface pressure. Finally, the compression reaches the collapse point, where the monolayer can no longer sustain further compression, causing the molecular structure to collapse or deform. These phases, depicted in the surface pressure vs. area plot, are essential for understanding the behavior of LB films and optimizing the conditions for producing well-ordered, high-quality films with desired properties.[80]

---

[80] *R. Kaur, G.K. Bhullar, K.K. Raina, Effects of silver nanoparticles doping on morphology and luminescence behavior of ferroelectric liquid crystals Langmuir–Blodgett films, Liq. Cryst. 43 (12) (2016) 1760–1767.*

Characterization Techniques

Fourier Transform Infrared (FTIR) Spectroscopy

FTIR was used to identify functional groups and molecular interactions. Characteristic peaks for PANI (C–N stretching, C=C aromatic ring vibrations) and metal oxides (M–O bonds) were analyzed to confirm composite formation.

UV-Visible Spectroscopy

UV-Visible Spectroscopy was used to study the optical properties and bandgap of the films. Shifts in absorption edges indicated strong interactions between PANI and metal oxides.

X-ray Diffraction (XRD)

XRD was analyzed the crystalline structure of the nanocomposites. Diffraction peaks for ZnO and TiO_2 confirmed their incorporation in the PANI matrix.

Photoluminescence (PL) Spectroscopy

Studied the emission properties of the films by using PL. Quenching or enhancement of photoluminescence provided insights into charge transfer between PANI and the metal oxides.

Atomic Force Microscopy (AFM)

AFM was used to analyze surface topography and roughness of films. To show whether film formation with nanostructured features is uniform.

Conductive AFM

Investigated local electrical properties of the films using CAFM. Correlated nanoscale conductivity with the distribution of metal oxide nanoparticles in the PANI matrix.

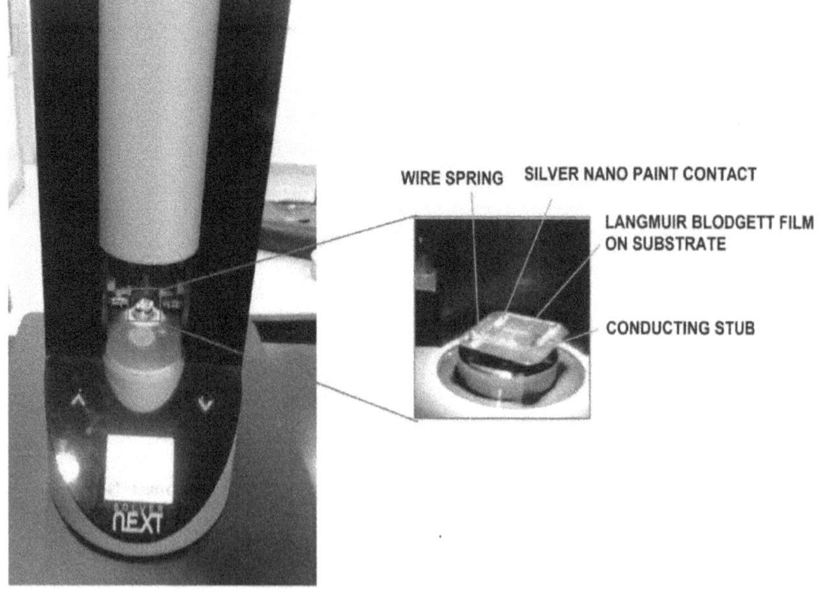

Figure 2. Sample holder view of Atomic Force Microscope for Conductivity measurements/imaging.

Results and Discussion

Structural Analysis (FTIR and XRD)

FTIR spectra showed characteristic peaks for PANI and metal oxides, confirming composite formation.

XRD patterns revealed peaks corresponding to ZnO, TiO_2, and PANI, indicating successful integration of the components.

Optical Properties (UV-Vis and PL)

UV-Vis analysis indicated a reduction in bandgap due to the interaction between PANI and metal oxides.[81] PL studies showed reduced emission intensity, suggesting effective charge transfer between PANI and the metal oxide nanoparticles. The hybrid films exhibited unique properties due to the interaction between PANI and TiO_2 nanoparticles, which enhanced their electrical and optical characteristics.

The combination of PANI and TiO_2 led to synergistic effects, improving the photocatalytic behavior of the films compared to the individual components.

Surface Morphology and Conductivity (AFM and Conductive AFM)

AFM images revealed smooth and uniform films with nanoscale features. The films showed good stability, uniformity, and high-quality surface morphology, making them suitable for various technological applications. Conductive AFM confirmed enhanced conductivity in regions with high metal oxide concentrations.

Applications

The enhanced electrical and optical properties of PANI-metal oxide composite films make them suitable for:

1. Optoelectronic Devices: Solar cells, light-emitting diodes.

2. Sensors: High sensitivity gas and chemical sensors.

3. Energy Storage: Supercapacitors and batteries.

---

[81] G.K. Bhullar, R. Kaur, K.K. Raina, *Electrical characterization of Polyaniline-ZnO nano-composite Langmuir-Blodgett thin films by conductive atomic force microscopy, Mater. Res. Soc. Symp. 1668 (2014) 834–835.*

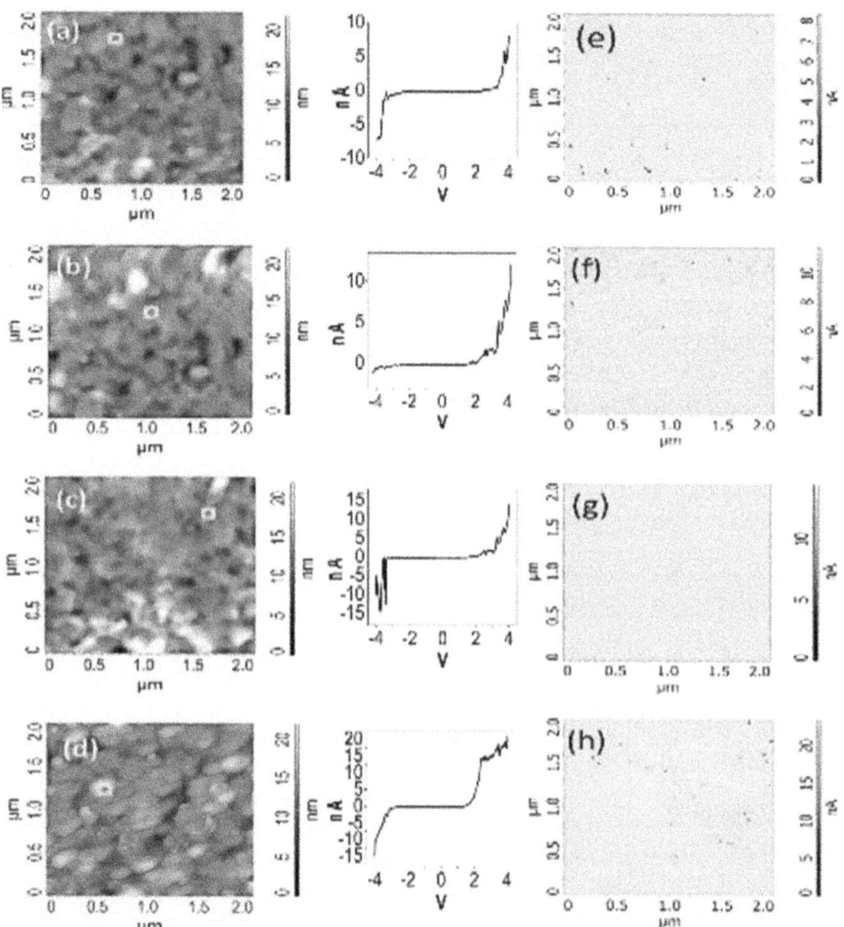

Figure. 3 AFM surface topography images in contact mode 2 × 2 µm2 (a) 5 wt%, (b) 10 wt%, (c) 15 wt%, (d) 20 wt% of TiO2 in PANi; and Single-point electrical I–V characteristics corresponding to the positions (squares) marked on images (a-d). Conductive data images, obtained with an applied bias voltage of 4 V for (e) 5 wt%, (f) 10 wt%, (g) 15 wt% and (h) 20 wt% of TiO2 in PANi on the ITO substrates recorded simultaneously with surface topography images (a-d).[82]

[82] *Gurpreet Kaur Bhullar, Ramneek Kaur, K.K. Raina, Enhanced luminescence and electrical conductivity of polymer ultrathin films doped with TiO2 nanoparticles Thin Solid Films 782 (2023) 140023*

Future Scope

PANI-metal oxide (ZnO, TiO$_2$) nanocomposite thin films prepared via the Langmuir-Blodgett technique exhibit excellent electrical and optical properties. The chemical synthesis route ensures uniform nanocomposite formation, while the LB technique facilitates the creation of highly ordered films. These materials hold significant potential for next-generation electronic and optoelectronic applications.

- Monolayers of polymer-nano-composite molecules can be examined at various pH values of the subphase and at various temperatures. As PANI exhibits both the electronic and ionic conductivity, the variation in subpahse pH levels may lead to variation in conductivity due to change in oxidation state. Hence, by monitoring changes in temperature along with pH can provides new innovations in electrtonic technology.

- Realization of electronic elements like diode based on organic–inorganic hybrid nano-composite LB films is possible as the local I-V characteristics resembles the diode characteristics. The growth of organized monolayers by the LB technique has led the research toward the goal of assembling singular molecules into highly ordered architectures.

6. DFT Study for the Substantial Properties of the Small ZnS and ZnSe Nanoclusters

- *Dheeraj Kumar Pandey*

Department of Physics, Ramashray Baleshwar College, Dalsingsarai

Nanoscience and Nanotechnology

In nanoscience, one deals with small structures or small-sized materials. The study on fundamental relationships between the physical properties and different types of phenomena of production and the determination of material's dimensions on the nanometer scale are also referred to as nanoscience. The nanoscience has a typical dimension span, which lies between subnanometers to several hundred nanometers. A nanometer is one billionth of a meter (i.e. 10^{-9} m). Micrometer-scaled materials mostly possess physical properties the same as that of bulk form, however, nanometer-scaled materials may have physical properties distinctively different from that of bulk. Thus, materials in this size range exhibit their unique physical properties.

Generally, Nanotechnology is the designing, fabrication, and applications of nanostructures and nanomaterials. It also includes the fundamental understanding of the physical properties and phenomena of production of nanomaterials and nanostructures.

Nanomaterials and Nanostructures

Nanostructures constitute a bridge between molecules and bulk systems. In general, nanostructures are considered to be a number of atoms or molecules bonded together within a radius less than hundred nanometer. Nanostructures can be modulated over nanometer length scales in zero to two dimensions. Thus, nanostructured materials are those with at least one dimension falling in nanometer scale. They can be divided into zero dimensional (Nanoclusters), one-dimensional (Nanowires and nanotubes) and two-dimensional (Thin films) based on their shapes.

A nanocluster is a non-periodic three-dimensional structure and is an intermediate state of matter between molecule and bulk, whose electronic and other properties may be exotic. The small nanocluster is analogous to a molecule and it has discrete energy levels. However, about the small sized nanoclusters the two fundamental facts are attributable instead of that their physical properties are very different from those of the bulk material. The first fact is that the excitons are confined in a dimension to the order of the nanocluster size resulting in a compression of the bulk exciton and a corresponding blue shift in the first excited state with decreasing size. This property is known as the quantum confinement effect. According to the technological point of view, the quantum confinement effect has created a great interest due to the unique ability to tune the optical properties by changing particle size. The second important fact of these quantum-confined nanoclusters is that the surface to volume ratio is much greater than that of the bulk and thus the nature of the surface influences more on the physical properties of these nanoclusters.

The procedures of the production of nanostructures underlying nanoscience and nanotechnology have two different approaches: one is the bottom-up approach, in other words, the miniaturization of the bulk material as articulated by Feynman[83] and the other is the

---

[83] *R. P. Feynman, Eng. Sci.,* **23** *(1960).*

approach of the self-assembly of atomic or molecular components to produce nanostructures. There are many other ways for fabrication and processing techniques such as top-down and bottom-up approaches, spontaneous and forced processes. Nanoclusters have been attracting a great deal of research interest due to their unique properties, characteristics of neither the molecular nor bulk and thus have potential to revolutionize the broad area of nanotechnology. The physical and chemical properties of nanoclusters can differ significantly from those of the bulk materials of the same composition. The uniqueness of the structural, characteristics, energetics and chemistry of nanostructures constitutes the basis of nanoscience. A nanocluster of a suitable properties and structure can be used in the fabrication of Nano-electromechanical systems (NEMS) and Micro-electromechanical systems (MEMS).

II–VI Semconducting Compounds

Among II-VI semiconducting compounds, Zinc Sulfide (ZnS) and Zinc Selenide (ZnSe) are well-known direct band gap semiconductors and promising multi-functional materials for fabricating photonic, optical and electronic devices[84][85][86][87][88]. These semiconductors have nearly similar fundamental physical properties. Due to their wide band gaps of 3.65 eV for ZnS and 2.80 eV for ZnSe at room temperature, these materials and their compound or composite structures are unique candidates for ultraviolet (UV) light lasers and detectors working in the 320- to 400-nm wavelength range[89][90][91].

---

[84] *R. H. Mauch, Appl. Surf. Sci. 92, 589 (1996).*

[85] *M. J. Leskela, J. Alloys. Compd. 275, 702 (1998).*

[86] *I. C. Ndukwe, Solar Energy Mater. Solar Cells 40, 123 (1996).*

[87] *A. Burnin, J. J. BelBruno, Chem. Phys. Lett. 362, 341 (2002).*

[88] *A. P. Alivisatos, J. Phys. Chem. 100, 13226 (1996).*

[89] *S. Hamad, C. R. A. Catlow, E. Spano, J. M. Matxain, J. M. Ugalde, J. Phys. Chem. B 109, 2703 (2005).*

[90] *S. H. Tolbert and A. P. Alivisatos, Annu. Rev. Phys. Chem. 46, 595 (1995).*

[91] *X. Wang, H. Xu, H. Liu, Z. A. Schelly, S. Wu, Nanotechnology 18,155604.1 (2007).*

Theoretical Work

It is quite obvious that the rapid development of Nanoscience and Nanotechnology will not be possible unless it is supported by a strong background of theoretical study in the same area. We may have a promising class of new but unknown materials. As an example, the Nanocomposites may have entirely new properties different from the properties of the individual compounds. These efforts have been intensified by the recent success in understanding the physics and the applications of quantum-confined two-dimensional electron gas structures.

Theoretical investigation of Nanostructures is of crucial importance since it allows one to both investigate fundamental physics and to optimize nanostructured devices. The advantage of theoretical studies is that the system is well-defined and that substantial properties beyond experimentally available can also be examined. Designing new materials and exploring the interesting electronic, optical, vibrational, magnetic, and other properties of existing materials at low dimensions are always challenging for researchers.

Theoretical Techniques

We have obtained the most stable nanoclusters of very small sizes up to five atoms of ZnS (n) and ZnSe (p), respectively. We have also predicted their substantial properties (like structural and electronic properties) and their variation with the size of the nanocluster (n/p). These established most stable Nanoclusters can have possible applications in the fabrication and design of Nondevices. There are several methods for calculating a wide range of physical properties of materials. In these methods, one requires only a specification of the ions present (by their atomic number) are usually referred to as ab-initio methods. No experimental data is employed in ab-initio methods. Among the different methods, one, the total–energy pseudopotential method stands alone. This method can model hundred-atom systems and can open up a wide range of interesting problems to quantum-mechanical calculations.

The linear combination of atomic orbitals (LCAO) is complicated when used as a first-principles method because when it is parameterized, one needs too many parameters for it and also the wave functions may be ill - defined. The LCAO methods, employing Gaussian orbitals, are seen to have some computational advantages but they need at least twice as many basis functions as the KKR method. The KKR and the linear augmented plane wave (LAPW) methods have proven highly accurate for Fermi surface calculations but they are numerically unwieldy and lack transparency. The linear muffin tin orbital (LMTO) method need less computation time, but suffer with the disadvantage that the forces on the atoms are not easily calculated correctly necessary for structural optimization.

Presently, the most widely used formulation for the simulation of electronic structure of the solids and molecules is the density functional theory (DFT). In the DFT, one can calculate the energy of a system of interacting electrons in terms of a set of single electron equations. The accuracies of DFT calculation and those of more computationally demanding quantum calculations are comparable. The density is determined from the electronic wave function which depends on 3N variable for a N electron system on the other hand, the charge density is a function of only 3 (4) variables. The DFT has its advantage because the ground state properties of a system can be obtained by the ground state density, which for a given number of electrons is a unique function of the potential.

All the geometrical structures are fully optimized employing the hybrid gradient-corrected functional (B3LYP)[92][93][94] within density

---

[92] A. D. Becke, *J. Chem. Phys.* **98,** 5648 (1993).

[93] A. D. Becke, *Phys. Rev. A* **38,** 3098 (1988).

[94] C. Lee, W. Yang and R. G. Parr, *Phys. Rev. B* **371,** 785 (1988).

functional theory framework[95] in the Gaussian-03 code[96]. The harmonic vibrational frequencies for each optimized structures are determined by analytical differentiation of gradients. The polarizable triple split valance basis set, 6-311G(3df) is used as the basic basis set in this study for the most precise calculation after selecting a large number basis set for each atom. The main advantage of this split valance basis set in comparison to others is that the orbital is allowed to change its size without making any change in its shape. The three d electrons and one f electrons of Zn and Se atoms are taken with the valence electrons as a polarized function due to their importance for the description of the ground state of each atom in three dimensions.

Zinc Sulfide And Zinc Selenide Nanoclusters

In the series of II-VI compounds, the Zinc Sulfide and Zinc Selenide, which possess bulk wide band gap have drawn great attention for their application in the fabrication of optoelectronic devices such as blue or UV light emitting diodes, emissive flat screens, laser diodes and n-window layers in solar cell technology. Different types of structures including the linear chains, rings, planer and three-dimensional ones have been investigated. Minimum energy for each structure is achieved by relaxing the atomic positions[97,98,99,100,101]. The convergence in the system energy upto 10^{-7} meV and the forces of 10^{-3} eV/Å on each atom were achieved. In order to have stability of nanocluster, we define the binding energy of the nanocluster. We

---

[95] B. Miehlich, A. Savin, H. Stoll and H. Preuss, Chem. Phys. Lett. **157,** 2000, (1989).

[96] Gaussian Inc. GAUSSIAN 03, Revision C.03 **(Pittsburgh, PA: Gaussian) (2003).**

[97] P. S. Yadav, D. K. Pandey, S. Agrawal and B. K. Agrawal, J. Nanopart. Res., **12,** 737 (2010).

[98] P. S. Yadav and D. K. Pandey, Adv. Sci. Eng. Med., **3,** 230 (2011).

[99] P. S. Yadav and D. K. Pandey, Applied Nanosci., **2,** 351 (2012).

[100] D. K. Pandey, P. S. Yadav, S. Agrawal and B. K. Agrawal, Adv. Mat. Res., **650,** 29 (2013).

[101] D. K. Pandey and P. S. Yadav, Adv. Sci. Eng. Med., **12(7),** 930 (2020).

subtract the total energy of a nanocluster from the sum of the energies of all the isolated atoms present in the nanocluster and divide the resultant quantity by the number of atoms. We name this as the binding energy (BE) per atom. For a more precise calculation, we have calculated the harmonic vibrational frequencies and the corresponding zero-point energy (ZPE) has been subtracted from the earlier calculated BE value to obtain the final binding energy (FBE) = BE - ZPE. Among all the complexes pertaining to a specific chemical formula (isomers) ZnS and ZnSe the configuration possessing the maximum value of BE is named as the most stable structure.

We discuss here all the possible 46 optimized structures for ZnS and 41 optimized structures for ZnSe. For the isolated two atoms S_2, ZnS and Zn_2 nanoclusters, the bond lengths are 1.90, 2.11 and 2.29 Å, respectively. The calculated value 1.90 Å of S – S bond length is in excellent agreement with the experimental value of 1.89 Å [102]. One may expect the minimum energies for those complexes which contain the maximum number of the S – S bonds followed by Zn – S and Zn – Zn bonds. The computed Se – Se, Zn – Se and Zn – Zn bond lengths are 2.18, 2.22 and 2.28 Å, respectively. The calculated value of Se – Se bond length is very close to the experimental value[103] of 2.15 Å, while that of Zn – Zn bond length is smaller than the experimental value[104] of 2.67 Å.

The variation of FBE with the nanocluster size (n/p) for the most stable ZnS and ZnSe nanoclusters is shown in the figure. We observe that the nanoclusters containing large number of S atoms for each 'n' is most stable in comparison with other nanoclusters of the same configuration. A perusal of Fig. 1 also reveals that the FBE of most stable nanoclusters with large number of S atoms also increases with

---

[102] B. Miehlich, A. Savin, H. Stoll and H. Preuss, *Chem. Phys. Lett.* **157**, 2000, (1989).

[103] R. C. Weast, D. R. Lide, M. J. Astle and W. H. Beyer, *CRC Handbook of Chemistry and Physics, 70th ed., Chemical Rubber, Boca Raton, 1990.*

[104] R. C. Weast, D. R. Lide, M. J. Astle and W. H. Beyer, *CRC Handbook of Chemistry and Physics, 70th ed., Chemical Rubber, Boca Raton, 1990.*

the nanocluster size (n). No experimental data is available for comparison.

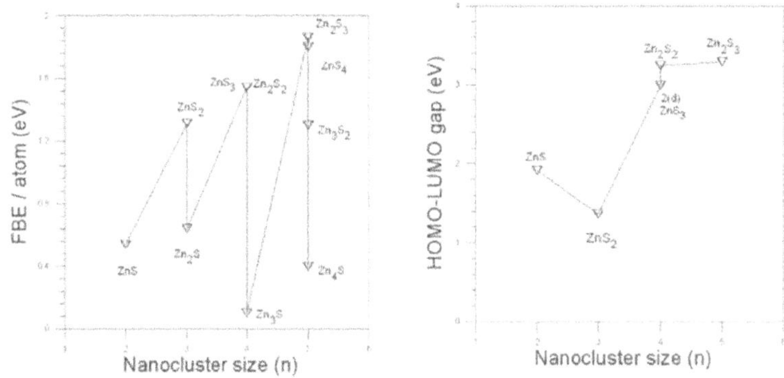

Fig. 1. Variation of FBE/atom and HOMO-LUMO gap with the nanocluster size (n) of ZnS nanoclusters.

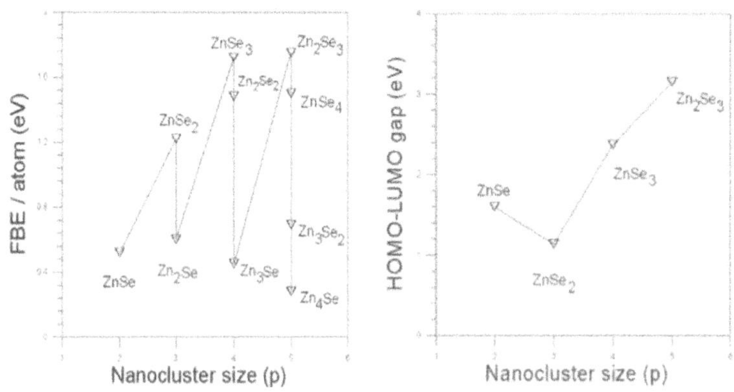

Fig. 2. Variation of FBE/atom and HOMO-LUMO gap with the nanocluster size (p) of ZnSe nanoclusters.

The variation of computed HOMO-LUMO gaps of ZnS and ZnSe nanoclusters with the nanocluster size (n/p) for the most stable configurations are also shown in the above Figs. The HOMO-LUMO gap first decreases up to n = 3 and then increases for n > 3 with nanocluster size of ZnS nanoclusters. While, for ZnSe nanoclusters, the HOMO-LUMO gap first decreases up to p = 3 and then increases for p > 3 with the size of nanocluster (p). The observed trend of the enhancement of the HOMO-LUMO gap with a decrease in the size of the nanocluster conforms with the quantum-confined behavior.

7. Unveiling Stellar Patterns: Photometric Insights into Galactic open cluster

-   *Apara Tripathi*

Department of Physics, Deen Dayal Upadhyaya Gorakhpur University

Introduction

Stars are fundamental units "atoms" of the universe and source of astronomical information. They serve as primary tracers of the structure and evolution of the universe and its contents ([105]Lada & Lada, 2003). Ancient sky watchers imagined them as prominent arrangements of stars which form patterns and called them "constellations". Ancient societies observed more, and integrated their knowledge of the heavens into their culture and mythology. The distribution of the stars in the sky was observed by a band of light spread across the night sky, i.e, the Milky Way. The dark patches of loosely connected stars and obscuration along the band of Milky Way had also been noted, and were given names according to their culture and mythology; the Pleiades in Taurus, Praesepe in Cancer and the Hyades in Taurus. The adventure of telescope made possible to resolve these mystery patches. Galileo Galilei (1564-1642) was the first to observe open clusters through a telescope. He believed that every nebulae in the sky could be resolved into individual stars. In his

---

[105] *Lada C. J. & Lada E. A. 2003, ARA&A, 41, 57*

words, **"the galaxy is nothing else but a mass of innumerable stars planted together in clusters"**.

Star clusters, in general, serve as the "laboratories" where all the stars are situated at nearly the same distance and all are created at almost the same time and move together ([106]Friel, 1995). Each cluster thus is a running experiment, where we can study the effects of composition, age, and environment. We are hobbled by seeing only a snapshot in time of each cluster, but taken collectively, we can understand the star formation process as well as their evolution. These clusters are found in all the three components, i.e halo, disk and bulge of our Galaxy. They are classified into two main types, namely globular clusters and galactic or open clusters. Open clusters and globular clusters, each with their own unique characteristics, are the keys in unlocking a deeper understanding of the universe.

Globular clusters are aggregates of approximately 10^4 – 10^6 gravitationally bound stars, highly concentrated to the center, spread over a volume ranging from a few tens to more than 300 light years in diameter. Only Hubble Space Telescope allowed astronomers to dig into the very central regions of many Galactic globular clusters. They constitute fossil tracers of the dynamical and chemical evolution of the parent Galaxy. Globular clusters represent the oldest generation of stars in the Milky Way.

Open clusters (OCs) stand out from their globular counterparts by generally younger and richer in elements heavier than hydrogen and helium (metals). They are typically found residing near the flat plane of our galaxy. Open clusters cover a broad spectrum in size and luminosity, ranging from groupings with few tens members with integrated magnitudes of M_v = -3 mag up to systems of many thousands of stars with integrated magnitudes as high as M_v = -9 mag (cf. [107]Sagar et al. 1983; [108]Pandey et al. 1989). Open clusters are not

---

[106] *Friel, E. D. 1995, ARA&A, 33, 381*
[107] *Sagar, R., Joshi, U. C., & Sinvhal, S. D. 1983, BASI, 11, 44*
[108] *Pandey, A. K., Bhatt, B. C., Mahra, H. S., & Sagar, R. 1989, MNRAS, 236, 263*

tightly bound as their density is 0.1-10 stars/pc3, only few open clusters therefore survive to old age; oldest clusters identified are of 10 Giga years (e.g. NGC 6791 and Be 17; Salaris et al. 2004[109]). OCs are moderately denser than the surrounding field and these groups are obvious against the general background (or foreground) of stars. Open clusters are families of usually several hundred to a few thousand member stars having roughly the same age, located within a diameter of 1 to 20 pc across. Young clusters are often associated with interstellar cloud and they usually contain bright main sequence stars, blue super-giants, and sometimes a few variable, either young Capheids or even younger pre-main sequence (PMS) T Tauri type stars. The open clusters have a wide spectrum of age, ranging from a few Myr to the age of Galaxy (a few times 10^9 year). As the spiral arms constitute major part of present-day star formation, the very young star clusters are generally found in these regions. [110]Becker (1963) pointed out the appearance of spiral structure in NGC 1232 ([111]Lynga 1980). Since then, many attempts have been made to get a better picture of the Galactic spiral arms by adding more information about young clusters.

The strong interest for the open clusters results from the unique fact that the stars in a cluster are at the same distance from the Sun, (the depth effects is negligible for open clusters at distances larger than 300 pc) and they have the same age. Open clusters have wide spectrum of mass, they offer many opportunities of investigating the dependence of astrophysical phenomena on the stellar masses or on ages. Open clusters are the ideal tools for many present-day astrophysical problems, but before taking the advantage of their diagnostic power several problems have to be solved e.g. attenuation of light by interstellar matter and field star contamination. Knowledge of basic parameters such as interstellar extinction (reddening), the distance, the age are essential.

---

[109]Salaris, M., Riello, M., Cassisi, S., & Piotto, G. 2004, A&A, **420**, 911
[110]Becker, W.: 1963, ZAp 57, 117
[111] Lynga, G.: 1980, in Star Clusters, eds. Hesser, J. E., Vol. of IAU Symposium, . 13

Several observations and theoretical attempts have been made to study star formation process, mass function and structure of open star clusters. However, various fundamental questions are still open. The primary aim of a general investigation of star formation is to obtain reliable measurements of the distribution of forming objects in mass, age, and spatial structure. A simultaneous aim of the investigation is to constrain the models used in determining these physical parameters. Further objective may include details of the time evolution of these properties and their dependence on other parameters. This chapter presents description of methodology used to determine the clusters basic parameters. We discuss the structural parameters of clusters.

Studying the stars within open clusters using techniques like astrometry and photometry allows us to determine properties that are challenging to measure in individual stars [112]Dias et al. (2021). This is a major reason why these stellar groupings are of such great scientific interest. This analysis is critical for piecing together the puzzle of star formation, evolution, and overall be havior ([113]Lada and Lada (2003); [114]Portegies Zwart et al. (2010)). Furthermore, by combining various parameters like distance, metallicity, and age with the motion of stars within open clusters, we can leverage them as powerful tools to investigate the formation and evolution of the Milky Way's disk itself ([115]Cantat-Gaudin, T. et. al. (2018)).

Observations & Data Reduction

NGC 1027 (αJ2000 - 02:42:40, δJ2000 +61:35:42; l ~ 135.758 and b ~ + 1.525), also known as Melotte 16, Collinder 30, OCL 357, MWSC 225 open star cluster, is located in the eastern part of Cassiopeia

---

[112] Dias, W. S., Monteiro, H., Moitinho, A., et al. 2021, MNRAS, 504, 356
[113] Lada, C. J. and Lada, E. A.: 2003, ARA&A 41, 57
[114] Portegies Zwart S. F. McMillan S. L. W. Gieles M., 2010, ARA&A, 48, 431
[115] Cantat-Gaudin, T., Jordi, C., Vallenari, A., et al. 2018, A&A, 618, A93

constellation near the northern celestial pole, adjacent to two prominent nebulae, the Heart (IC 1805) and Soul Nebulae (IC 1848).

NGC 1027 is not physically associated with these two nebulae as they are more distant (d ~ 2.1 kpc; [116]Chauhan et al., 2011; [117]Panwar et al., 2017) compared to the NGC 1027 (d~ 1 kpc; [118]Maciejewski & Niedzielski, 2007). [119]Ruprecht (1966) considered this cluster as class iii 2 p, i.e., a less populated open cluster with noticeable concentration and a medium range in magnitude of the stars [120]Trumpler (1930).

Photometric studies of OCs are found to be fundamental tools for determining their structural parameters. These parameters play an important role towards understanding galactic structure and evolution. However, most of the OCs are affected by field star contamination. Therefore, finding out member stars of the cluster becomes necessary to look into the cluster properties ([121]Carraro et al., 2008; Cantat-Gaudin, T. et al., 2018). Proper motion diagram is a reliable tool to identify cluster members on the basis of astrometric precision and membership determination on kinematic method. This precise learning of cluster membership gives information about distribution of stellar mass in the OCs and throw light on dynamic evolution of star clusters. Numerous research studies have obtained present-day MF for a number of OCs, yet, it is still not clear weather initial mass function (IMF) is universal in time and space or depends upon different star forming conditions. Study of the distribution of low and high mass stars towards the cluster region provides a clue to the mass segregation in OCs

The sequence of observation is to take the target field, the standard field and calibration frames. UBVRcIc photometric observations. On

---

[116]Chauhan, N., Pandey, A. K., Ogura, K., et al. 2011, MNRAS, 415, 1202

[117]Panwar, N., Samal, M., Pandey, A., et al. 2017, MNRAS, 468, 2684

[118] Maciejewski, G., & Niedzielski, A. 2007, A&A, 467, 1065

[119] Ruprecht, J. 1966, Bulletin of the Astronomical Institute of Czechoslovakia, vol. 17, .98, 98

[120] Trumpler, R. J. 1930, Lick Observatory Bulletin, 420, 154

[121] Carraro, G., V´azquez, R. A., & Moitinho, A. 2008, A&A, 482, 777

eliminating unwanted frequencies, fine details of an object is obtained. Therefore, filters in astronomy are used either to reduce the overall intensity or to restrict the wavelength range of light used. Detectors available now have a wider wavelength response and/or improved sensitivity in comparison to the earlier photographic plate detectors. So, the role of filters has become more important. Choosing a proper filter, standard pass bands are sampled for the total flux from the astronomical sources at different wavelengths, providing information about temperature, luminosity etc. Different filters are needed while doing photometry to measure the magnitude of stars to a standard, internationally agreed system with precision. Photometry (measurement of flux, or intensity) of an astronomical object is done using photometers. For accurate photometric studies, electronic devices, like CCDs, are preferred above photographic plates and photomultiplier tubes. CCD has quickly won over the astronomical community as it combines the advantages of both the photographic plates and the photomultiplier tubes.

To remove the atmospheric, instrumental and CCD electronics signature from the image, these are pre-processed. Strong atmospheric turbulence, poor focusing or the presence of charge diffusion in the detector can cause image spread. Image processing compensates for this deformation and restores the original image. CCD is affected from by different noises which are superimposed on the images. Extraction of useful information from this kind of environment is one of the main purposes of image reduction. To carry out these tasks, several image processing packages have been developed world-wide such as MIDAS, IRAF, DAOPHOT etc. There are three basic stages of image processing in the case of photometric measurements,

1. Preprocessing

2. Reduction photometry

3. Calibration photometry

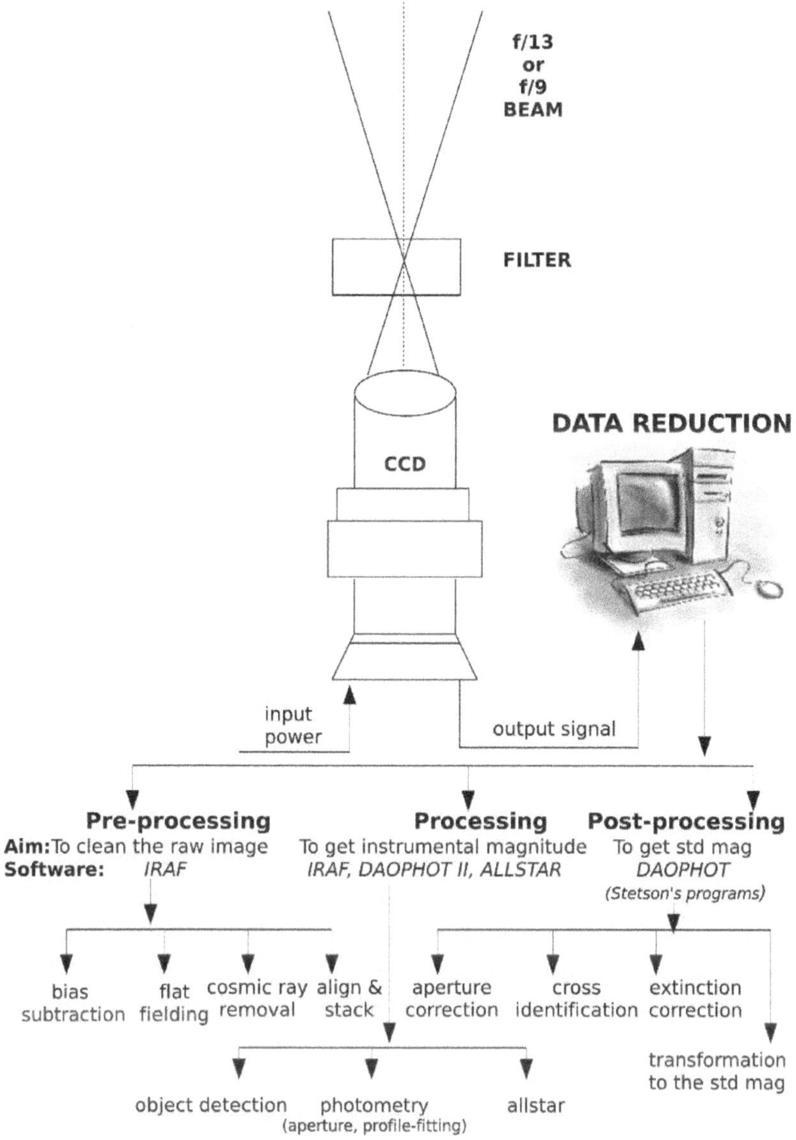

Figure 1. A chart summazing whole data reduction process.

A raw image from CCD cannot be analysed directly. Several steps are taken to preprocess the data prior to analysis. To clean the images, number of bias and twilight flat-field frames are taken in all the filters. Multiple short and long exposures are obtained for all chosen clusters. To calibrate the magnitude of stars in cluster field, standard field are also observed. The spread in the Point Spread Function (PSF) caused by seeing can be approximated by a central Gaussian and the large outer part by a power law. A commonly used measure for the angular size of the PSF is the diameter where the flux falls to half its central value, i.e, full width at half maxima (FWHM). Data is reduced using IRAF data reduction package. Initial processing of data frames includes bias subtraction, flat fielding and cosmic ray removal. To obtain quantitative values for the brightness of stars aperture photometry and profile fitting photometry is done. Isolated bright stars are selected to get a profile fitting function. The obtained PSF is applied to all the stars with the help of ALLSTAR routine of DAOPHOT II. Then aperture corrected magnitudes are applied to the PSF magnitudes to get the aperture instrumental magnitudes. For cross-identification of the stars measured on different frames of the cluster DAOMASTER program is used. Magnitudes of bright stars saturated in deep exposure frames are taken from short-exposure frames. For translating the observed aperture magnitudes to the standard magnitudes least-square linear regressions outlined by Stetson (2000) are fitted. The accuracy of the morphology and position of the cluster features in CMDs depends on the variation of photometric errors with magnitudes. Photometric errors are approximated to be related with the signal-to-noise ratio of the source. ALLSTAR evaluates the error as the mean square root of the residuals of the fittings of a PSF to the profile of the central part of each star.

The basic step to provide the celestial coordinates of all the stars in J2000.0 is to get the astrometric solution. To obtain this solution, SkyCat tool is used. We found bright stars per field for which we have both the celestial coordinates and the corresponding pixel coordinates. Then by using IRAF task CCMAP and CCTRAN, we found the corresponding transformation between the two coordinate systems and computed the individual celestial coordinates for all the detected stars.

Data Analysis & Results

Cluster Center and Radial Density Profile

To obtain the cluster parameters, first we estimate the cluster center using the Python Kernel density estimation (KDE). For this, we use the Gaia data for the sources within 40 arcmin radius around the cluster. Our analysis shows the cluster center at α, δ ~ 02:42:43.9, +61:39:34 which is about 2 arcmin away from the center mentioned in WEBDA. Cluster radius (rcl) is taken as the distance from cluster center to where the average cluster contribution becomes negligible with respect to the background stellar field. Cluster radius as well as extent of field-star contamination is estimated using spatial surface density profile of stars. To estimate the structural parameters, [122]King (1962) surface density profile is fitted to the radial distribution of stars. The fit is done using non-linear least squares fit routine which uses the errors as weight. The radial density profile can be represented by

$$f(r) = \frac{f_0}{1+\left(\left[\frac{r}{r_c}\right]\right)^2} + f_b$$

where f_0 is the central density region, r_c is the core radius of the cluster and f_b is the background density.

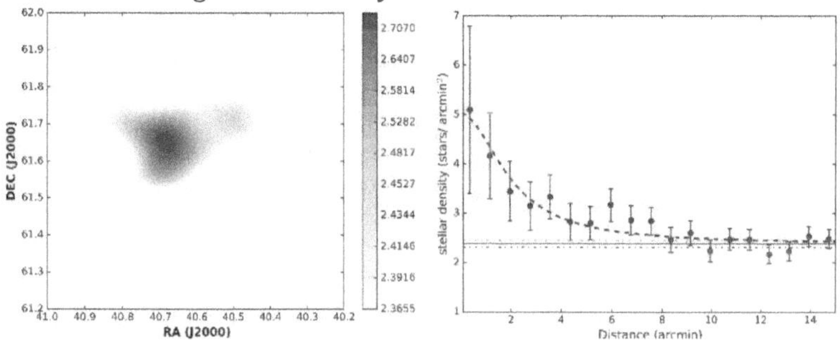

Figure: 2 Left panel: The color maps are two-dimensional kernel density estimations (KDEs) of the spatial distribution of the bright GAIA EDR3 sources (G ≤ 17 mag). Right panel: The radial density profile for the bright stars in the region. Dashed curve represents the least-square fit of the King (1962) profile to the observed data points. The error bars represent ±√N errors. The black line indicates the density of field stars.

---

[122]King, I. 1962, AJ, 67, 471

The best fit solution along with uncertainties for density distribution is shown in Figure 2. The radial density profile of the cluster NGC 1027 decreases and flattens around 8 arcmin. Therefore, for further analyses we have considered the cluster radius as 8 arcmin, which is lower than 10.3 arcmin, the value reported before by Maciejewski & Niedzielski (2007). For NGC 1027, f0 = 2.2 stars/arcmin^{-2}, rc = 2.4 arcmin and fb = 2.3 stars/arcmin^{-2}.

Member stars of the cluster

We use Gaia data for the sources within the cluster region to select the cluster members and to determine mean proper motion of cluster NGC 1027 (radius ≤ 8 arcmin). We use the proper motion in RA (μ^*_α) and proper motion in declination (μ_δ) for the stars within the cluster radius to generate the vector point diagram (VPD). The VPD for those sources is shown in Figure 3.

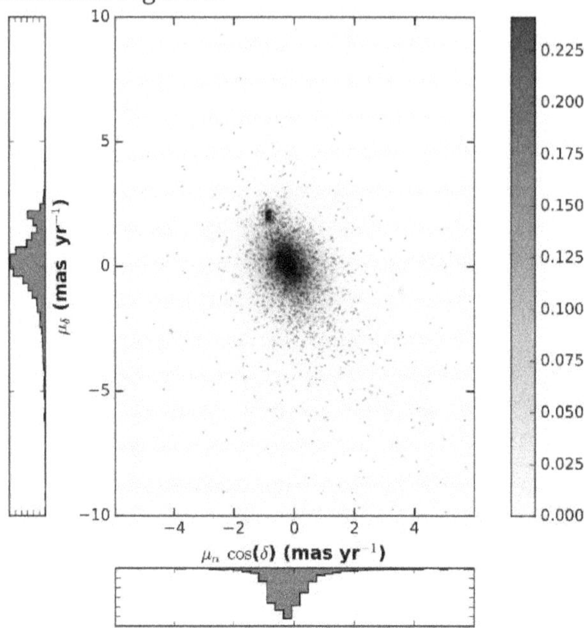

Figure 3. *Proper motion vector-point diagram for the Gaia sources located within the cluster radius. Blue color bar shows the distribution of the proper motions for the stars in the control field of the similar area.*

The over-density of sources can be easily noticed. The proper motion of the stars in the cluster region peaks at $(\mu^{*}_{\alpha}, \mu\delta) \sim (-0.84, 2.04)$ mas yr^{-1}. A circular area of radius 0.7 mas yr^{-1} around the peak of the over-density in the VPD is used to select the probable cluster members, and the remaining sources in the VPD are considered as field stars. Assuming a distance of ~ 1.14 kpc and a radial velocity dispersion of 1 km s^{-1} for open clusters, a dispersion (σ_c) of ~ 0.19 mas yr^{-1} in the PMs of the cluster can be obtained.

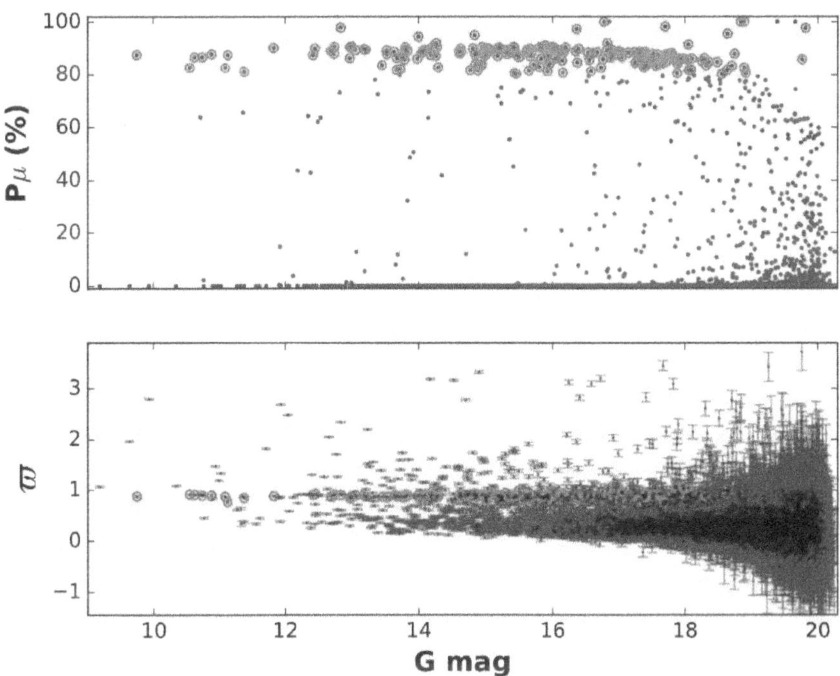

Figure: 4 Top Panel: Membership probability for the stars located within the cluster area (radius ~ 8)) plotted as a function of G-band magnitude. Bottom panel: The blue dots show the distribution of parallax values for the Gaia sources within the cluster as a function of G magnitude.

We obtain $\mu_{xf} = -0.08$ mas yr^{-1}, $\mu_{yf} = -0.33$ mas yr^{-1}, $\sigma_{xf} = 1.05$ mas yr^{-1} and $\sigma_{yf} = 2.02$ mas yr^{-1} for the probable field members. These values are further used to construct the frequency distributions of the cluster stars (φ^v_c) and field stars (φ^v_f). In Figure 4 (upper panel), we have plotted the estimated membership probability for all the Gaia sources within the cluster radius as a function of G-band magnitude as blue dots. Gaia sources with high membership probability ($P\mu > 70\%$) are shown with red circles. 217 stars has been found with ($P\mu > 70\%$). There is a clear separation between the cluster members and field stars toward the brighter part, supporting the effectiveness of this technique.

A high membership probability extends down to $G \sim 19$ mag, whereas toward the fainter limits, the probability gradually decreases. A majority of the stars with high membership probability follow a tight distribution in the VPD. We have also plotted the parallax for all the Gaia sources as a function of G-band magnitude (dots in Figure 4, bottom panel). We estimate the cluster distance using the parallax values of the cluster members having high membership probability ($P\mu > 70\%$) and good parallax accuracy ($\sigma > 5$). These sources are shown with the red circles in Figure 4 (bottom panel). The median parallax value of these sources is 0.892 ± 0.088 mas. We estimate the cluster distance after correcting the median parallax value for the known parallax offset of ~ -0.015. The distance estimate for the cluster using Gaia data comes out to be $\sim 1.14 \pm 0.11$ kpc, which is in agreement with that reported by ([123]Cantat-Gaudin & Anders, 2020)). Using a matching radius of ~ 1 arcsec, we get ~ 1610 optical UBV R_cI_c counterparts of Gaia sources with membership probability information within the cluster radius. Out of these, about 160 stars are cluster members.

Reddening toward the NGC 1027 (U-B)/(BV) Color-Color Diagram

 Knowledge of reddening is essential for estimation of distance and age of the cluster. The reddening, $E(B-V)$ in the cluster region is determined using the two color diagram (TCD) (U-B) versus (B-V) for the member stars within 8 arcmin (Figure 5). We adopt the slope of the reddening vector $E(U-B)/E(B-V) = 0.72$ and fit the intrinsic zero-

---

[123]*Castro-Ginard, A., Jordi, C., Luri, X., et al. 2020, A&A, 635, A45*

age-main sequence (ZAMS) with the solar metallicity (Schmidt-Kaler, 1982) for main-sequence stars by shifting the ZAMS for different color excesses. The best fit corresponding to E(B-V)=0.36 mag is shown with the thick curve in Figure 5. The dashed curve shows the ZAMS shifted for a reddening E(B-V) of 0.7 mag. Our estimated value of color excess E(B – V) = 0.36 ± 0.04 mag is comparable to E(B – V) = 0.41± 0.12 mag estimated by Maciejewski & Niedzielski (2007). Line-of-sight extinction, A_G, and the reddening, $E(G_{BP} - G_{RP})$, are estimated using the relations given in (Wang & Chen, 2019). We use A_G = 1.21 and $E(G_{BP} - G_{RP})$ = 0.35 for the further analyses of Gaia data.

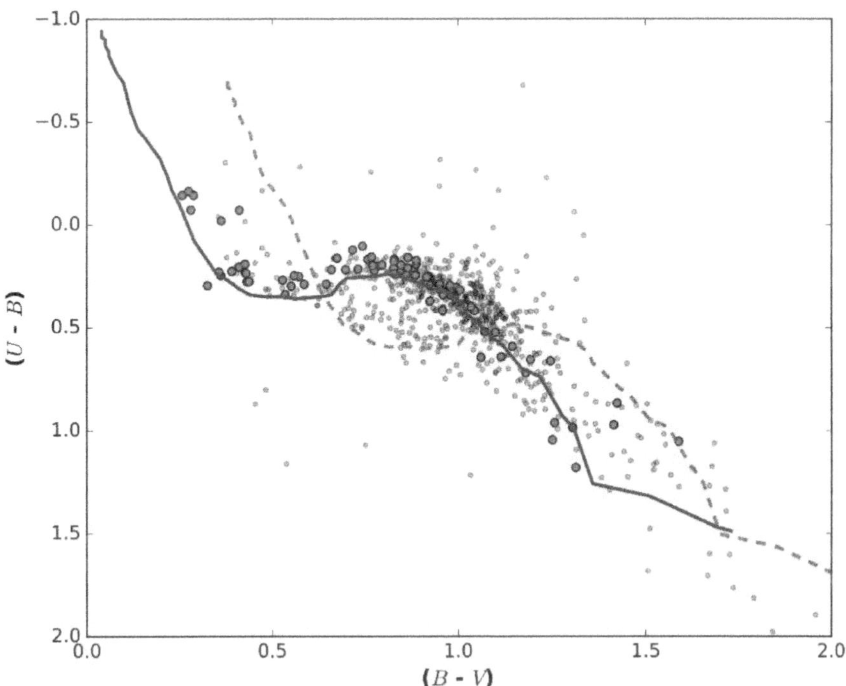

Figure: 5 Two color diagram for NGC 1027. Red color circle denotes member stars present within 8 arcmin radius.

Age and distance of the cluster

The CMDs are important tools to estimate the cluster's age and distance. We have constructed the optical CMDs using cluster members from our optical catalogue and Gaia data. V vs (B – V) and V vs (V − I) color-magnitude diagrams for the sources in the cluster region (black dots) along with the member stars (red circles) shown in the Figure 6. $G_{BP} − G_{RP}$ 7 is plotted using the cluster members with membership probabilities $P\mu > 70\%$. The CMDs of target cluster show a well-defined narrow main sequence (MS) that extends from V ∼10.5 mag to V ∼20 mag. It is seen that the field star contamination becomes more evident for stars V ≥ 17 mag. Distance and age estimation of the cluster have been derived by using MS isochrone for solar metallicity taken from

Padova PARSEC version 1.2S database of stellar evolutionary tracks & isochrones of (Pastorelli et al., 2020). This is corrected for the derived reddening values from the TCD. We tried to fit the MS isochrones of different ages over the member stars (shown with the red circles in Figure 6 and 7). The visual best fit of the MS to the blue part of the intrinsic CMDs gives distance modulus $(V - M_V)$.

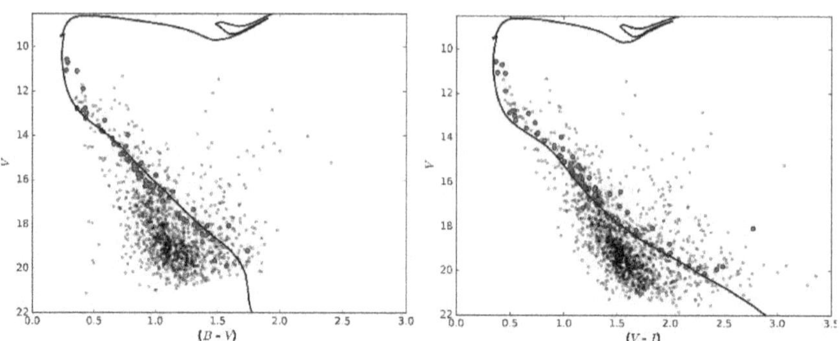

Figure: 6 V/(B − V) (left panel) and V/(V-I) (right panel) color magnitude diagrams for the stars in the cluster NGC 1027 (radius ≤ 8 arcmin). The red circles represent high membership probability members from Gaia.

The best fit isochrone yields a distance modulus $(V - M_V)$ = 10.28 mag indicating a distance of ∼ 1.14 Kpc for the cluster and a log age of 8.11 (∼ 130 Myr) corrected for the adopted distance and reddening. Our estimated distance for the target field is comparable to the value of 1.03 Kpc whereas the age estimation is lower than the value 252 Myr derived by (Maciejewski & Niedzielski, 2007). 3.5 Luminosity Function and Mass function Stellar mass cannot be measured directly.

Stellar models are required to transform magnitude of a star in a given wavelength into masses. With the help of CMDs, we derive luminosity function (LF) of probable main sequence cluster members and MF using mass-luminosity relation from theoretical evolutionary models. We have used Gaia high membership probability members to determine LFs for the cluster.

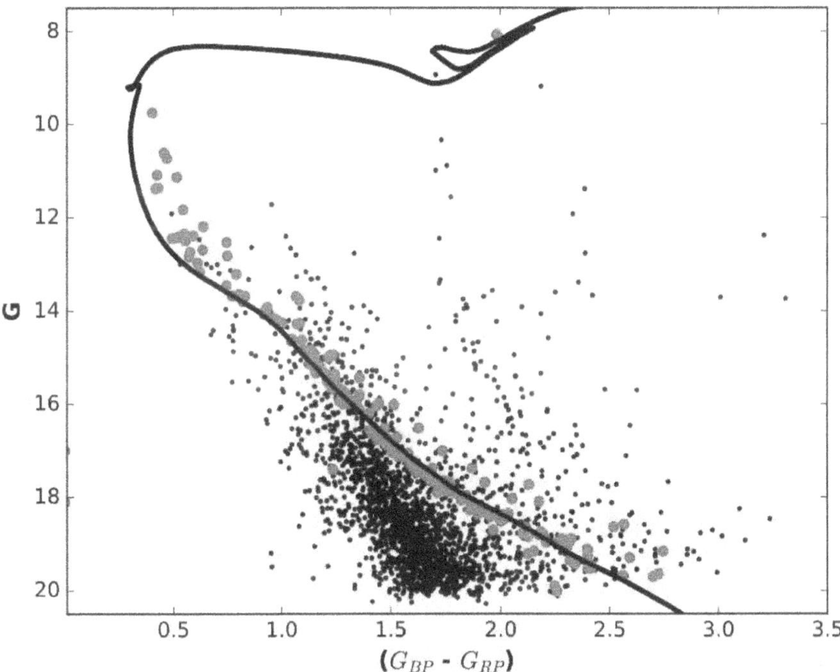

Figure: 7 G/(G_{BP}-G_{RP}) color-magnitude diagram for the stars in the cluster region. The red circles represent Gaia sources with Pμ > 70. The thick curve represents the main sequence isochrone (Padova-Parsec) for log age of 8.11 corrected for the adopted distance and reddening

We have used G versus (G_{BP} – G_{RP}) CMD to construct the LF. Field star contamination and membership uncertainty affects luminosity and mass function of open star clusters (Scalo, 1998), therefore, to avoid the contribution of the field stars in our sample of cluster members, we have used only kinematic and photometric confirmed members of the cluster for the LF and MF estimation. To determine the completeness of the data, we constructed the magnitude histogram method (Panwar et al., 2017). Using the magnitude histogram, we found that completeness of the data limits to G ~ 18.5 mag. For estimation of LF, magnitude of the MS stars was converted to absolute magnitudes using estimated distance modulus and reddening.

Conversion of LF into present day MF is done using the latest version of the theoretical isochrones of Padova's stellar evolutionary tracks and isochrones ([124]Pastorelli et al., 2020). To construct MF, we have converted absolute mag bins to mass bins. Consequently, we transform the LF to MF for all the main-sequence stars (~ 180 stars) having mass $0.55 \leq M/M \leq 2.1$. MF slope is given by using a power-law $\Gamma = d \log N(\log m)/d \log m$ (3) where $N(\log m)$ is the number of stars per unit logarithmic mass interval. dN is the probable cluster members in a mass bin dM with central mass M. Observational results suggest that the MF slopes is similar to that given by [125]Salpeter (1955), that is, $\Gamma = -1.35$. The resulting mass function for our target cluster is shown in Figure 8. For the cluster NGC 1027, we obtain that the mass distribution has a best-fitting slope $\Gamma = -1.46 \pm 0.15$, similar to the Salpeter value.

Discussion

Observational investigation of the OCs reveals that in general, massive stars are concentrated toward the nucleus in comparison to low-mass stars which are mostly distributed in the corona region of the cluster. This segregation of massive stars towards cluster's center can happen due to the equipartition of energy (dynamical evolution) or due to the star formation processes itself. We have analysed the radial distribution of probable member stars (with membership probability > 70 %) in two mass bins, i.e., stars with masses < 1.2 M), suggesting mass segregation effect in the NGC 1027 cluster. To investigate

---

[124] Pastorelli, G., Marigo, P., Girardi, L., et al. 2020, MNRAS, 498, 3283
[125]Salpeter, E. E. 1955, ApJ, 121, 161

whether the mass segregation in this cluster is due to star formation processes or due to dynamical relaxation, we estimated the dynamical relaxation time (TE), i.e., time in which the individual star exchange sufficient energy to achieve the velocity distribution of a Maxwellian equilibrium. We have used the method given by [126]Binney & Tremaine (1987) to estimate the dynamical relaxation time (TE), i.e., TE = N 8logN × Tcross (4) where, Tcross = D/σV is the crossing time, N is the total number of stars in the cluster region of diameter D, and σV is the velocity dispersion, with a typical value of 3 km s−1 ([127]Sharma et al., 2020; [128]Bisht et al., 2017). Using the above equation, we estimated the value of TE as ~10 Myr for the NGC 1027 cluster. Comparing the cluster age (~130 Myr) with its dynamical relaxation time (~10 Myr), we found that the cluster is dynamically relaxed and the observed mass segregation is due to the result of dynamical evolution. Due to the mass segregation process, low-mass members may become more vulnerable for evaporation and hence ejected out of the cluster more easily. This stellar evaporation results in a continuous decrease of the total mass of the cluster, and hence the gravitational binding energy of the cluster. However, external disturbances, e.g., the tidal force from nearby giant molecular clouds or star clusters, passages through Galactic spiral arms or disks, or a shear force by Galactic differential rotation, increase the stellar evaporation of the cluster. For a cluster, the tidal radius is the defined as a distance at which two gravitational forces; one towards the Galactic center and another towards the cluster center; balances. Thus, tidal radius is estimated to separate gravitationally bound and unbound stars to a cluster. The tidal radius of a star cluster in the solar neighborhood is given by the equation: rt = GMC 2(A − B) 2 1/3 (5) where, G is the gravitational constant, MC is the total mass of the cluster, and A, B are the Oort constants where A = 15.3 ± 0.4 km s−1 kpc−1, B = -11.9 ± 0.4 km s−1 kpc−1 (Bovy, 2017). For the total cloud mass of ~164 M estimated from the MF distribution, the corresponding tidal radius comes out to be ~7.8 pc. If we assume that ~ 50% of the cluster mass is missed due to data

[126] *Binney, J., & Tremaine, S. 1987*
[127]*Sharma, S., Ghosh, A., Ojha, D. K., et al. 2020, MNRAS, 498, 2309*
[128]*Bisht, D., Yadav, R., & Durgapal, A. 2017, New Astronomy, 52, 55*

incompleteness, the tidal radius will be ~9 pc. Therefore, the tidal radius of the cluster is much larger than the present estimate of the cluster radius (Rcl ~2.65 pc), or in other words, this cluster is already started to lose its low-mass members due to dynamics. Thus, there is a possibility of finding member stars beyond the observed cluster boundary. For this, we searched for the stars sharing the similar proper motion and distance as cluster members, outside the observed cluster boundary. We estimated the membership probability and found ~460 stars with membership probability > 70% upto a radius of 40 arcmin (cf. Figure 8). To study the cluster dynamics and mass segregation, we divided these stars into two mass bins, stars having mass less than 1.2M and stars having mass greater than 1.2M, and created the respective stellar density distribution maps. The stellar density distributions for above two mass bins are over-plotted on a DSS2-R band image shown in the Figure 8. There is a clear evidence of mass segregation as the stars having mass greater than 1.2M are concentrated toward the center compared to the relatively low-mass stars. The spatial distribution of the low mass members in the cluster NGC 1027 shows slightly tailed structure (cf. Figure 9, right panel). This might have caused due to the tidal striping of member stars from the cluster. Tidal striping of stars can happen in a cluster due to the tidal forces from a nearby massive object, disk crossing, or differential rotation of the Galaxy. Thus, the tidal stripping depends on the mass and age of a cluster. The ratio of the number of cluster inside the tidal radius to those outside, can tell us about the amount of tidal stripping already done in a cluster. For example, for Blanco 1 (age ~ 100 Myr) cluster, it is found to be ~3 ([129]Zhang et al., 2020), whereas, for Coma Berenicesa cluster (age ~ 700 Myr) this ratio is estimated as 0.6 ([130]Tang et al., 2019). However, in case of an old massive star cluster Hyades (age ~ 800 Myr), this ratio is estimated as ~1.1 ([131]Röser et al., 2019). NGC 1027 is relatively young and appears to be more dynamically bound. The observed radius of the cluster suggest that it is a dynamically relaxed cluster that show mass-segregation and has

---

[129] Zhang, Y., Tang, S.-Y., Chen, W. P., Pang, X., & Liu, J. Z. 2020, apj, 889, 99

[130] Tang, S.-Y., Pang, X., Yuan, Z., et al. 2019, ApJ, 877, 12

[131] Röser, S., Schilbach, E., & Goldman, B. 2019, Astronomy & Astrophysics, 621, L2

already lost some of its member stars and currently it is in the process of dissolution due to the influence of external tidal interactions.

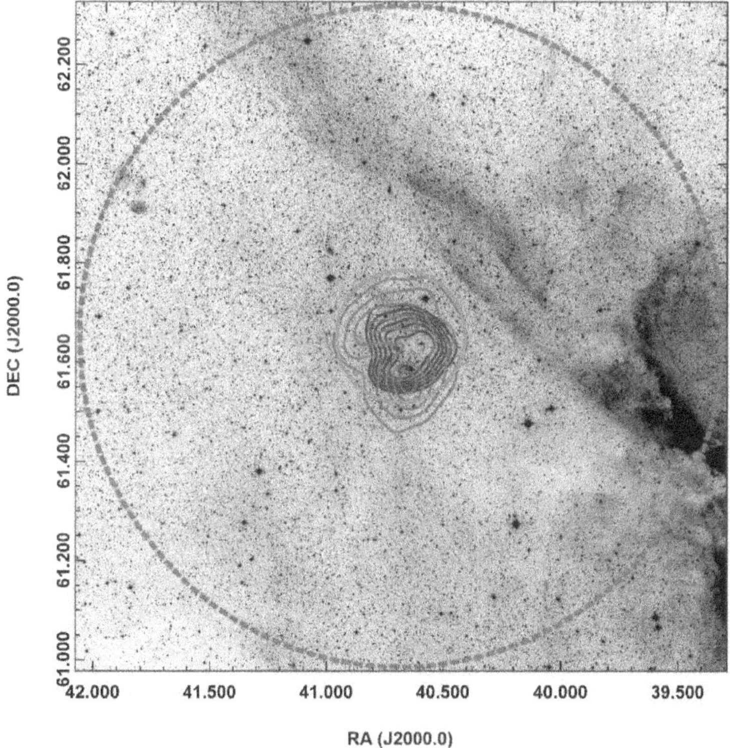

Figure 8: DSS2-R image of the open cluster NGC 1027. The red and blue contours show the density distribution of low-mass (< 1.2 M⊙) and relatively higher-mass (≥ 1.2 M⊙) members, respectively. The green circle shows the cluster radius and magenta dashed circle represents the area (radius ∼ 40 arcmin), used for the search of kinematic members outside cluster radius.

Summary and Conclusion

We present the photometric and kinematic study of the open cluster NGC 1027 using UBVRIc data taken with 1.04m Sampurnanand telescope and Gaia data. Using two-dimensional KDEs analysis of the Gaia EDR3 data, we have obtained the cluster center that is about 2 arcmin away from the center mentioned in WEBDA. The cluster extent is estimated to be about 8.0 arcmin. The distribution of proper motion of the stars in the cluster region shows a clear separation between the cluster members and field stars. The mean proper motion for the cluster has been estimated to be $(\mu^*_\alpha, \mu\delta)$ = (- 0.84, 2.04) mas yr^{-1}. Based on the membership analysis, 217 member stars are identified (Pμ > 70%) in the cluster region. Their mean parallax value is 0.892 ± 0.088 mas corresponding to a distance of ~ 1.14 kpc. The (U-B)/(B-V) color-color diagram for the cluster members give a reddening E(B-V) ~ 0.36 ± 0.04 mag towards the cluster. The CMDs for the cluster members, constructed using UBVRI photometric data and Gaia EDR3 data, show that NGC 1027 is an intermediate age OC with an age ~ 130 Myr and located at a distance of ~ 1.14 kpc. The LFs and MFs are determined by considering the members selected from Gaia proper motion database and photometry. The mass function slope for the cluster, Γ =-1.46 ± 0.15, is in good agreement with that given by Salpeter (1955) for the Galactic OCs. We have studied the radial distribution of stellar masses within the cluster region and found that relatively massive stars are dominantly distributed in the inner regions of the cluster suggesting mass segregation. We report presence of astrometric members of the target field outside the cluster's radius. The observed small size of the cluster as compare to its tidal radius, indicates mass segregation, slightly elongated morphology and a comparison of dynamical relaxation time with the age of cluster.

8. Quantum Chemical Investigation on Vibrational Dynamics and Ground State Electronic Properties of a Non-Linear Optical Material

- *Parag Agarwal*

Department of Physics, Teerthanker Mahaveer University, Moradabad

Introduction

A detailed quantum chemical study of 2-hydroxy-3-methoxy-N-(2-chloro-benzyl)-benzaldehyde-imine (HMCBI) has been discussed in this book chapter. 2-hydroxy-3-methoxy-N-(2-chloro-benzyl)-benzaldehyde-imine(HMCBI) is a non-linear organic material. Nonlinear optical (NLO) materials are at the forefront of current research because of their importance in providing the key functions of frequency shifting, optical modulation, optical switching, optical logic, and optical memory for the emerging technologies in areas such as telecommunications, signal processing, and optical interconnections[132]. The organic NLO crystals have attracted attention because of the low cost and flexibility of molecular design, which we need for applications with, using suitable donor and acceptor. Nonlinear optical effects arise from the interactions of electromagnetic fields in various media to produce new fields altered in phase, frequency, amplitude or other propagation characteristics from the incident fields. For materials to show nonlinear optical

---

[132]D. Sajan, H. Joe, V. S. Jaikumar and J. Zaleski, J. Mol. Struc. **785** (2006) 43.

effects[133] in the solid state, it is essential that the molecules are packed in such a way as to produce a nonzero macroscopic electric dipole moment.

Quantum chemistry is the field in which solutions to the Schrodinger equation are used to predict the properties of molecules and solve chemical problems. Many of the central properties of chemistry, such as molecular structure, relative energies of different structure and spectroscopic observables may in principle be predicted from quantum mechanics. It treats molecules as collection of nuclei and electrons, without any reference to chemical bonds. The solution to the Schrodinger equation is in terms of electrons, which in turn leads directly to molecular structure and energy among other observables, as well as to information about bonding. However, the Schrodinger equation can not actually be solved for any but a one electron system and approximations need to be made. Quantum chemical models differ in the nature of these approximations and span a wide range, both in terms of their capability and reliability and their "cost".

The quantum chemical method used here is the density functional theory (DFT). DFT attempts to calculate ground state electronic energy and other ground state molecular properties from the ground state electron density $\rho_0.$ This is becausethe ground state molecular energy wave function, and all other molecular electronic properties are uniquely determined by the ground state electronic probability density ρ_0 (x, y, z)[134]. The importance of this theory lies in the fact that (within the Born-Oppenheimer approximation) any atomic, molecular or condensed matter system is completely described by the number of electrons in it and by the types and positions of nuclei in it. DFT is presently the most successful approach to compute the electronic structure of matter. Its applicability ranges from atoms, molecules and solids to nuclei and quantum and classical fields. It enhances our understanding by relying on relatively simple physically

---

[133]J. Zyss, Ed., Molecular Nonlinear Optics, Materials, Physics and Devices (Academic Press), New York, 1994.
[134]P. Hohenberg, W. Kohn, Phys. Rev. **B864** (1964) 136.

accessible quantities that are easily visualized even for very large systems[135].The interpretation of experimental vibrational spectra for large molecules is greatly assisted by quantum chemical predictions, particularly in the region below 1800 cm^{-1} where the high density of states result in spectral congestion[136].

Vibrational spectroscopy is an advantageous analytical tool for providing information about composition, structure, conformation and intra-molecular interactions of complex molecules.Vibrational spectroscopy comprises of two complementary techniques: infrared (IR) and Raman spectroscopy.In contrast to X-ray diffraction which is sensitive to long range order, vibrational spectroscopy is sensitive to short range structure of molecular solidsSince the vibrational energy levels are unique to each molecule, the IR and Raman spectra provide a "fingerprint" of a particular molecule. The frequencies of these molecular vibrations depend on the masses of the atoms, their geometric arrangement, and the strength of their chemical bonds. The spectra provide information on molecular structure, dynamics, and environment. Infrared and Raman spectroscopy involve the study of the interaction of radiation with molecular vibrations but differs in the manner in which photon energy is transferred to the molecule by changing its vibrational state.

Normal mode analysis (NMA) is a technique for studying the vibrational properties of various molecular structures at the atomic level. The frequencies in the IR spectra can be assigned empirically to various vibrational modes of the molecule or groups within it but assignment of modes, which are mixtures of group modes, may not be straightforward. In such cases calculations of normal modes and eigen vectors of the secular equation become necessary. The frequencies can be used to relate observed vibrational spectra to details of molecular structure and dynamics[137].

---

[135]S. Kummel and L. Kronik, Rev. of Mod. Phys.**80** (2008) 3.
[136]M. D. Halls, J. Velkovski and H. B. Schlegel, Theor. Chem. Acc. **105** (2001) 413.
[137]D. I. Bower and W. F. Maddams, "The Vibrational Spectroscopy of Polymers" (Cambridge University Press, Cambridge) (1989).

Methodology

For both the molecule;2-hydroxy-3-methoxy-N-(2-chloro-benzyl)-benzaldehyde-imine (HMCBI) and 2, 6 – dichlorobenzonitrile (DCBN), the optimized geometry, harmonic vibrational wave-numbers, absolute Raman scattering activities and infrared absorption intensities have been calculated by density functional theory (DFT) with B3LYP functionals using extended basis set 6-311++G(d,p). A complete vibrational assignment is provided for the observed FT-IR and FT-Raman spectra. Isoelectronic molecular electrostatic potential surface (EPS) has been used for predicting sites and relative reactivities towards electrophilic attack. The HOMO, LUMO analysis has been done to elucidate information regarding charge transfer within the molecule.

The normal coordinate analysis was performed and the PED was calculated among symmetry coordinates for the molecule. For this purpose, a complete set of 93 symmetrized internal coordinates was defined with help of Pulay's recommendations. The vibrational assignments of the normal modes were provided on the basis of the calculated PED by using the program GAR2PED. It is well known that the harmonic frequencies by DFT calculations are usually higher than the corresponding experimental etc., they were scaled down by the wave number linear scaling procedure (WLS) of Yoshida et al.[υ_{obs} = $(1.0087-0.0000163\upsilon_{cal})$ υ_{cal} cm^{-1}].

Computational details

The entire calculations were performed at density functional theoryusing Gaussian 03 program[138], invoking gradient geometry

---

[138]M.J. Frisch, G.W. Trucks, H.B. Schlegel, G.E. Scuseria, J.R. Cheeseman, J.Montgomery, TV, J. C. Burant, J. M. Millam, S. S. Iyengar, JT, B. Mennucci, M. Cossi, G. Scalmani, NR, H. Nakajima, Y. Honda, OK, M. Klene, X Li, J.E. Knox, H.P. Hratchian, J. B. Cross, C. Adamo, J. Jaramillo, R. Gomperts, R. E. Stratmann, A. J. Austin, R.Cammi, C. Pomelli, J.W.Ochterski, K. Morokuma, G.A. Voth, P. Salvadorm, J. Jnnenberg, S. Dapprich, A.D. Daniels, M.C. Strain, Malick, A.D. Rabuck, KR, J.V. Ortiz, Q. Cui, A.G. Baboul, SC, B.B. Stefanov, G. Liu, A. Liashenko, P P, R.L. Martin, D.J. Fox, T. Keith, M.A. Al-Laham, A. Nanayakkara, M.

optimization. Geometry optimization was performed using the Becke's three parameter hybrid functional, a combination that gives rise to the well known B3LYP method [139 140 141 142]. The 6-311++G(d,p) extended basis set. The absolute Raman scattering and infrared absorption intensities were calculated from the derivatives of the polarizability and dipole moment associated with each normal mode, respectively.

Experimental Details

Infrared spectra were recorded in the region 3200 – 500 cm^{-1} on Bruker FTIR spectrometer, model ALPHA equipped with Diamond ATR module by averaging 24 scans with spectral resolution of 4 cm^{-1}. The FT-Raman spectra were recorded on Senterra Raman Spectrometer at 785 nm excitation line in the region 3200 – 100 cm^{-1}. The spectral resolution of the instrument was 3 cm^{-1}.

Results & Discussion

2-hydroxy-3-methoxy-N-(2-chloro-benzyl)-benzaldehyde-imine (HMCBI) is a promising non-linear organic crystal. It belongs to orthorhombic crystal system and space group Pbca. The single crystal XRD study reveals that the lattice parameters are a = 7.068(6) Å, b = 13.727(8) Å and c = 27.600(9) Å; α = 89.88(3) Å and β = γ = 90.14(6) Å[143]. It has a higher second harmonic efficiency and emits a green radiation using Nd: YAG laser as the source[144].

Challacombe, M.W. Gill, W. Chen, M.W. Wong, C. Gonzalez and J.A. Pople, Gaussian 03, Revision C.02.2003.

[139]*C. T. Lee, W. T. Yang, R. G. Parr, Phys. **Rev.B 37**(1988) 785.*

[140]*R. G. Parr, W. Yang, Density Functional Theory of Atoms and Molecules; (OxfordUniversity Press: New York) (1989).*

[141]*A. D. Becke, J. Chem. Phys. **98** (1993) 5648.*

[142]*P.J. Stephens, F.J. Devlin, C.F. Chabalowski, M.J. Frisch, J.Phys. Chem.**98** (1994) 11623.*

[143]*S. Singh and B. Lal, J. of Cryst. Growth**312** (2010) 301.*

[144]*H. Unver, A. Karakus and A. Elmali, J. Mol. Struct.**702** (2004) 49.*

Geometry Optimization and Energies

Initial geometry generated from single crystal X-ray diffraction parameters was minimized at DFT level employing B3LYP/6-311++G(d,p) without any constraint to the potential energy surface. The optimized geometry is shown in figure 1 (a). The optimized and experimental structures of the molecule were compared by superimposing them [figure 1 (b)] using a least squares algorithm that minimizes the distances of the corresponding non-hydrogen atoms.

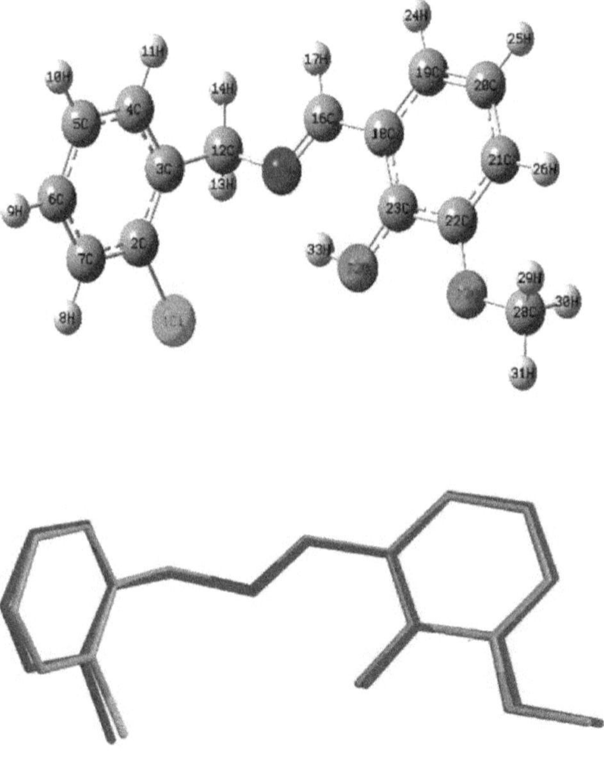

Figure 1 (upper): Optimized Structure of HMCBI; (lower): Comparison of the experimental (in blue) and the optimized (in grey) structure of HMCBI (hydrogen atoms are not shown).

Conformational Analysis

In order to investigate the possible conformations of HMCBI, potential energy scans were performed for the dihedral angles D12 (N15-C12-C3-C4), D13 (C16-N15-C12-C3), D16 (C19-C18-C16-C15) and D25(C28-O27-C22-C21) at the B3LYP/6-31G level of theory. The conformational stability of HMCBI was further checked by performing two-dimensional potential energy scans for same dihedral angles taking two at a time. The variation of potential energy for the pair of torsions D13 (C16-N15-C12-C3) and D16 (C19-C18-C16-N15) is presented in figure 2. Although there will be many conformers, the results obtained by two-dimensional scan D13-D16 combined with one dimensional scan reveal six conformers (Figure 2).

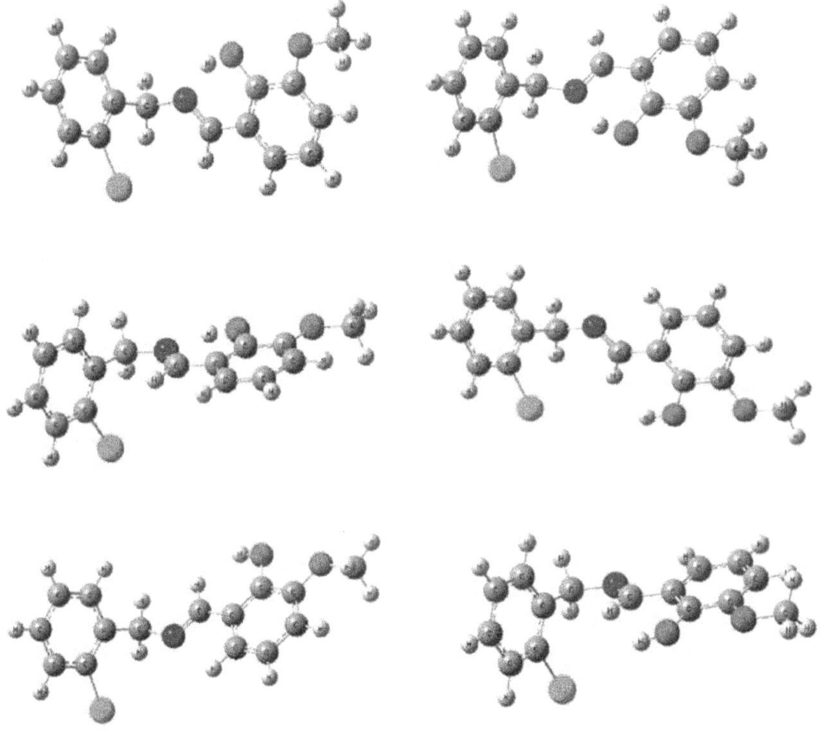

Fig. 2: Conformers of HMCBI based on 1D and 2D potential energy scan results.

Among these six, the parameters of conformer 2 are the same as obtained by optimizing the experimental parameters of XRD. So the present work is based on this conformer.

Molecular Electrostatic Potential

The MEP plot of HMCBI (Figure 3) reveals that the oxygen atoms of the hydroxyl group and the methoxy group exert the most negative potential (dark red) and are major active electrophilic centre whereas the chlorine atom seems to exert almost neutral electrostatic potential (green color).

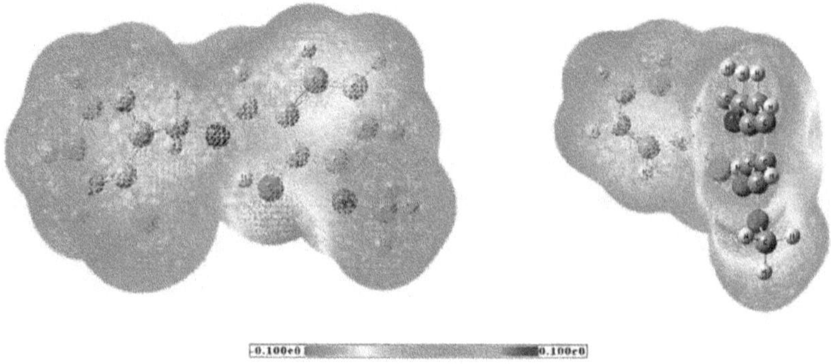

Fig. 3: Molecular Electrostatic Potential mapped on to isodensity surface (a) along the molecular plane (b) in prependicular plane, for HMCBI.

Electronic Spectra and solvent effect

The electronic spectra of HMCBI were computed in the gas phase and in different polar solvents - chloroform, THF and in methanol and the results are presented in table 1. It is evident from the table that the positions of absorption maxima are slightly shifted by solvent effects i.e. HMCBI exhibits positive solvatochromism. With increase in solvent polarity, bathochromic shift (red shift) is seen. A close agreement has been obtained between the experimental and calculated values of transition energies. The calculations show that the lowest energy transition takes place mainly as the transition from Highest Occupied Molecular Orbital (HOMO) to Lowest Unoccupied Molecular Orbital (LUMO).

Table 1: Calculated absorption wavelengths, energies and oscillator strengths of HMCBI using TD-DFT method

	Transition type	λ (nm) Exp[a]	λ (nm) Cal	Transition energy E(ev)	Oscillator strength (f)	Assignment
Gas Phase	H→L	—	335.88	3.6914	0.0567	π, π^*
	H-1→L	—	257.75	4.8103	0.3394	π, π^*
Chloroform	H→L	333.22	328.47	3.7746	0.0681	π, π^*
	H-1→L	264.0	258.94	4.7881	0.3652	π, π^*
THF	H→L	332.7	326.81	3.7938	0.0658	π, π^*
	H-1→L	264.0	258.24	4.8012	0.4012	π, π^*
Methanol	H→L	331.3	323.74	3.8297	0.0615	π, π^*
	H-4→L	296.3	265.89	4.6631	0.0425	π, π^*
	H-1→L	262.1	257.16	4.8213	0.4151	π, π^*
	H→L+3	219.0	211.77	5.8545	0.5453	π, π^*
	H-2→L+1	201.3	204.2	6.0717	0.0376	π, π^*

[a] Experimental absorption wavelengths have been taken from reference[145].

The calculations in the gas phase as well as in solvents assigned the frontier level HOMO to the molecular orbital number 72 with 'A' symmetry and the LUMO to the molecular orbital number 73 with the same 'A' symmetry. The transition from HOMO-1 to LUMO is strong having high oscillator strength in all the solvents. Another strong transition (oscillator strength 0.5453) is calculated at 212 nm and may be correlated to the experimental band at 219 nm in methanol. All these transitions are π, π* which are generally considered as indicative of molecular first hyperpolarizability with non-zero valueand are shown in figure 4.

[145] H. Unver, A. Karakus and A. Elmali, J. Mol. Struct. **702** (2004) 49.

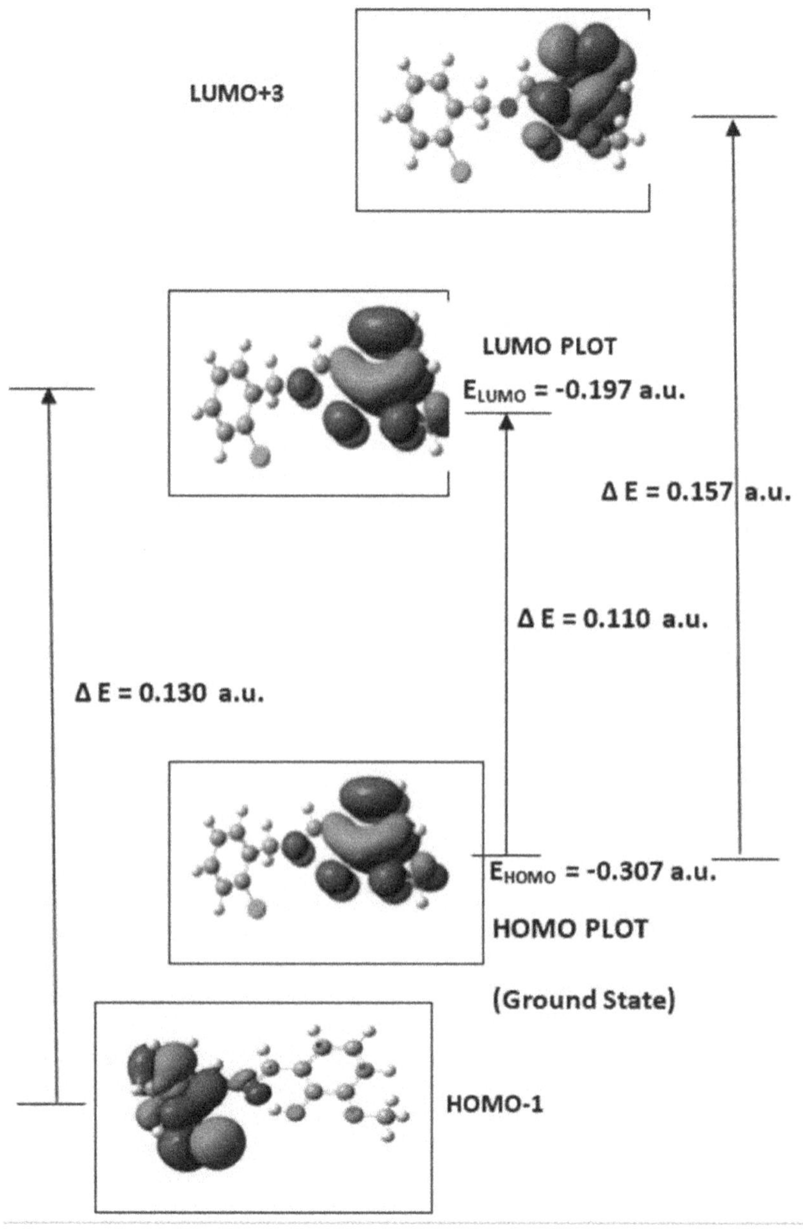

Fig. 4: The atomic orbital compositions of the molecular orbitals and the electronic transitions for HMCBI.

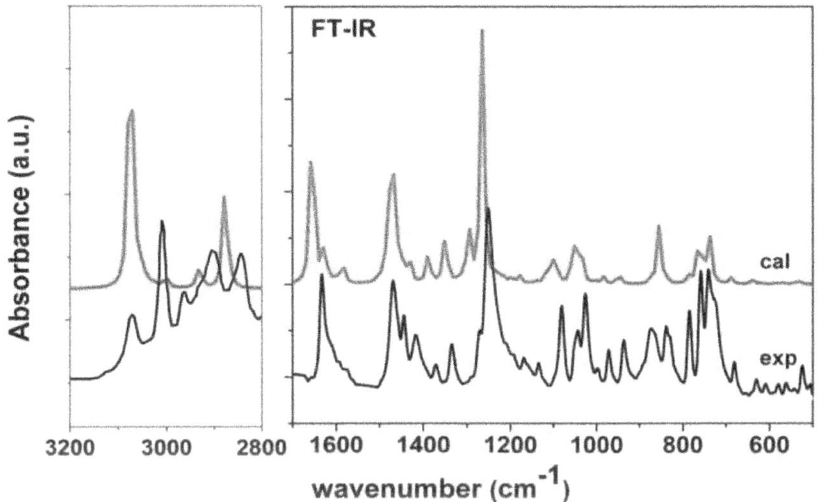

Fig. 5: Experimental and calculated (scaled) FT-IR spectra of HMCBI. (Lower and higher frequency region spectra are normalized separately)

Vibrational Analysis

A complete vibrational analysis of the 93 fundamental vibrational modes of HMCBI has been done on the basis of its experimental infrared and Raman spectra and DFT/B3LYP/6-311++G(d,p) quantum chemical calculations. The optimized structural parameters were used in the vibrational frequencies calculation to characterize all stationary points as minimum. The assignments are given as per the internal coordinate system recommended by Pulay et al[146]. The experimental and the theoretically predicted infrared spectra in 3200 – 500 cm⁻¹ region and corresponding Raman spectra in 3200-100 cm⁻¹ region are given in figure 5 and 6, respectively.

---

[146]P. Pulay, G. Fogarasi, F. Pang, J. E. Boggs, J. Am. Chem. Soc101 (1979) 2550.

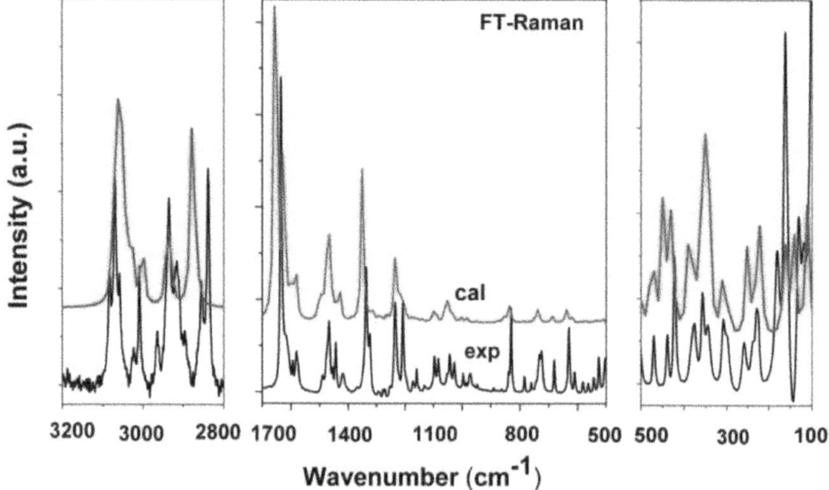

Fig. 6: Experimental and calculated (scaled) FT-Raman spectra of HMCBI. (Lower and higher frequency region spectra are normalized separately)

A close agreement between the scaled and experimental frequencies and intensities of the infrared and Raman bands may be noticed from these figures. The vibrational dynamics can be discussed in following categories.

Phenyl ring vibrations

The carbon hydrogen stretching vibrations give rise to bands in the region 3100-3000 cm^{-1} in all the aromatic compounds[147]. The ring C-H stretching vibrations appear to be very weak. This is due to steric interaction that induces effective conjugation and charge carrier localization resulting in twisted phenyl ring[148]. In this region, the bands are not affected appreciably by the nature of the substituent. As in the present case, both the phenyl rings have different substituents but C-H stretchings are nearly at same frequencies. These are localized modes and have almost 100% contribution in potential

---

[147] B. Smith, *Infrared Spectral Interpretation, A Systematic Approach, (CRC press, WashingtonDC) (1999).*

[148]C. James, A. Amal Raj, R. Raghunathan, V. S. Jayakumar and I. Hubert, Joe, *Spectrochim Act.**A 70** (2008) 1208.*

energy distribution. The absorption bands arising due to C-H in plane bending vibrations, interacting somewhat with C-C stretching vibrations, are observed as a number of medium-strong intensity sharp bands in the region 1500-1100 cm[-1]. As evident from PED, the asymmetric, asymmetric', puckering and trigonal deformation modes of ring 1 and ring 2 appear as highly coupled modes with other vibrational modes.

Chloro-phenyl vibrations

The C-Cl stretching modes generally appear in the range 800-1000 cm[-1][149]In general, the ν(C-Cl) local mode spreads out between two or more normal modes[150]. Besides C-Cl stretching, contribution from ring (C-C-C) in plane bending in all these modes is supported by Varsanyi[151]. It has been observed by him that in benzene derivatives, the C-X (X= halogen atom) stretching vibrations are strongly coupled with C-C-C bending vibrations.

Methylene Group Vibrations

The C-H stretching of the methylene group is at lower frequencies than those of the aromatic C-H ring stretchings. The asymmetric CH_2 stretching vibrations are generally observed in the region of 3000-2900 cm[-1][152], while the CH_2 symmetric stretch appears in the region 2900-2800 cm[-1][153]. The four bending vibrations of the methylene group are referred as scissoring, twisting, wagging and rocking. The scissoring mode is characterized by the strong IR band at 1468 cm[-1] and the FT-Raman band at the same value which is computed at 1465 cm[-1]. The vibrational bands corresponding to the twisting, wagging and rocking of the methylene group appear in the region 1371 – 947

---

[149]E. F. Mooney, Spectrochim. Acta**20** (1964) 1021.
[150]S. Sudha, N. Sunderganesan, M. Kurt, M. Cinar and M. Karabacak, J. Mol.Struct. **985** (2011) 148
[151]G. Varsanyi, Vibrational Spectra of Benzene Derivatives, (Academic Press, New York and London) (1969)
[152]D. Sajan, J. Binoy, B. Pradeep, K. Venkata Krishna, V.B. Kartha, I. Hubert Joe and V.S. Jayakumar, Spectrochim.**Act. A 60** (2004) 173.
[153]K. Furic, V. Mohacek, M. Bonifacic and I. Stefanic, J. Mol. Struct. **267** (1992) 39.

cm^{-1}. In the present assignment the CH_2 bending modes follow in decreasing wave-number, the general order CH_2 scissoring > CH_2 wag > CH_2 twist > CH_2 rock. All the bending modes have been observed and analyzed, supported by DFT computations.

Imine group vibrations

The vibrations of imine bridge are highly sensitive to the degree of charge transfer between the donor and acceptor groups, and therefore such modes are of particular interest for spectroscopists. It is difficult to identify the C=N and C-N stretching from other vibrations. Rofouei et al[154]have assigned the bands at 1681 cm^{-1} and 1258 cm^{-1} in FT-Raman to C=N and C-N stretching respectively in N, N′–di (2-methoxyphenyl) formamidine. In our work, the strong FT-Raman bands appearing at 1636 cm^{-1} and 1043 cm^{-1} are ascribed to C=N and C-N stretching respectively. The C=N stretching mode is calculated at 1654 cm^{-1} having mixed contribution of C-C stretching and phenyl C-H in plane bending. The large deviation of this value from the experimental one may be attributed to the hydrogen bonding. The calculated value of C-N stretching 1036 cm^{-1} shows a good agreement with the experimental one.

Methoxy group vibrations

For a molecule containing a methoxy group, the electronic charge is back donated from the lone pair of electrons on oxygen atom to the σ^* orbital of C-H bonds causing weakening of the C-H bonds. This is followed by an increase in C-H bond distance and the decrease in C-H force constant. This can result in enhancement of IR band intensities of the C-H stretching modes. In the title molecule, the CH_3 asymmetric stretching vibration is observed as strong peak at 3008 cm^{-1} in FT-IR spectra and at 3009 cm^{-1} in FT-Raman spectra.

---

[154]M.K. Rofouei, N. Sohrabi, M. Shamsipur, E. Fereyduni, S. Ayyappan and N. Sunderganesan, Spectrochimi. **Act. A 76** (2010) 182.

The CH_3 rocking modes calculated at 1196 and 1155 cm^{-1} are in good agreement with the bands observed at 1195 and 1169 cm^{-1} in FTIR spectra and at 1209, 1159 cm^{-1} in FT-Raman spectra. The relatively large value of IR and Raman wave-number of the rocking mode suggests the presence of hyperconjugation.

When the CH_3 group is directly attached to an oxygen atom, the C-H stretching and bending bands can shift position due to electronic effects. This causes the $O-CH_3$ stretching bands to spread over a larger region than that of $C-CH_3$ group. In the present case, this spreading is observed between 1100 and 950 cm^{-1}.

Hydroxyl Group Vibrations

The hydroxyl stretching vibrations are sensitive to hydrogen bonding. The non-hydrogen bonded or free hydroxyl group absorbs strongly in the region 3600-3550 cm^{-1}, whereas the existence of hydrogen bond can lower the O-H stretching wave-number to the 3550-3200   cm^{-1} region with an increase in IR intensity[155]. In the title molecule, the O-H stretching is observed as a broad peak at 3448 cm^{-1} in the FTIR reported by S. Singh et al. DFT calculations predict this mode at 3074 cm^{-1}. This significant theoretical underestimation of the associated O-H stretching wave-number is due to the failure of the harmonic approximation in describing vibrations of atomic groups involved in hydrogen bond. This type of interaction causes a significant anharmonicity in the potential in which the atomic groups involved in hydrogen bonds vibrate. The O-H in plane deformation vibration usually appears as strong band in the region 1440-1260 cm^{-1} in the IR spectra, which gets shifted to higher wave-numbers in the presence of hydrogen bonding. The calculations show that the O-H in plane bending vibration is mixed with the phenyl ring C-C stretching and C-H in plane bending vibrations.

---

[155]N.B. Colthup, L.H. Daly, S.E. Wiberley, *Introduction to infrared and Raman Spectroscopy*, (Academic Press, New York) (1990).

NLO Activity and its Vibrational Correlation

Quantum chemical methods are presently routinely used for predicting the molecular NLO properties of different molecules[156] [157]. Theoretical determination of hyperpolarizability is quite useful both in understanding the relationship between the molecular structure and nonlinear optical properties. It also provides a guideline to experimentalists for the design and synthesis of organic NLO materials. The calculated dipole moment, polarizability and hyperpolarizability of HMCBI by HF/6-311++G(d,p) are given in table 2. The calculated first hyperpolarizability of the title compound is 4.74 $*10^{-30}$e.s.u., which is comparable with the reported values of similar structures[158] [159] [160] [161] [162] (table 3) but experimental evaluation of this data is not readily available. The value of hyperpolarizability is about two times greater than urea[163] using as standard[164], thus illustrating the potential of HMCBI for the application as NLO material.

The large value of hyperpolarizability β, which is measure of the non linear optical properties of the molecular system, is associated with the intramolecular charge transfer, resulting from the electron cloud movement through π conjugate framework from electron donor to electron acceptor groups.

---

[156]A. Subhashini, R. Kumarvel, S. Leela, H.S. Evans, D. Sastikumar and K. Ramamurthi, Spectrochim. Act.**A 78(3)** (2011) 935.

[157]R.T. bailey, T.J. Dines and M.C. Tedford; J. Mol. Struct. **992(1-3)** (2011) 52.

[158]T. Vijaykumar, I. Hubert Joe, C.P. Reghunandhan Nair and V.S. Jaikumar, Chemical Physics**34** (2008) 83.

[159]N. Subramanian, N. Sunderaganesan and J. Jayabharathi, Spectrochim. Act.**A 76** (2010) 259.

[160]S. Sebastian, N. Sundaraganesan, B. Karthikeiyan and V. Srinivasan, Spectrochim. Act.**A 78** (2011) 590.

[161]L. Sinha, O. Prasad, V. Narayan and S. R. Shukla, Molecular Simulation**37 (2)** (2011) 153.

[162]Z. Weiqun, L. Kuisheng, Z. Yong and L Lu, J. Mol. Struct. **657** (2003) 215.

[163]C. Cassidy, J.M. Halbout, W. Donaldson and C.L. Tang, Opt. Communic.**29 (2)** (1979) 243.

[164]J. Ledoux and J. Zyss, Chem. Phys.**73** (1982) 203.

*Table 2: The electric dipole moment μ (Debye), the average polarizability$<\alpha>$(e.s.u.*10^{-30}) and firsthyperpolarizability β_{tot} (e.s.u.*10^{-30}) of HMCBI.*

μ_x	0.9029	β_{xxx}	2.004
μ_y	0.0420	β_{xxy}	0.295
μ_z	1.3033	β_{xyy}	-0.316
μ	1.5860	β_{yyy}	2.499
α_{xx}	1.854	β_{xxz}	0.121
α_{yy}	1.698	β_{xyz}	-0.031
α_{zz}	1.603	β_{yyz}	1.707
α_{xy}	0.342	β_{xzz}	0.607
α_{xz}	0.054	β_{yzz}	0.290
α_{yz}	1.603	β_{zzz}	2.084
$<\alpha>$	1.718	β_{total}	4.740

*Table 3: A comparison of the electric dipole moment μ (Debye) and first hyperpolarizability β_{tot} (e.s.u.*10^{-30}) of HMCBI and some other molecules.*

	HMCBI	DANS[a]	VA[b]	4M2CBP[c]	3B5CU[d]	N4CBN'2T[e]	Urea[f]
μ	1.5860	9.97	---	4.74	4.75	----	4.56
β_{total}	4.740	43.54	2.815	0.6305	2.93	1.88	2.3

[a] DANS → 4-[N,N-Dimethylamino]-4'-Nitro Stilbene[26]
[b] VA → 1, 2 – bis (3-methoxy-4-hydroxybenzylidene) hydrazine[27]
[c] 4M2CBP→ 4-methyl-2-cyanobiphenyl[28]
[d] 3B5CU→3- benzoyl-5-chlorouracil[29]
[e] N4CBN'2TN→ (4-chloro)benzoyl-N'-2-tolylthiourea[30]
[f]Urea[31]
a, b, c, d, e are the calculated values and f is the experimental value.

The electron cloud is capable of interacting with an external electric field and thereby increasing the asymmetric electronic distribution in either or both the ground and excited states, thus leading to an increased optical non-linearity[165]. The analysis of the wave function indicates that the electron absorption corresponds to the transition from ground to first excited state and is mainly described by one electron excitation from the HOMO to LUMO. The atomic orbital compositions of the frontier molecular orbitals sketched in figures 6 shows that the highest occupied molecular orbitals are localized mainly on the ring containing hydroxyl and methoxy groups, On the other hand, the lowest unoccupied molecular orbitals are localized on the whole molecule. These two orbitals significantly overlap on the imine group in the π-conjugated system, which is an inherent condition to achieve the charge transfer transition and, consequently the non-linear optical response of a NLO chromophore. However, the CH_2 group lacks any conjugation; hence there is no π-conjugation between the two phenyl rings. This prevents the molecule to exhibit very efficient second order NLO property. The electronic coupling between the imino nitrogen lone pair electrons and the phenyl ring π – system creates phenyl-N-conjugation. This phenyl-N conjugation brings about ICT[166] and this leads to superior performance in material chemistry such as hyperpolarizability[167], hole transport[168] electroluminescence[169] etc.

Conclusion

A systematic study has been conducted on the structural and spectral characteristics of non-linear molecule HMCBI by experimental spectroscopic methods and quantum chemical calculations. Molecular geometry parameters calculated by density functional theory agree

[165] V.G. Dimitriev, G.G. Gurzadyan, D.N. Nikogosyan, *Handbook of Nonlinear Optical Crystals*, (Springer, Berlin) (1991).

[166] L.H. Ma, Z.B. Chen, Y.B. Jiang, *Chem. Phys. Lett.* **372** (2003) 104.

[167] C. M. Whitaker, E. V. Patterson, K. L. Kott. R. J. MacMohan, *J. Am. Chem. Soc.* **118** (1996) 9966.

[168] Z .G. Liu, H. Nazare, *Synth. Mat.* **111** (2000) 47.

[169] A. Yamamori, C. Adachi, T. Koyama, Y. Taniguchi, *J. Appl. Phys.* **86** (1999) 4369.

with the experimental value within 0.06 Å in bond lengths, 3.5° in bond angles and 6.0° in dihedral angles. Plots of infrared and Raman spectra of the molecule based on DFT calculations show reasonable agreement with the experimental spectra. Any discrepancies noted between the observed and calculated frequencies are due to the fact that the calculations have been actually performed on single (or isolated) molecule in the gaseous state. Thus some reasonable deviations from the experimental values seem to be justified. The computed ^{1}H chemical shift of hydroxyl proton supports the resonance stabilization of HMCBI in enolic form. MEP contour has been plotted in order to predict sites and relative reactivity towards electrophilic attack. A complete assignment of the experimental absorption peaks in the near ultraviolet region of the electronic spectra of the HMCBI has been made by calculating transition energies, oscillator strengths of the singlet ground states by time dependent density functional theory (TD-DFT). Nonlinear optical NLO behavior of the examined molecule was investigated by the determination of the electric dipole moment μ, the polarizability α and the hyperpolarizability β. Rather large hyperpolarizability derived by theoretical calculations suggests the possible future use of this compound for non-linear optical applications. The study suggests the importance of π conjugated systems for non-linear optical properties and the possibility of charge transfer interactions. We hope that the results of the present study of HMCBI are of assistance in development of new efficient materials for technological applications.

9. Study of atmospheric molecule of environmental importance: CO_2

-    *Prabhunath Prasad*

Department of Physics, Deen Dayal Upadhyaya Gorakhpur University, Gorakhpur

Introduction

The universe is full of molecules. They are the building blocks of all matter including biological matter. The most abundant molecule in the universe is Hydrogen (H_2) but it is absent from the terrestrial atmosphere. The presence of distant molecules is interpreted only through the application of spectroscopic techniques. Till date more than 320 molecules have been confirmed to be detected in the interstellar medium or circumstellar shells[170]. Most of these are carbonaceous organic molecules with the largest being a 13 atomic linear cyanopolyene. Larger and more complex molecules, like fullerenes and aromatic hydrocarbons, have also been indicated by certain observations. While molecules in the earth's atmosphere are easier to detect, their abundance estimation is complex due to continuous formation and destruction. The present work is aimed to study the spectroscopic properties of important molecules for remote sensing of their concentrations. The astrophysical molecules are always observed remotely but the environmental molecules can be detected directly, by local sampling, and also remotely through satellites. In this introduction a brief outline of the atmosphere and its

---

[170] *CDMS, CDMS classic documentation, https://cdms.astro.uni-koeln.de/classic/molecules#.*

constituents is presented. The need for remote sensing and constraints towards this task are also addressed.

Atmosphere of the Earth

Earth is the only planet where life is possible. This is mainly due to its atmosphere which is the thin layer of gases that separate the earth's surface from space and is held in place by gravitation. The constituents of the atmosphere, columnar temperature and pressure, distance from the sun etc. all factors together make earth's environment suitable for life. The major components of the earth's atmosphere, molecular nitrogen and molecular oxygen, contrast with those of its nearest neighbours Mars and Venus, whose atmosphere is primarily composed of carbon dioxide. Earth's atmosphere has by volume roughly 78% nitrogen (N_2), 21% oxygen (O_2), 0.9% argon (Ar), and other gases in trace amounts. The major components of these trace gases that take part in atmospheric chemistry are: 420 ppmv (part per million by volume) carbon dioxide (CO_2), 1922 ppbv (part per billion by volume) Methane (CH_4), 336 ppbv nitrous oxide (N_2O), 100 ppbv carbon monoxide (CO) and 70 ppbv ozone (O_3). Although the mixing ration of these trace gases is small, they play an important role in atmospheric physics, climate change and weather. The trace gases also play important role in the greenhouse effect, which is discussed in the next section. Besides these the atmosphere also contains aerosols, clouds and a huge variable amount of water vapour, which averages around 0.40% overall and varies from 1-4% at the surface of the earth. Other physical parameters that characterize the atmosphere are atmospheric pressure and temperature.

The Greenhouse Effect

An atmospheric process by which the earth is warming up is greenhouse effect. Roughly one-third of the incoming solar energy that reaches top of the atmosphere is reflected back to the space and the remaining two-third is absorbed by the atmosphere, land cover and ocean. The absorbed energy warms the earth's surface which emits energy back to the space at longer wavelengths in the infrared. Most of these TIR are absorbed by atmospheric gases and re-radiated in all directions including back towards the earth. This process is called the greenhouse effect. The atmospheric gases, which are largely transparent to incoming solar radiation and partially opaque to the outgoing TIR, are called greenhouse gases (GHGs). The natural greenhouse effect warms the earth enough to aid growth and sustenance of life. At present, the average temperature of the earth is about 15^0C. But without the GHGs the surface would have mean temperature of about -18^0C, which is 33^0C less than the actual global mean surface temperature. However, human activities have gradually changed the population of the atmospheric components, and intensified the natural greenhouse effect, causing global warming[171]. The atmospheric gases which contribute to the greenhouse effect, are water vapour (H_2O), carbon dioxide (CO_2), methane (CH_4), ozone (O_3) and nitrous oxide (N_2O). It is also identified that carbon monoxide (CO) is an important indirect greenhouse gas. The three main constituents of the atmosphere: nitrogen (N_2), oxygen (O_2) and argon (Ar) do not take part in the greenhouse effect.

Industrialization and other anthropogenic activities have increased the global amount of GHGs. Four most important long lived anthropogenic GHGs are CO_2, CH_4, N_2O and chloro-fluoro-carbons (CFC; hydrocarbons gases containing Fluorine and Chlorine). Measured records show that atmospheric abundances of almost all GHGs and aerosols reached highest values during the 1990s altering the energy balance of the climate system. The IPCC predicts further increases in GHGs that will result in warmer climate and increased global average air and ocean temperature. This will cause melting of snow and ice, and rise in global average sea level. The climate change as a consequence will impact negatively on the world's water resources, food, eco-system and health. If the trend of global warming

---

[171] *IPCC2001, Climate Change 2001: The Scientific Basis. Contribution of Working Group I to the Third Assessment Report of the IPCC, Cambridge University Press, Cambridge, United Kingdom and New York, (2001).*

continues the situation will worsen. Continuous monitoring of the atmosphere and exploring various mitigation policies is essential.

Our current knowledge about climate system, future GHGs emission scenarios and its source and sinks are limited[172]. The IPCC Spatial Report on Emission Scenarios (SRES)[173] describes four scenarios families, A1, A2, B1 and B2, based on alternative development pathways, covering wide range of technological, demographic and economic driving forces and their impact on emission of the GHGs.

Broadly *A1* assumes very rapid economic growth, increasing global population, and introduction of new and more efficient technologies. A1 is further divided into three groups based on energy technologies: fossil intensive (A1FI), non-fossil energy sources (A1T) and balanced across all energy sources (A1B). *A2* describes a heterogeneous world with growing population, but slow economic growth and slow technological development. In the scenario *B1* a convergent world with same population as in A1 is considered but with rapid changes in economic structures towards a service and information economy. The scenario *B2* describes intermediate population and economic growth, emphasizing local solutions to economic, social and environment sustainability. The projected growth of CO_2 concentration and temperature projection from 1900 to 2100 is shown in Figure 1[174]. The climate change is quantified in terms of radiative forcing (RF), which is a measure of the energy balance of the earth atmospheric system.

---

172 *B. B. Stephens, K. R. Gurney, P. P. Tans, C. Sweeney, et al., Sci. 316 (2007) 1732-1735.*
173 *N. Nakicenovic, J. Alcamo, G. Davis, B. de Vries, et al., Special Report on Emissions Scenarios : a special report of Working Group III of the IPCC, Cambridge University Press, New York, NY (US), United States, (2000).*
174 *CSSR, Climate Science Special Report, https://science2017.globalchange.gov.*

Emissions, Concentrations, and Temperature Projections

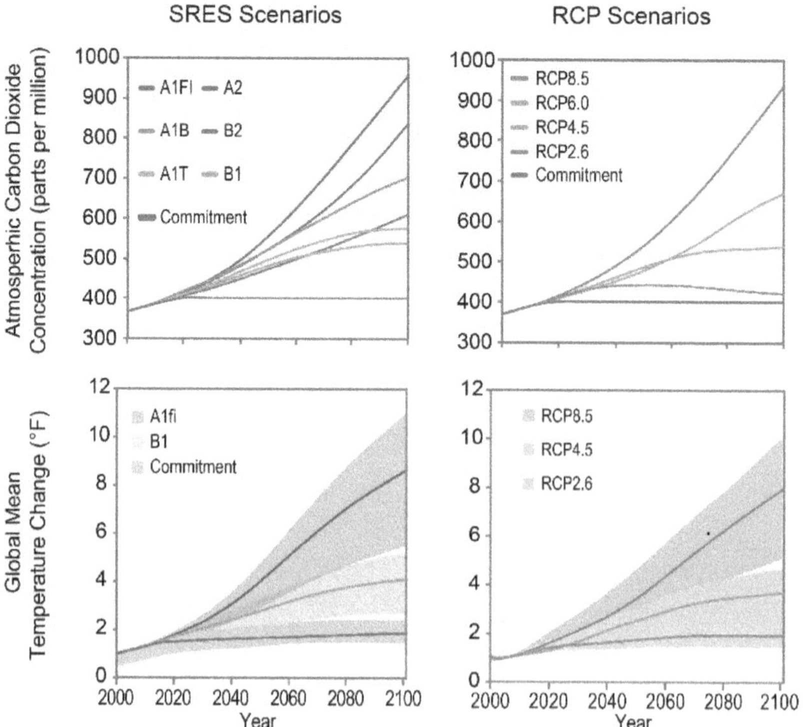

Figure 1: Concentration of CO$_2$ according to SRES scenarios projected up to year 2100[175].

RF is the rate of energy change per unit area of the globe as measured at the top of atmosphere in Watts per square meter (Wm^2). A positive RF means increase in energy of the system thus tending to warmer climate, while negative RF tends to cool the climate system. Other than GHGs, aerosols and clouds also influence the climate.

The influence of various atmospheric components on the climate is measured in terms of the RF due to that component. This is shown in Figure 2, from the 6th assessment report[176] on climate change (AR4)

---

[175] *IPCC, SRES vs. RCP Projections,*
https://science2017.globalchange.gov/chapter/4#fig-4-1, 2017.
[176] *IPCC2021:Fig7.6, IPCC Sixth Assessment Report Figure 7.6,*
https://www.ipcc.ch/report/ar6/wg1/figures/chapter-7/figure-7-6, 2021.

by IPCC 2021. The reference year for RF by different atmospheric components is taken to be near the beginning of the industrial era i.e. 1750.

Atmospheric Trace Gases: Carbon dioxide

Among the GHGs CO_2 is the most abundant and its RF on the climate is greater than the RF of all other GHGs put together (Figure 2). The abundance of CO_2 has increased from pre-industrial times by about 140 ppmv (50%) over the last 270 years. Its concentration increases primarily due to fossil fuel, land use changes such as deforestation, cement production and biomass burning[177]. This anthropogenic emission is perturbing the natural global carbon cycle of the complex carbon exchange between the main carbon reservoirs (atmosphere, ocean, terrestrial biosphere and sediments). Prior to 1750, for about 10000 years, the atmospheric concentration of CO_2 was stable between 260 to 280 ppmv. Since 1750, atmospheric CO_2 concentration has risen from 280 to 420 ppm in 2021.

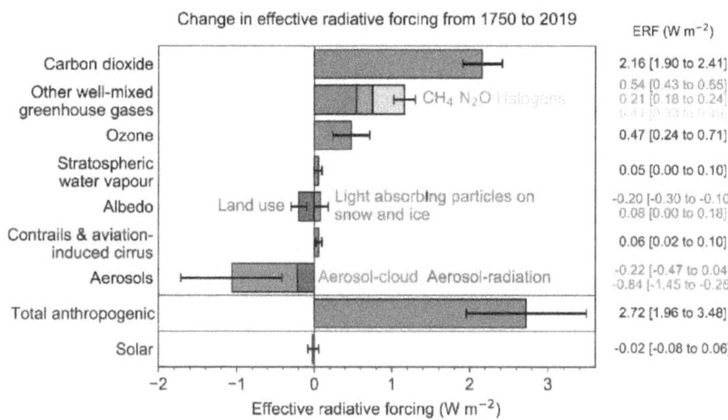

Figure 2: Radiative forcing of climate by different components. Taken from IPCC 2021[178].

---

[177] *IPCC2007, S. Solomon, D. Qin, M. Manning, et al., Climate Change 2007: The Physical Science Basis: Working Group I Contribution to the Fourth Assessment Report of the IPCC, Cambridge University Press, Cambridge (UK), New York (USA), (2007).*
[178] *IPCC2021:Fig7.6, IPCC Sixth Assessment Report Figure 7.6, https://www.ipcc.ch/report/ar6/wg1/figures/chapter-7/figure-7-6, 2021.*

The CO_2 concentration has increased at an even faster rate in the last few decades. It is a long-lived gas and due to its continuous cycling between atmosphere, ocean and land biosphere its specific lifetime is difficult to estimate. The IPCC:2001 technical report estimates 5 to 200 years lifetime for atmospheric CO_2.

Different carbon reservoirs prefer different isotopes of C. From the abundance information of the two stable carbon isotopes, 13C and 12C, available within the atmosphere, it is possible to distinguish between the type of emission sources and sinks of CO_2. The atmospheric CO_2 contains about 99% of 12C and nearly 1% of 13C. Emission of CO_2 from fossilized fuel like wood, coal, oil and gas combustion have 13C/12C isotopic ratio less than that in atmospheric CO_2. This is because during photosynthesis CO_2 containing 12C is preferred. Therefore, the 13C/12C isotopic ratio keeps on falling on increase in emissions from fossil fuels[179].

Other strong source of CO_2 is cement production which is steadily increasing, emissions from land use change is ongoing. Terrestrial biosphere and ocean are natural CO_2 sinks which are important and without these the amount of CO_2 in the atmosphere would have grown to much higher values.

Rising of CO_2 concentration is the cause of global warming and this warming reduces the efficiency of the terrestrial biosphere and ocean to work as CO_2 sink. The positive feedback leads to longer atmospheric CO_2 increase and greater climate change. Therefore, reliable estimation and prediction of atmospheric CO_2 and associated climate change require a good understanding of CO_2 source and sinks and their distribution spatially and temporally.

---

[179] R. F. Keeling, S. C. Piper, A. F. Bollenbacher, J. S. Walker, *Monthly atmospheric 13C/12C isotopic ratios for 11 SIO stations. In Trends: A Compendium of Data on Global Change,* 2010.

Spectral bands of carbon dioxide

CO_2 plays a significant role in the absorption and emission of atmospheric radiation. Due to its long life time and chemical inertness it is well mixed within the atmosphere and its distribution is influenced by transport process. As a linear tri-atomic molecule it has four normal modes of vibration (3N - 5) -a symmetric and an antisymmetric C=O stretching vibration and two degenerate bending vibrations. The fundamental stretching modes appear at 2349 and 1388 cm^{-1} (4.26 and 7.20 μm) while the degenerate bending appears at 667 cm^{-1} (14.99 μm) (Figure 3).

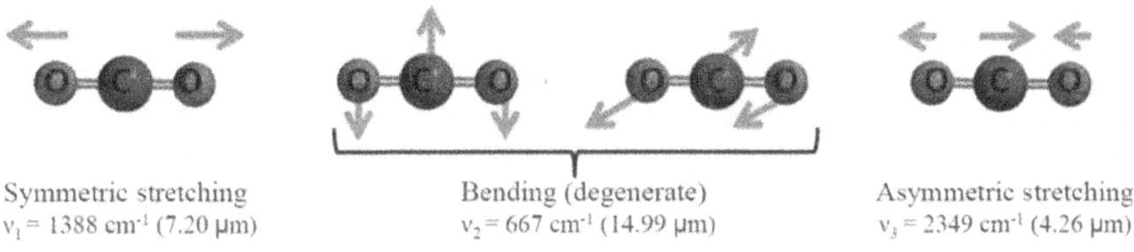

Figure 3: Normal modes of vibration of CO_2.

Assuming that the CO_2 concentration is fixed through the whole atmosphere[180][181], the strong emission bands at 14.99 and 4.26 μm are used to derive atmospheric temperature profile[182][183][184]. In both the bands sensitivity of observed radiances towards emission temperature is much larger than sensitivity to CO_2 concentration. In addition, water vapour significantly interferes in absorption at these bands. Beyond these fundamental frequencies there are several absorptions bands of CO_2 due to overtones and combinations of the fundamentals. For CO_2 in the NIR region there are two band families at around 2.0 μm and 1.6 μm. This NIR region is much less sensitive to temperature making these bands suitable for remote sensing of CO_2. In the 2.0 μm range there is a Fermi triad[185] with bands at 4853, 4978

[180] H. E. Fleming, L. M. McMillin, Appl. Opt. 16 (1977) 1366-1370.
[181] L. M. McMillin, H. E. Fleming, ibid.15 (1976) 358-363.
[182] W. L. Smith, ibid.9 (1970) 1993-1999.
[183] M. T. Chahine, J. Atmos. Sci. 27 (1970) 960-967.
[184] C. D. Rodgers, Rev. Geophys. Space Phys. 14 (1976) 609.
[185] C. E. Miller, L. R. Brown, J. Mol. Spectrosc. 228 (2004) 329-354.

and 5099 cm^{-1} which are strongly influenced by water vapour absorption features. In the 1.6 µm range there is a Fermi tetrad having four strong bands that appear at 6076, 6228, 6348 and 6503 cm^{-1}. In the Fermi tetrad the less intense 6076 and 6503 cm^{-1} bands are due to $(6v_2 + v_3)$ and $(3v_1 + v_3)$, while the stronger bands at 6228 and 6348 cm^{-1} are due to $(v_1 + 4v_2 + v_3)$ and $(2v_1 + 2v_2 + v_3)$ overtone combination modes[186]. These bands at 6228 and 6348 cm^{-1} (1.606 and 1.576 µm) are not affected by any other molecular absorption. Sensitivity studies[187] to explore the feasibility of space-based measurement in the 6348 cm^{-1} band also point to the suitability of this spectral region for CO_2 detection.

Research Methodology

Trace Gas Monitoring and Estimation

Reliable measurements for correct estimation and prediction of the trace gases are essential for understanding the associated global climate and its change. Our current knowledge of GHGs and their variability, based on sporadic local measurements, is very limited and insufficient[188]. There are several in-situ air sampling network observatories that provide accurate estimation of GHGs. Such measurements are temporally and spatially limited on the globe and provide inadequate information for use in understanding and predicting global climate. Such measurements are also limited in their vertical profiling and give good concentration estimates only in the boundary layer and the lower troposphere. Satellite observations are capable of continuous monitoring over the whole globe. Their limitation is the enormous cost and the effectiveness of the detector. Usually, detectors show good sensitivity in a narrow spectral range and thus limit the detection to a few species in few bands.

---

[186] A. B. Binder, D. P. Cruikshank, Astrophy. J. Let. 152 (1968) L7.

[187] J. Mao, S. R. Kawa, Appl. Opt. 43 (2004) 914-927.

[188] B. B. Stephens, K. R. Gurney, P. P. Tans, C. Sweeney, et al., Sci. 316 (2007) 1732-1735.

Ground measurements

In-situ CO_2 measurement and sampling are accurately obtained by several networks such as the NOAA ESRL (National Oceanic and Atmospheric Administration, Earth System Research Laboratory), carbon cycle greenhouse gas cooperative air sampling network, CDIAC (Carbon Dioxide Information Analysis Centre) etc. There are more than hundred land sites that provide regular observational information. These fixed measurements are complimented with ship and aircraft measurements. Collectively on the global scale they are sparse and have inhomogeneous geographical distribution[189]. A majority of these observatories are over the US and Europe and only limited numbers are in the southern hemisphere[190]. The seasonal and annual variation of the trace gases concentrations obtained from ground based instruments cannot provide accurate knowledge of their sources and sinks. Yet, ground based measurements are important and provide accurate information for validation of remote or indirect observations. The understanding of CO_2 concentration and its role in global climate change require wider spatial and temporal information[191].

Satellite instruments

Satellite based measurement is an effective approach to obtain and monitor the global distribution of greenhouse gases at high spatial and temporal resolution[192]. Since the most important trace gases are CO_2, a majority of instruments are dedicated to its measurement. Due to the detector sensitivity few satellite-based instruments take broadband observations of atmospheric CO_2 in thermal infrared (TIR). More

---

[189] *M. P. Barkley, U. Frieß, P. S. Monks, Atmos. Chem. Phys. 6 (2006) 3517-3534.*
[190] *M. Reuter, M. Buchwitz, O. Schneising, J. Heymann, et al., Atmos. Meas. Tech. 3 (2010) 209-232.*
[191] *M. P. Barkley, U. Frieß, P. S. Monks, Atmos. Chem. Phys. 6 (2006) 3517-3534.*
[192] *D. F. Baker, H. Bösch, S. C. Doney, D. O'Brien, D. S. Schimel, ibid.10 (2010) 4145-4165.*

reliable and accurate estimates are made by spectral measurements in the near-infrared/shortwave-infrared (NIR/SWIR) spectral region.

Global observations of atmospheric carbon dioxide in the near-infrared wavelengths were first conducted by SCIAMACHY onboard ENVISAT[193]. From 2009 onwards, several satellites were launched for CO2 measurement, including the Greenhouse Gases Observing Satellites (GOSAT and GOSAT-2)[194]. GOSAT became the first satellite dedicated to atmospheric greenhouse gas observations, contributing significantly to the quantification of emissions, particularly over high-latitude regions[195]. TROPOMI also provides high-latitude coverage for CO2 measurements[196]. OCO-2 and OCO-3 are also high-precision CO2 observation satellites, after GOSAT[197].

Spectral Simulation

A plot of 1.6 μm spectral range for some selected resolutions at 400 ppmv CO_2 concentration are presented in Figures 4. At fine resolutions the rotational features are visible that gradually average out in lower resolution simulations along with decrease in peak absorption. At the resolution of 0.2 nm the R branch rotational features totally smooth out with peaks at 1.6025 μm. Lower resolutions show similar smooth bands but the insensitive central regions between the P and R branches get affected and show absorption[198].

The sensitivity of this bands with respect to concentration is analysed by taking percent transmittance change per unit change in atmospheric CO_2 column in ppmv. Thus, sensitivity is calculated at all

[193] M. Buchwitz, R. de Beek, J. P. Burrows, H. Bovensmann, et al., ibid.5 (2005) 941-962.
[194] A. Kuze, H. Suto, M. Nakajima, T. Hamazaki, Appl. Opt. 48 (2009) 6716.
[195] S. Baray, D. J. Jacob, J. D. Maasakkers, J. X. Sheng, et al., Atmos. Chem. Phys. 21 (2021) 18101-18121.
[196] J. P. Veefkind, I. Aben, K. McMullan, H. Förster, et al., Remot. Sens. Environ. 120 (2012) 70-83.
[197] R. Doughty, T. P. Kurosu, N. Parazoo, P. Köhler, et al., Earth Syst. Sci. Data. 14 (2022) 1513-1529.
[198] P. Prasad, S. Rastogi, R. P. Singh, S. Panigrahy, Spectrochimica Acta Part A: Molecular and Biomolecular Spectroscopy 117 (2014) 330-339.

different resolutions and plotted in Figures 5 for some selected resolutions, as in Figure 4. The wavelengths of peak sensitivity coincide with the wavelengths showing maximum absorption i.e. R branch 1.6025 μm. At 0.2 nm and lower resolutions the sensitivity around the peak wavelength position remains constant. This implies that in concentration retrieval for these resolutions the exact identification of the peak wavelength is not essential[199].

Result and Discussion

The study of GHGs from satellites is a relatively new field of earth observation. Spectroscopic detection of the atmospheric trace gases is limited by the detector characteristics/resolution and sensitivity[200].

A detector material usually is sensitive to only a small region of the electro-magnetic spectrum. Spectroscopic information puts further restrictions on the required wavelength resolution. In recent years satellite instruments covering the UV/vis/NIR spectral range have evolved from having a few discrete channels with low spectral resolution, to instruments with wide and continuous spectral coverage at moderate spectral resolution[201]. While the latter can usually resolve the relevant structures in the UV and visible range, they cannot resolve the rotational line spectra, in particular in the NIR. The NIR spectral region is highly suitable for satellite-based observations of CO_2 because its spectral bands occur in this spectral window.

At good resolutions the rotational features associated with these NIR bands can be identified and their variations can be studied.

---

[199] P. Prasad, *Study of Aromatic Molecules of Astrophysical and Environmental Importance, Physics Department, DDU Gorakhpur University Gorakhpur, Gorakhpur, 2014, pp. 159.*
[200] *Ibid.*
[201] A. Richter, T. Wagner, *The Use of UV, Visible and Near IR Solar Back Scattered Radiation to Determine Trace Gases, in: J. P. Burrows, P. Borrell, U. Platt (Eds.), The Remote Sensing of Tropospheric Composition from Space, Springer Berlin Heidelberg, Berlin, Heidelberg, (2011), 67-121.*

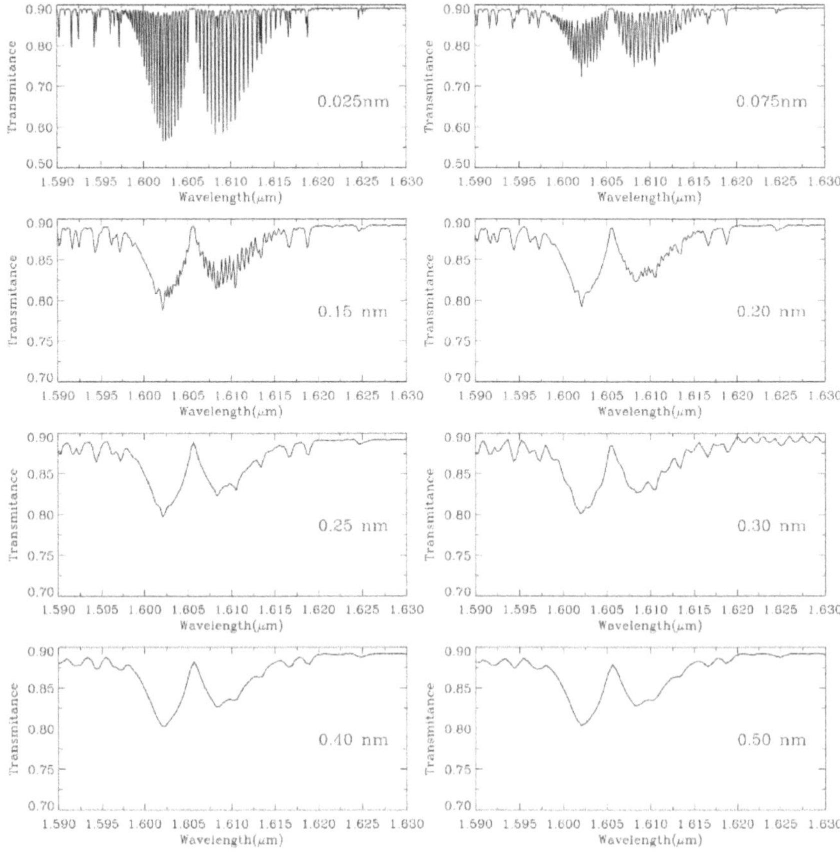

Figure 4: Transmittances for the 1.606 μm band at resolutions mentioned in the graphs. At low resolutions the y-scale is enlarged to show the absorption features clearly.

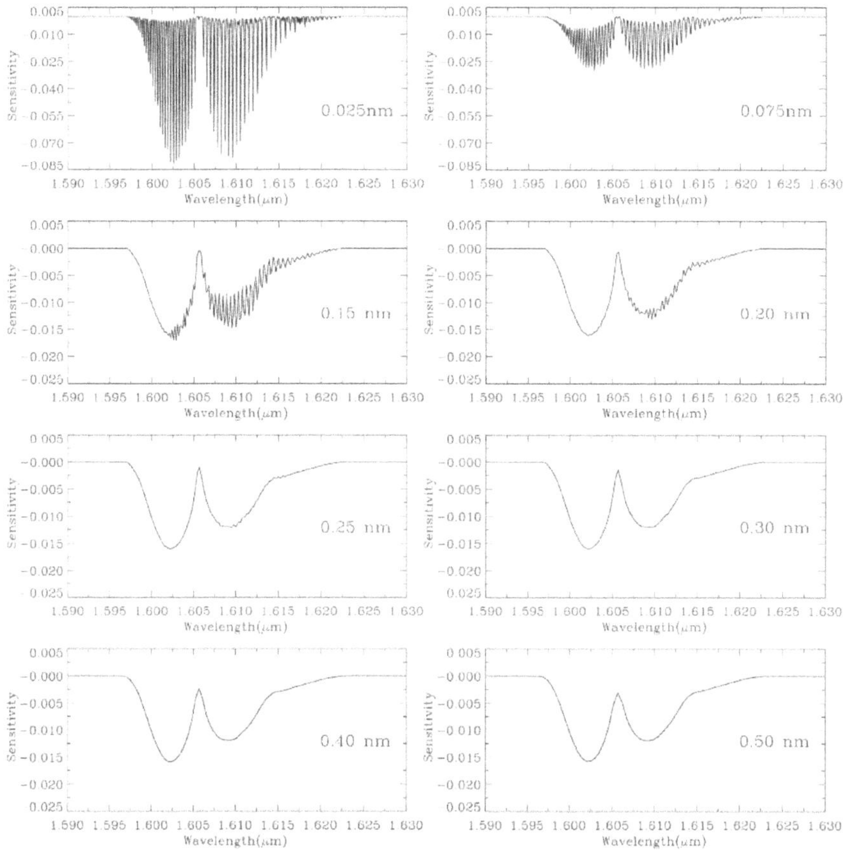

Figure 5: Sensitivity of the 1.606 μm spectral band to concentration, as percent transmittance change per ppmv concentration. At low resolutions the y-scale is enlarged for better visualization of sensitivity change.

To study a specific gas and estimate its concentration appropriate fitting windows need to be selected where the differential absorption structures of the molecule of interest is maximized and the impact from interfering signals is minimized. The detector requirement, therefore, is that it must be sensitive enough in the wavelength window to be able to detect absorption features of the specie even at low concentrations. For effective concentration retrieval the detector must also be able to resolve the spectral features. Any detector functions best if the energy being detected is high, which is possible if the wavelength window, is broad. If this is the case the resolution will be low and spectral band details will not be detected and may hamper concentration retrieval.

The choice of suitable sensor characteristics is thus the main factor of consideration for spectrometer designers and users. For better resolution suitable FTIR based dispersive instruments have also been considered useful, but their deployment in space and maintain spatial resolution is difficult[202]. The primary motive of the present study was to identify suitable limits of resolution, which can be utilized for accurate enough concentration retrieval. With this aim study of the NIR bands of CO_2 has been made and its important bands in the 1.6 µm wavelength region are studied. Such studies on identification of spectral windows and their feasibility for concentration retrieval are rare. The study shows that the 1.6 µm spectral band is suitable for observing CO_2 through remote sensing or ground-based observations. However, for reliable concentration measurements, the resolution should not be coarser than 0.2 nanometre.

---

[202] *A. M. Piters, B. Buchmann, D. Brunner, R. Cohen, et al., Data Quality and Validation of Satellite Measurements of Tropospheric Composition, ibid., 315-364.*

10. Study of Intermolecular Interaction of Pyridine and HO-(CH2)n-O-C6H4-C6H4-CN (HnCBP) Liquid Crystal Molecules by using AIM Calculations

- *Jitendra Kumar*

Department of Physics, Babasaheb Bhimrao Ambedkar University, Lucknow

Introduction

Matter exists in three forms i.e. solid, liquid and gas in which solid may exist either in crystalline form or in amorphous form.[203] The crystalline solids have a regular arrangement of the molecules over a large distance compared with the molecular dimensions and such order is called a long range order.[204,205,206,207,208] When a solid is heated, it transforms into an isotropic liquid and again on cooling it

---

[203] I.C. Khoo, "Liquid Crystal" A Johan Wiley & sons, inc., Publication (2007).

[204] D. Demus, J. Goodby , G. W. Gray, H. W. Spiess and V. Vill"Handbook of Liquid Crystals"Deutsche Bibliothek Cataloguing Publication (1998).

[205] P. J. Collings, M. Hird, Introduction to Liquid Crystals; Chemistry and Physics, Taylor and Francis London (2009).

[206] D.A. Dunmur, S. Singh, Liquid Crystals, World Scientific Publishing Company, Singapore (2002).

[207] K. Fontell "X-Ray diffraction by liquid crystals-Amphilic systems" in Ellis Horwood series in physical chemistry "Liquid crystals and Plastic crystals", Halsted, N. Y. vol 2 (1974) pp. 80.

[208] D. Demus, and L.Richfer, Texture of Liquid Crystals, Verlag Chemistry N. Y. (1978).

gets transformed to crystalline solid[209,210].There are certain materials which does not directly transform from crystalline solid to isotropic liquid and vice versa but take on an intermediate structure in which they can flow like liquid with maintaining the anisotropic physical properties similar to crystalline solids. This intermediate phase of material is termed as liquid crystal, liquid crystalline phase, mesophase or mesomorphic phase and such materials are called mesogens, liquid crystalline or mesomorphic substances[211,212,213,214]

Liquid crystals show different phases with heating or cooling the solid and crystalline liquid materials. These different phases appear due to their different orientation and positional order. According to the order there are mainly two type of liquid crystal found basically i.e. nematic and smectics. Later several more phases were derived depending on the molecular properties[215]

The name nematic liquid crystal was first used by Friedel[216] from the Greek word which means thread and refers to the tread like defects absorbed in nematics. Molecules in the nematic liquid crystal phase have a preferred direction of orientation order. The orientation order called the director is denoted by vector **n**. The director is long axes point in one direction and the molecule can rotate by both the axes, because their high mobility, they possess an isotropic like properties in term to optical property, viscosity, electrical susceptibility, magnetic susceptibility, electrical conductivity and thermal conductivity[217].

[209] W. Goodby, Mol. Cryst. Liq. Cryst., **92**, 171 (1983).

[210] H. Sackann, Liq., Cryst., **5**, 43(1981).

[211] S. Chandrasekhar, B.K. Sadashiva and K. A. Suresh, Pramana, **9**, 471(1977).

[212] J. Billard, J.C. Duois, N.H. Tinh and A.Z. NouveanJ.Chim.,**2**, 535(1978).

[213] L. Komitov, Mol. Cryst. Liq. Cryst., **608**, 246 (2015).

[214] A. Yamaguchi, A. Yoshizawa, I. Nishiyama, J. Yamamoto, H. Yokoyama, Mol. Cryst. Liq.Cryst., **439**, 85 (2005).

[215] G. Friedel, Ann. Physique, **18**, 273 (1922).

[216] W. Hamley, Introduction to Soft Matter, John Wiley and Sons Ltd., England, (2000).

[217] S. T. Lagerwall, FLC and Anti FLC, Wiley, VCH,Weinhelm, (1999).

The other one is cholesteric phase, also known as blue phase, is like the nematic phase in having long-range orientation order but no long-range order in positions of the centers of mass of molecule. The first blue phase of cholesteric liquid crystal (cholestericbenzoate) was discovered by the Renitizier in year 1888. He reported a bright blue-violet reflection right below the clearing point for a narrow range of temperature between the isotropic phase and nematic phase[218]and the another one is the smectic liquid crystals are layer structures of the side chain polymers and are characterized by the parellel arrangement of the side groups in layers and unoriented main chains. The smectic phases are periodic three-dimensional objects in one direction[219] and smectic phases have lamellar structure. The smectic layers are always long-range orientation order but not have the positional order the same in all layers. The SmA, SmC, SmB, SmI, and SmF are five different smectic liquid crystal mesophases. On the basis of chirality in molecules smectics can be divided in two groups: achiral smectic and chiral smectic.

Although the role of intermolecular association energy had always been considered to be important with respect to the behavior of materials, but the quantitative evaluation with actual molecular geometry started in early 80s. estimated the variation of total energy of a pair of nematic liquid crystal molecules with respect to change in the relative orientation of the molecules and obtained a curve agreeing with the Maier-Saupetheory. The energy values clearly indicated that the molecules had a strong tendency for alignment along the long molecular axis. Similar results were obtained by Sanyal et. al. in case of a number of nematogens [220,221,222,223,224].

---

[218]H. Sackmann, Liq. Cryst. **5, 43 (1989).**

[219]P. J. Collings, Liquid crystals, 1 edn., Princeton University Press, Princeton, New Jersey, USA, (1990).

[220] M. Roychoudhury& D. P. Ojha, Mol. Cryst. Liquid Cryst., 213, (1992) 73.

[221] M. Roychoudhury& D. P. Ojha, Nat. Acad. Sci. Lett., 16, (1993) 303.

[222] M. Roychoudhury, D. P. Ojha & N. K. Sanyal, Indian J.Phys., 32, (1994) 440.

[223] D. P. Ojha, D. Kumar & M. Roychoudhury, Proc. Nat. Acad. Sci. India, 65A, (1995) 115.

[224] M. Roychoudhury & D. Kumar, Materials Sci. Forum Transtec Publ., Switzerland, 13,222-223, (1996).

Physicochemical properties of liquid crystalline 2, 5-disubstituted pyridine derivatives, the effect of the introduction of the pyridine 2,5-diyl fragment into the molecular core of some liquid crystals have attracted attention of scientists working in the field of liquid crystals.[225,226,227]Petrove and Polueheuko[228] have presented a comparative study of 60 compounds of this class and pointed out some peculiar structure- property relationships. It has been observed that in the case of two ring alkyl alkoxyl pyridines, the variations of length in alkyl chain or positions of hetro atoms in the ring affects the mesogenic characters significantly.[229] The molecular structure of the 2,5-disubstituted pyridine derivatives, position and quantity of their pyridine ring, and position of the nitrogen in the pyridine ring plays important role on their mesomorphic properties. The geometrical and electronic structure of the pyridine ring[230,231] plays a crucial role in the intra- and inter-molecular interactions which affect the packing of the molecules and which also influences mesophase stability.[232,233,234]

In this work, a probability distribution of the configuration has been computed using Maxwell- Boltzmann statistics in order to obtain a

[225] R. Buchecker, A. I. Pavluchenko, V. F. Petrov, M. Schadt, N. I. Smirnova, V.V. Titov EUr. Pat. Appl., EP0361 157, (1990).

[226] A. I. Pavluchenko, V.V. Titonv, N. I. SmirnvaAdvances in Liquid Crystal Research and Applications, L. Bata ed., Pergamon-Press-AkademiaiKiado, Oxfort-Budapest, pp. 1007 (1980).

[227] A. I. Pavluchenko, G. V. Purvanyatskas, N. I. Smirnova, M. F. Grebenkin, V. F. Petrov, M. I. Barnik, A. V. Ivaschenko, N. I. Korotkova, E. I. Kovshev, A. Z. Rabinovich, N. A. Bumagin, N. P. Andrjukhova, I. P. Beletskaya, S. D. Maltsev, V. V. Titov, PCT WO 88/07992, (1988).

[228] V. F. Petrov, A. I. Pavluchenko, and N. I. Smirnova Mol. Cryst. Liq. Cryst., 265, 47 (1995).

[229] M. F. Grebyonkin, V. F. Petrov, V. V. Belyaev, A. I. Pavluchenko, N. I. Smirnova, E. I. Kovshev, V. V. Titov, A. V. IvashchenkoMol. Cryst. Liq. Cryst., 129, 245 (1985).

[230] A. I. Pavluchenko, V. F. Petrov, S. Takenaka, IDW'98, Proc. Fifth Int. Display Workshops, December 7-9, Kobe, Japan, pp. 835 (1998).

[231] A. I. Pavluchenko, V. F. Petrov, M. F. Grebenkin, A. V. Ivaschenko, N. I. Korotkova, N. I. Smirnova, L. V. Krjuchkova, L. A. Karamysheva, I. F. Agafonova, P. P. Dakhnov, R. Kh. Geivandov, E. P. Pozhidaev, B. M. Bolotin, Eur. Pat. Appl., EP 0 374 849, (1989).

[232] V. F. Petrove and A. I. Polueheuko, Mol. Cryst. Liq. Cryst. ,383, 63 (2002).

[233] C. G. Le Fevre, R. J. W. Le Fevre, J. Chem. Soc., 2750 (1955).

[234] B. Schanker, J. Applequist, J. Phys. Chem., 100, 3879 (1996).

better insight. Thus, in a particular interacting condition, say rotation of a molecule about an axis perpendicular to the molecular plane during stacking, let us suppose energy at any orientation is ε_1 the probability of finding the molecular system in this orientation P_i will be given by

$$P_i = \frac{e^{\frac{-\nabla\varepsilon_i}{kT}}}{\sum\limits_{i} e^{\frac{-\nabla\varepsilon_i}{kT}}}$$

Where, the summation is over all the possible orientations, k is the Boltzmann constant and T denotes absolute temperature. $\Delta\varepsilon_i$ is the difference in energy from the minimum energy value for the particular set. Hence, calculation of probability for each orientation enables to evaluate to the probability distribution with respect to the angle between two molecules. The relative preference for alignment may be examined through this curve. To compare the preference for alignment between different molecules, one may introduce a parameter (similar to the order parameter) by measuring the angular separation of two points at half-maximum probability.

Similarly, the tendency to form layers or the molecular freedom to move under aligned condition etc. may also be examined with the help of the study of probability distribution during sliding.

In this section, I am calculating the charge density and Laplacian charge density of the interacting molecules. I study the interaction of stacked pairs of some pyrideen molecules and the other the some 4, 4' - disubstituted biphenyls of formula HO $(CH_2)_6OC_6H_4C_6H_4R$ with R = cyano and nitro terminal groups have been determined including co-crystallized materials of both of the compounds.

Method of calculation

Calculation of interaction has been done using Atomic in molecules (AIM) method. AIM analysis incorporates various graphical techniques including population analysis. It has been designed to examine the minor effect caused by the boundary in the primarily featureless electron density.

This is done by calculating the gradient and Laplacian of the electron density. Interaction of each pair of molecule is different for different interacting sides. The entire process is carried employing a computer program-based AIM calculation. For the given pair of molecules, program would calculate the number of interaction sites (atom of each molecule taking part in interaction). A Global search of the different configuration is difficult and time consuming since it would involve many non-physical configurations which could be avoid by choosing suitable path for calculation. Since most of the systems under study have long and flat molecular structure, the interaction scheme comes under the category of stacking interaction.

In stacking interaction, a flat strip like molecule has two surfaces say Side A and Side B (See in Figure 1). For a molecular pair, the staking may be visualized in following way (a) Side A of the first facing of the second (b) Side A of the first facing Side B of second facing or Side B of the first facing of the Side A of the second. Under all the condition mentioned above, the following variation may be required to be investigated.

- ❖ Translational of one molecule with respect to with respect other perpendicular to the plane of molecule.
- ❖ Rotation of one molecule about the long molecular axes.
- ❖ Rotation about an axis perpendicular to the plane of the molecule.
- ❖ A small rotation may also be required about an axis perpendicular to the molecular axes and in the plane of the molecular axis and in the plane of the molecule to obtain a proper contact.

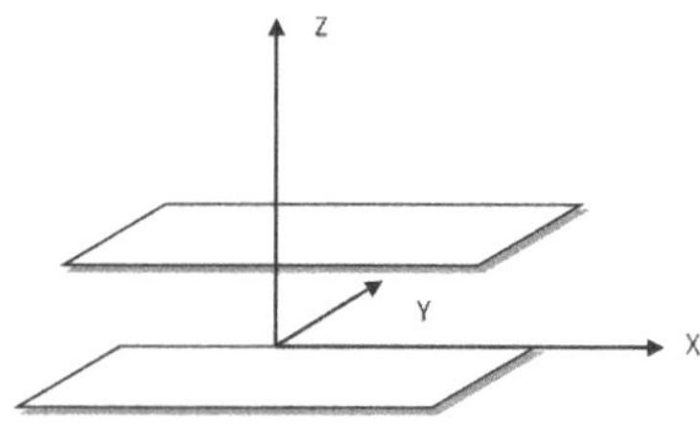

Fig. 1: the mode of stacking interaction of molecular pair.

Results and Discussion

(a) Pyridine molecules

The molecular structure of the 2, 5-disubstituted pyridine derivatives as well as position of the nitrogen in the pyridine ring play important role on their mesomorphic properties. The geometrical and electronic structures of the pyridine ring also play crucial role in the inter-molecular interactions, which affect the packing of the molecules and influence mesophase stability. In this section, I have study pyridine and its substituent group. The substituent group play a crucial role in Liquid Crystal. The interaction of pyridine molecule is stacking both sides, pyridine side one stacking Side A (PD_01_ST_01) and the other pyridine staking Side B (PD_01_ST_02). there molecular interactions are as follows:

(b) Bipolar, mesogenic biphenyls

Bipolar, mesogenic biphenyls show very good intermolecular interaction. The interaction of atom is defined here by the charge density as well as Laplacian charge density; they play an important role in the molecular atomic interaction. Here I discuss the biphenyl mesogenic property of molecule HnCBP (n=4-8) and detect the short and long alkyl terminal group. These molecular interactions study the liquid crystalline state. The homologs series of this compound exists in nematic phase. An analysis of the Laplacian of the charge density shows that the direction of the maxima which characterize local charge concentrations around the oxygen atoms.

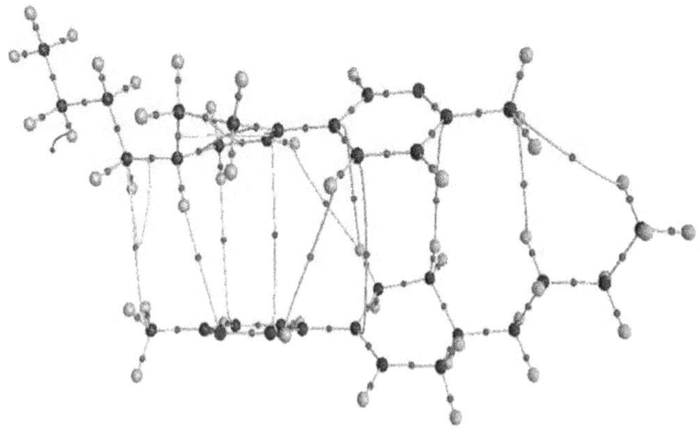

Fig. 2: AIM representation of PD_01_ST_01 molecule.

In Figure 2, the structure defined the stacking interaction of side one. In this, there are nine atoms interacting with each other. The minimum interaction charge density is 0.005 between atom no. 32 and no. 53 but atom pairs 37-75, 30-72, and 11-72 interact strongly in side A.

Table 1: Electron density and Laplacian of electron density of PD_01_ST_01.

S. No	Atom No.	(ρ)	$\nabla^2 l$
1.	25-57	0.002	-0.002
2.	32-53	0.005	-0.003
3.	29-55	0.002	-0.001
4.	37-75	0.001	-0.001
5.	30-72	0.001	-0.001
6.	11-72	0.001	-0.001
7.	14-73	0.002	-0.002
8.	39-63	0.003	-0.003
9.	39-58	0.002	-0.002

Fig. 3: AIM representation PD_01_ST_02 molecule.

Table 2: Electron density and Laplacian of electron density of PD_01_ST_02

S. No	Atom No.	(ρ)	$\nabla^2 l$
1.	22-60	0.004	-0.003
2.	25-63	0.003	-0.002
3.	25-73	0.003	-0.002
4.	29-48	0.002	-0.001
5.	30-52	0.002	-0.001
6.	13-80	0.001	-0.001

In Figure 2 the structure defined the stacking interaction of side B. In this, there are six atoms interacting with each other. Interaction between atom no. 22-60 is weakest while interaction of atom no. 13-80 is strongest. The atom No 13-80 interaction plays a crucial role in the molecular system.

Side A possesses better interaction properties in compare the side B because it has a greater No. of interacting atoms which leads to enhanced physical and chemical properties.

Figure 3 and Table 3 show the Side A stacking. Atoms no 54-109, 39-75, and 37-95 have the strongest interaction while atom no. 32-87, 35-87, and 35-91 interact in a comparatively weaker manner.

The charge density plays an important role in intermolecular interaction. The Laplacian charge density of atoms No. 37-95, 39-75, and 54-109 is very important as they have the highest value of charge density at a particular point.

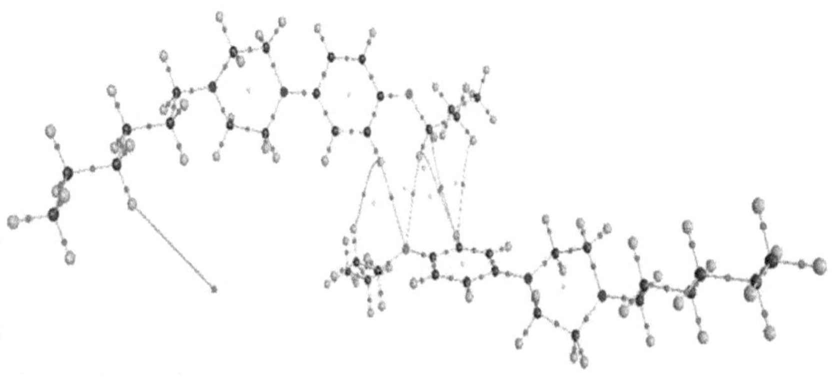

Fig. 4: AIM representation PD_02_ST_01 molecule.

Table 3: Electron density and Laplacian of electron density of PD_03_ST_01

S. No	Atom No.	(ρ)	$\nabla^2 l$
1.	32-87	0.0004	-0.0003
2.	35-87	0.0004	-0.0003
3.	35-91	0.0004	-0.0003
4.	37-95	0.001	-0.001
5.	39-75	0.001	-0.001
6.	45-74	0.003	-0.002
7.	46-76	0.003	-0.003
8.	54-109	0.001	-0.001
9.	23-112	0.0003	-0.003

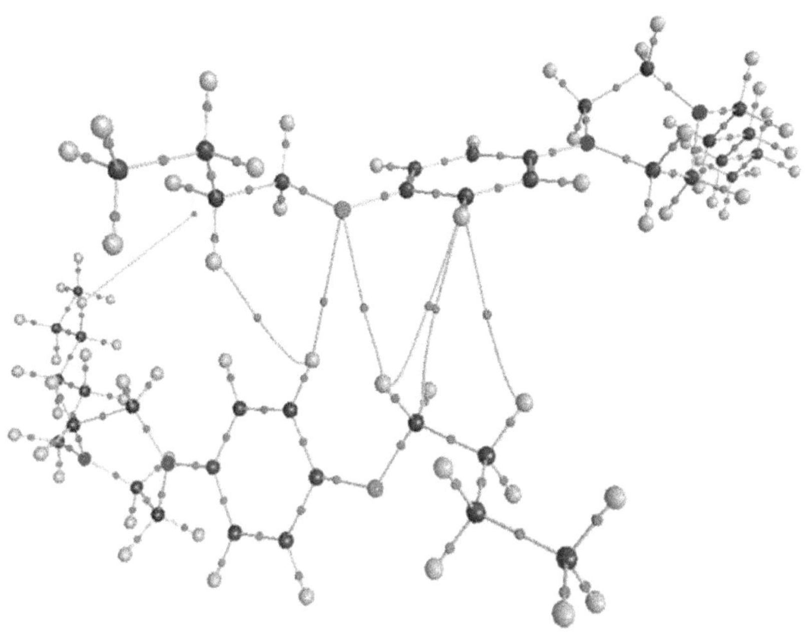

Fig. 5: AIM representation of PD_02_ST_02 molecule.

Table 4: Electron density and Laplacian of electron density of PD_02_ST_02

S. No.	Atom No.	(ρ)	$\nabla^2 l$
1.	109-47	0.002	-0.002
2.	76-47	0.004	-0.003
3.	76-49	0.003	-0.003
4.	103-49	0.002	-0.002
5.	103-20	0.002	-0.002
6.	103-51	0.002	-0.001

Figure 4 and Table 4 show the charge density of interacting atoms and Laplacian charge, which are very weak. Therefore, it is to be concluded that the intermolecular property of staking side A is better in comparison to side B.

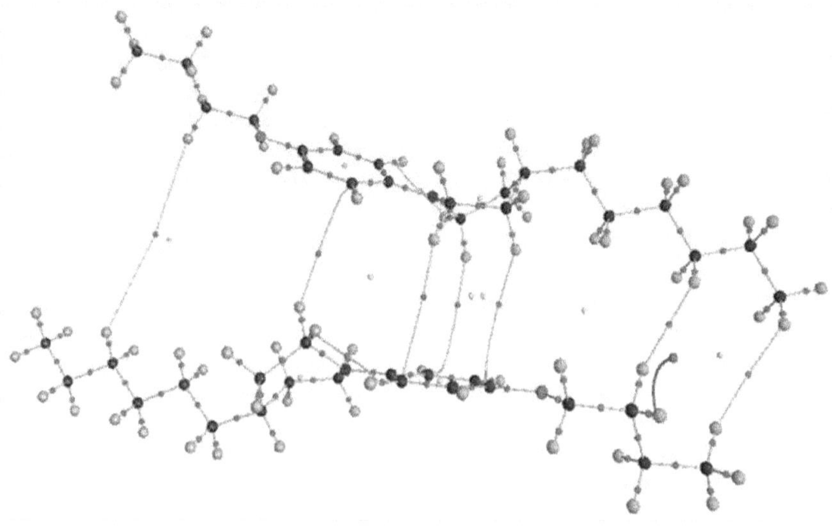

Fig. 6: AIM representation of PD_03_ST_01 Molecule.

Table 5: Electron density and Laplacian of electron density of PD_03_ST_01

S. No.	Atom No.	(ρ)	$\nabla^2 l$
1.	36-82	0.003	-0.002
2.	36-87	0.001	-0.001
3.	17-101	0.001	-0.001
4.	50-100	0.002	-0.001
5.	50-76	0.002	-0.001
6.	54-73	0.004	-0.003

In the interaction of side A of the PD03 molecule, no. of interacting atoms is six. The pair 54-73 has the lowest interaction. The point of maximum interacting charge density is 0.001.

Table 6: Electron density and Laplacian of electron density of PD_03_ST_02

S. No.	Atom No.	(ρ)	$\nabla^2 l$
1.	111-29	4.838	-3.580
2.	72-43	0.002	-0.001
3.	67-18	0.002	-0.001
4.	101-14	0.002	-0.001
5.	97-16	0.002	-0.001
6.	88-53	0.001	-0.001
7.	84-56	0.001	-0.001

In the PD03 side B interaction, the No. of interacting atoms are seven which is greater in comparison to side A.

Table 7: Electron density and Laplacian of electron density of PD_04_ST_01

S. No.	Atom No.	(ρ)	$\nabla^2 l$
1.	27-80	0.0002	-0.0002
2.	27-56	0.0003	-0.0002
3.	36-64	0.002	-0.001
4.	12-68	0.002	-0.001
5.	11-95	0.003	-0.002
6.	13-97	0.001	-0.001
7.	47-101	1.617	-1.280

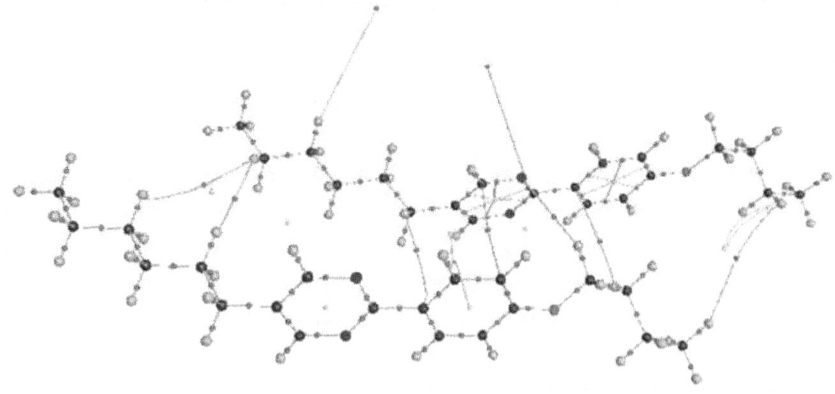

Fig. 7: AIM representation of PD_03_ST_02 Molecule.

Fig. 8: AIM representation of PD_04_ST_01 molecule.

In the molecule PD04 No of interact atoms is six, in this interact atom No. 13-97 is a strong interact atom and 47-101 is very less. Atom No. 13-97 is a higher value of the charge density of the interaction point. The total No. of interact atom is seven the atom changes the symmetry of the atom; change in symmetry is the change in the physical property of the atom.

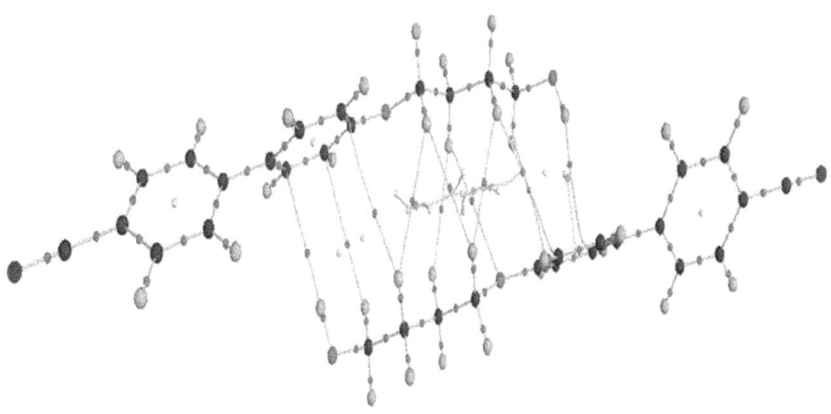

Fig. 9: AIM representation of PD_04_ST_02 molecule.

Table 8: Electron density and Laplacian of electron density of PD_04_ST_02

S. No.	Atom No.	(ρ)	$\nabla^2 l$
1.	28-98	2.335	-1.866
2.	35-64	0.002	-0.001
3.	12-59	0.002	-0.001
4.	8-63	0.002	-0.002
5.	13-87	0.002	-0.001
6.	47-76	2.466	-2.071

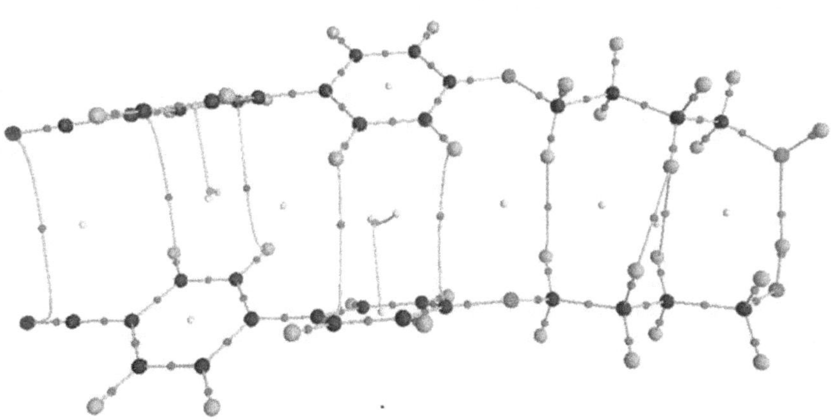

Fig. 10: AIM representation of H4CBP_ST_01 molecule.

Table 9: Electron density and Laplacian of electron density of H4CBP_ST_01

S.No.	Atom No.	(ρ)	$(\nabla^2\rho)$
1.	14-58	0.004	-0.003
2.	13-59	0.002	-0.001
3.	12-61	0.002	-0.001
4.	28-61	0.001	-0.001
5.	28-65	0.002	-0.001
6.	24-65	0.002	-0.002
7.	24-48	0.002	-0.001
8.	24-47	0.004	-0.003
9.	26-63	0.003	-0.002
10.	26-52	0.002	-0.002
11.	22-49	0.005	-0.004

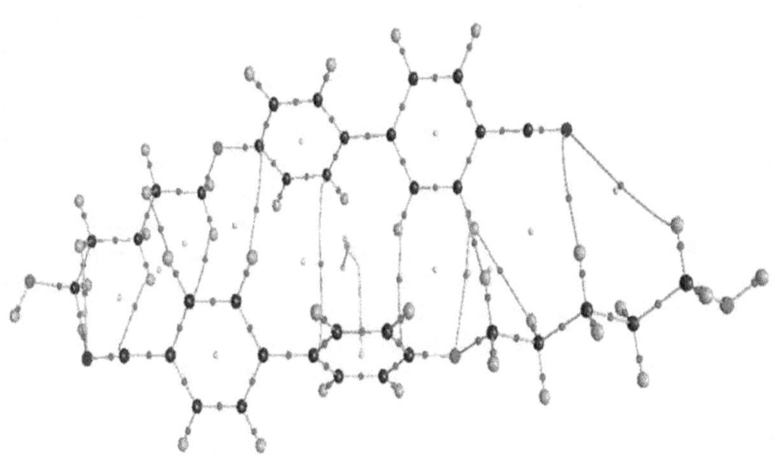

Fig. 11: AIM representation of H4CBP _ST_02 molecule.

Table 10: Electron density and Laplacian of electron density of H4CBP_ST_01

S.No.	Atom No.	(ρ)	$(\nabla^2\rho)$
1.	1-38	0.001	-0.001
2.	4-40	0.002	-0.001
3.	34-44	0.002	-0.001
4.	14-68	0.003	-0.002
5.	12-67	0.002	-0.002
6.	28-66	0.006	-0.004
7.	26-62	0.004	-0.003
8.	24-62	0.006	-0.004
9.	21-57	0.023	-0.022

For staking side B of PD04, there are only six interacting atoms this six-interacting atom charge density is high which means these atoms show very weak interaction properties; therefore, side A is good for intermolecular interaction.

On side A of molecule H4CBP, no. of interacting atoms is eleven and in side B, the no. of interacting atoms is nine so the H4CBP.

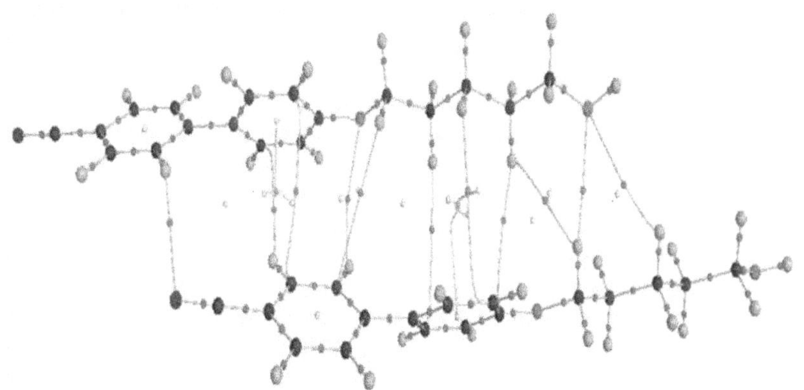

Fig. 12: AIM representation of H5CBP_ST_01 molecule.

Table 11: Electron density and Laplacian of electron density of H5CBP _ST_01

S.No.	Atom No.	(ρ)	$(\nabla^2\rho)$
1.	37-61	0.006	-0.005
2.	38-61	0.005	-0.004
3.	34-60	0.003	-0.003
4.	33-62	0.003	-0.002
5.	30-42	0.002	-0.001
6.	10-63	0.001	-0.001
7.	8-47	0.0005	-0.0004
8.	23-50	0.002	-0.001
9.	2-70	0.002	-0.002
10.	22-53	0.002	-0.002
11.	22-73	0.002	-0.002
12.	21-74	0.001	-0.001
13.	21-78	0.001	-0.0007

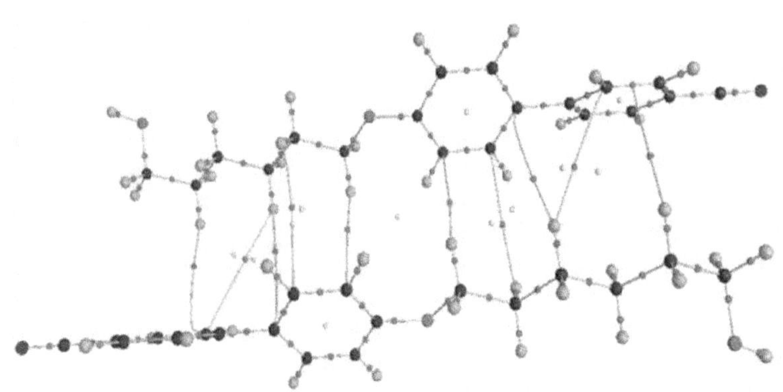

Fig. 13: AIM representation of H5CBP _ST_02 molecule.

Table 12: Electron density and Laplacian of electron density of H5CBP _ST_02

S.No.	Atom No.	(ρ)	$(\nabla^2 \rho)$
1.	23-61	0.005	-0.003
2.	12-65	0.003	-0.002
3.	9-46	0.003	-0.002
4.	30-45	0.001	-0.001
5.	13-64	0.002	-0.002
6.	33-66	0.002	-0.001
7.	34-49	0.001	-0.001
8.	37-50	0.003	-0.002
9.	37-71	0.002	-0.002
10.	19-71	0.006	-0.004
11.	19-75	0.002	-0.002

In the side A of molecule H5CBP, the no. of interacting atoms are thirteen but for the side B, only eleven.

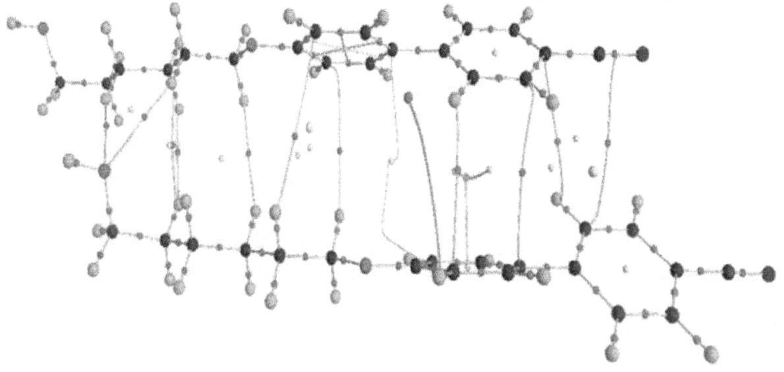

Fig. 14: AIM representation of H6CBP _ST_01 molecule.

Table 13: Electron density and Laplacian of electron density of H6CBP _ST_01

S.No.	Atom No.	(ρ)	$(\nabla^2\rho)$
1.	20-51	0.002	-0.001
2.	36-51	0.001	-0.0008
3.	36-47	0.001	-0.0008
4.	33-48	0.001	-0.0008
5.	32-49	0.002	-0.001
6.	6-75	0.002	-0.001
7.	5-76	0.002	-0.001
8.	4-79	0.001	-0.001
9.	27-79	0.001	-0.0008

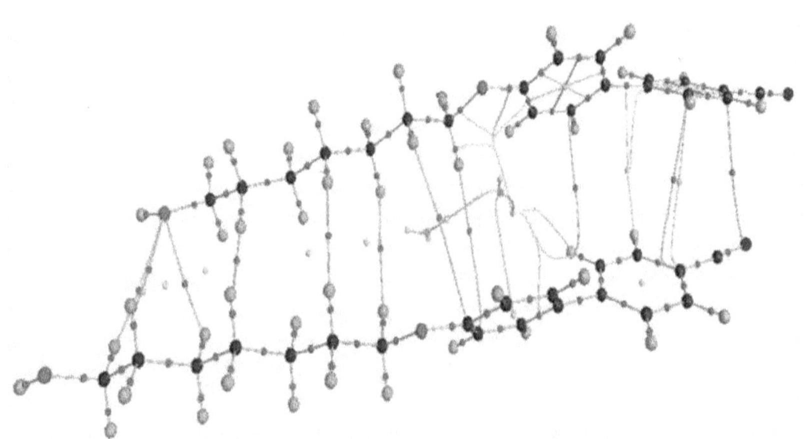

Fig. 15: AIM representation of H6CBP_ST_02 molecule.

Table 14: Electron density and Laplacian of electron density of H6CBP _ST_02

S.No.	Atom No.	(ρ)	$(\nabla^2\rho)$
1.	37-65	0.006	-0.004
2.	33-65	0.005	-0.004
3.	33-82	0.002	-0.002
4.	36-82	0.001	-0.001
5.	32-78	0.001	-0.001
6.	2-77	0.001	-0.0001
7.	6-74	0.002	-0.0009
8.	27-45	0.002	-0.001
9.	9-47	0.002	-0.002
10.	10-73	0.002	-0.002
11.	14-55	0.002	-0.002

In the H6CBP molecule, side A has nine interaction sites and side B has eleven. The no. of interaction atom is high therefore the H6CBP possesses higher homologous packing. Side B has better interaction properties than side A.

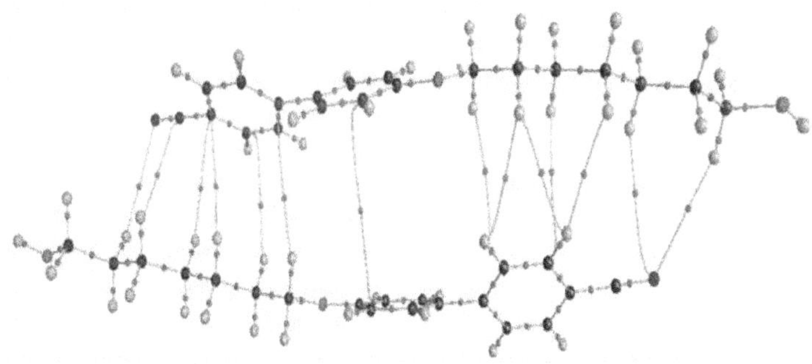

Fig. 16: AIM representation of H7CBP _ST_01 molecule.

Table 15: Electron density and Laplacian of electron density of H7CBP _ST_01

S. No.	Atom No.	(ρ)	$(\nabla^2\rho)$
1.	23-88	0.003	-0.002
2.	22-87	0.002	-0.002
3.	1-83	0.002	-0.002
4.	1-84	0.003	-0.002
5.	280	0.003	-0.002
6.	3-79	0.001	-0.001
7.	11-55	0.0007	-0.0005
8.	33-71	0.001	-0.001
9.	34-71	0.002	-0.001
10.	33-74	0.002	-0.001
11.	38-70	0.002	-0.002
12.	37-48	0.002	-0.002
13.	41-69	0.002	-0.001
14.	45-69	0.002	-0.002

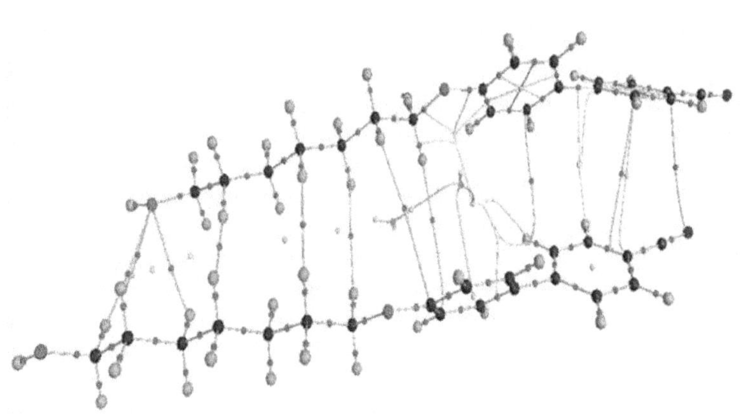

Fig. 17: AIM representation of H7CBP _ST_02 molecule.

Table 16: Electron density and Laplacian of electron density of H7CBP _ST_02

S. No.	Atom No.	(ρ)	$(\nabla^2\rho)$
1.	21-91	0.002	-0.002
2.	21-88	0.003	-0.003
3.	21-87	0.004	-0.003
4.	43-84	0.008	-0.006
5.	39-80	0.002	-0.002
6.	36-79	0.001	-0.001
7.	35-56	0.0004	-0.0004
8.	32-55	0.0006	-0.0005
9.	8-71	0.002	-0.001
10.	5-47	0.002	-0.001
11.	6-69	0.003	-0.002

In side A of H7CBP, no. of interacting atoms are fourteen while side B has eleven. The no. of interacting atoms is high, therefore the packing H7CBP molecules for the higher homologous series HnCBP is good.

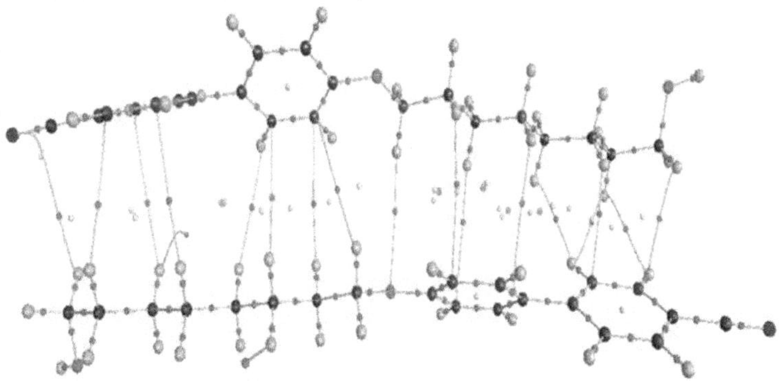

Fig. 18: AIM representation of H8CBP _ST_01 molecule.

Table 17: Electron density and Laplacian of electron density of H8CBP _ST_01

S.No.	Atom No.	(ρ)	$(\nabla^2\rho)$
1.	24-96	0.001	-0.001
2.	6-95	0.002	-0.002
3.	2-92	0.001	-0.0009
4.	5-91	0.002	-0.001
5.	29-88	0.001	-0.001
6.	8-87	0.001	-0.001
7.	9-84	0.001	-0.001
8.	9-83	0.001	-0.001
9.	34-62	0.001	-0.001
10.	38-60	0.002	-0.001
11.	35-58	0.001	-0.001
12.	39-56	0.002	-0.001
13.	42-76	0.005	-0.004
14.	46-76	0.003	-0.003
15.	46-77	0.003	-0.003
16.	42-54	0.002	-0.005

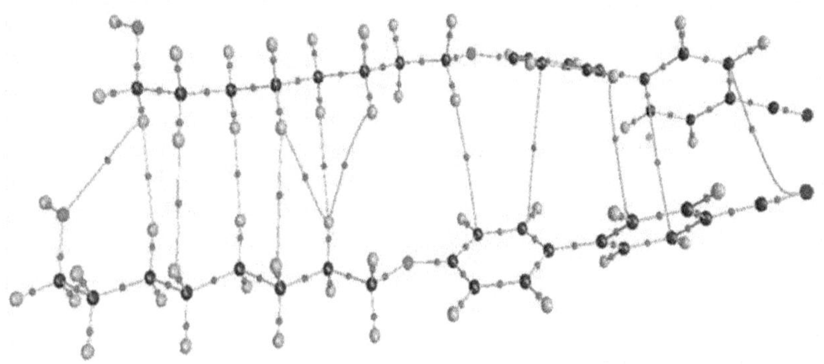

Fig. 19: AIM representation of H8CBP _ST_02 molecule.

Table 18: Electron density and Laplacian of electron density of H8CBP _ST_02

S.No.	Atom No.	(ρ)	$(\nabla^2\rho)$
1.	47-71	0.003	-0.003
2.	43-89	0.007	-0.005
3.	47-93	0.004	-0.003
4.	46-90	0.003	-0.002
5.	42-86	0.002	-0.002
6.	42-85	0.002	-0.002
7.	39-85	0.002	-0.002
8.	38-85	0.001	-0.001
9.	34-60	0.002	-0.001
10.	9-61	0.002	-0.001
11.	29-52	0.002	-0.001
12.	4-55	0.001	-0.001
13.	2-73	0.002	-0.001

Side A of H8CBP has sixteen interacting atoms and side B has thirteen. Side A has greater no. of interacting atoms than side B. In side A the charge density is high in comparison to side B.

Conclusion

In the summary of this work, the AIM calculation provides the HnCBP molecule interaction of the different stages and different sides of this series molecule. The interaction energies for the stacking side A and the stacking side B of molecules were found asymmetrical. These calculations confirm that the HnCBP molecule stacking interaction increases with increases in the chain of the molecule.

11. Electrical Transport Study of Potassium Metaborate: KBO_2

-   *Kripa Mani Mishra*

Department of Physics, D.D.U. Gorakhpur University, Gorakhpur

Introduction

Numerous researchers [235] have studied the electrical conductivity of some potassium-based salts in an effort to find potassium-ion conducting superionic solids, but no major attempt had been made in estimating the relative contribution of electronic & ionic conductivities in them, that is required to assess their capacity for use in electro-chemical devices. Additionally, the majority of research on these mentioned compounds is restricted to either the phase of superionic, which is located slightly below the melting-point, or the low conduction of the β-phase. They haven't been thoroughly studied using a broad variety of temperatures (through their room temperature to the melting-points). Given the scarcity of research, we decided to re-evaluate these salts from the aforementioned perspectives. This research makes an effort in that approach by studying the solidified melt of KBO_2. Additionally, new findings on the electrical transport of potassium-based superionic solids have been presented. These results obtained are very useful to solid state potassium based rechargeable batteries. The next generation of solid-state rechargeable batteries uses very low cast, very safe batteries. Solid electrolytes from potassium sources are essential for enhancing

---

[235] A. BENRATH and K. DREKOPF, Z. Phys. Chem. 99 (1921) 55.

the performance for all batteries of solid-state. Due to the limited supplies of conventional fossil fuels, it is now essential to develop renewable energy sources like nuclear, solar, and wind. However, these renewable sources cannot provide a consistent supply of electricity since they are erratic in terms of time and location. As a result, the goal has been changed towards the electrical storage of energy to mitigate the intermittent nature of sources of energy. A rechargeable battery may efficiently transform chemical energy into electrical energy by storing it. Rechargeable batteries have developed into an industrial product during the last 20 years, and they are now employed in portable energy storage systems and electrical vehicles, among other commonly used electronic goods. Energy storage from sources of renewable energy, including wind turbines &solar cells, is crucial. Therefore, rechargeable batteries are required to prevent climate change, a problem that affects the whole world today.

Material Preparation and Experimental technique

K_2CO_3 with stated 99.99% purity procured through the M/S rare and Research chemical Bombay, India and B_2O_3 (with stated 99.99% purity) procured through the M/S chempure, Calcutta, India. No specific chemical impurities have been given by the supplier within 0.01% and we have made no attempt to know them. Starting materials were divided into equal portions based on molecular weight, carefully mixed, and burned in air for 60 hours with one intermediate grinding and the firing temperature was 1000K.On a solidified melt, electrical conductivity was measured. For this, a self-made sample holder was used. It is composed of a test tube with a flat bottom made of corning glass & two parallel, flat silver electrodes that are the same size and have the same surface area. Two substantial silver cables are used to link these two electrodes to the outside world. A sample container is filled with the substance whose conductivity has to be determined, then pressed. Then it is cooled until the salt within dissolves. It cools to room temperature gradually. The measurement device is then linked to the outside electrodes. Using the sample container and method described elsewhere, the measurement of σ was carried out [236].

Result and Discussion

KBO_2 produced in various batches have had their thermoelectric power S and electrical conductivity (σ) evaluated as temperature function. The measurements were taken throughout heating & cooling cycles respectively. No considerable variations has been noticed in S & σ value in the cooling and heating cycles. The findings have been given in the fig-1 Log σ T Vs T^{-1}& S Vs T^{-1} curves. Ion or electron migration, or perhaps both, contribute to electrical conductivity. The ionic and electronic contributions have quite distinct underlying hypotheses. Therefore, it is necessary to determine whether the conductivity is primarily ionic or electronic in order to give any relevant discussion of electrical conduction. There are standard ways to do this, but measuring σ_{dc} as a time function using an electrode that inhibits ionic but not electronic conduction is a far simpler technique.If the electrodes being used to test this conductivity are able to stop the flow of ions, a time-dependent dc electrical conductivity will often be seen in solids with ionic conduction. Positive ions flow in the field direction whereas negative ions move in the reverse direction at the time when electric field has been applied to the two electrodes using a potential difference. Ions cannot discharge at electrodes because electrodes are impeding their passage, therefore they start to accommodate there instead. Thus, as more ions are unable to reach the electrode and as the d.c. source of current falls, the net force exerted on the ions seeking to flow in that direction diminishes. Over time, the opposing field tends to rise and eventually catch up to the applied field (t→∞). Therefore, the d.c. current in pure ionic solids declines with time and eventually tends to zero out.[237]

---

[236] *A. KVIST and A. LUNDEN, Z. Naturforsch. 20a (1965) 235.*
[237] *I. D. RAISTRICK, C. HO and R. A. HUGINS, Mater. Res. Bull. 11 (1976) 953.*

If the aforementioned argument is applied to the example of a mixed ionic conductor, one would anticipate a steady drop in the current that would eventually tend to reach a constant value. This current develops because the polarization caused by the ions prevents the electric field from being zero. When these transients have passed, the remaining constant amount of current may be completely attributed to the electron. The transient is caused by ionic charges. The entire current produced by both ions and electrons is known as the initial current (current at t=0). Thus, we may assess the overall conductivity as well as the ionic and electronic components from time-dependent current measurement. At low but constant temperatures and electric fields, we conducted time-dependent research of σ. Fig-1 displays typical plots (2). Plots with different temperatures are of a similar kind. The graphic shows that, generally, σ declines wit course of time and has a tendency to remain constant.At lower temperatures, the tendency of consistency takes a little while to emerge, but it becomes stronger as the temperature rises.The electronic component(σ_e) of the conductivity is the constant value of $\sigma_{d.c.}$ over a long period (t→∞), and the value of $\sigma_{d.c.}$for t→0 is the total conductivity (ionic + electronic). σ was tested at a few affixed frequencies to see whether $\sigma_{d.c.}$ (0) correlate to true conductivity. The results are shown in Fig-4. This graphic demonstrates that there is no distinction between $\sigma_{d.c.}$(0) and $\sigma_{a.c.}$ values. This leads one to believe that the samples do not have any holes in them and that the impacts of grain boundaries are not substantial. At each of the 6 or 7 broadly separated temperatures used in the time-dependence research of $\sigma_{d.c.}$, $\sigma_{d.c.}$(0) and $\sigma_{d.c.}$(∞) were obtained. These numbers have been used to calculate the ionic ratio to electronic conduction ($r=\sigma_i/\sigma_e$) by utilizing this given relation,

$$r = \frac{\sigma_i}{\sigma_e} = \frac{\sigma-\sigma_e}{\sigma_e} = \frac{\sigma_{d.c.}(0)-\sigma_{d.c.}(\infty)}{\sigma_{d.c.}(\infty)} \tag{1}$$

The graph in Fig-3 displays the log r against temperature. By applying the relation, one can estimate from this value the contribution of ionic and electronic conductivity for overall conductivity at the point of any given temp.

$$\sigma_i = \left(\frac{r}{r+1}\right)\sigma \tag{2}$$

$$\sigma_e = \left(\frac{1}{r+1}\right)\sigma \tag{3}$$

The proportion of electronic and ionic contribution to σ in the material under study at various temperatures is shown in the table to further illustrate this (1). We have distinguished the conductivity through electronic (σ_e) and ionic (σ_i) components by utilizing the log r against plots of T. Their variation having the temperature displayed in Fig-1. For KBO_2 as Log σ_iT and Log σ_eT against T^{-1} plots. Fig-1 depicts their temperature fluctuation KBO_2 as plots of Log σ_iT and Log σ_eT against T^{-1}. It is more acceptable to give the analysis of these plots individually since the electronic and ionic transportation theories are quite distinct from one another.[238]

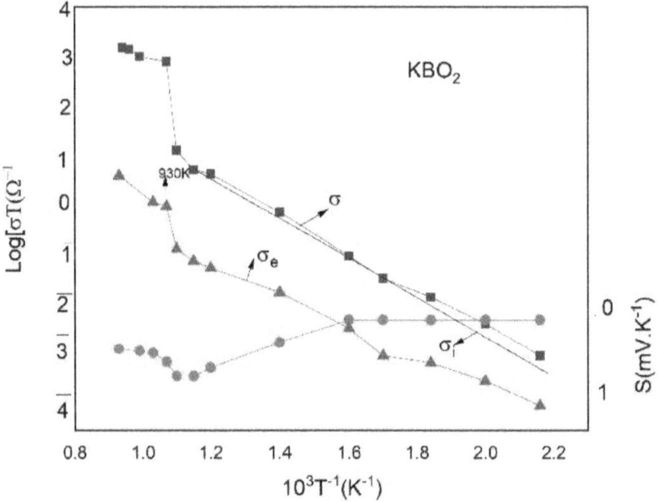

Fig. 1. Variation of the logarithmic product of conductivity and temperature with inverse of temperature. The variation of thermoelectric power is also displayed.

---

[238] J. B. BOYCE and J. C. MIKKELSEN Jr, *Solid State Commun. 31(1979) 741.*

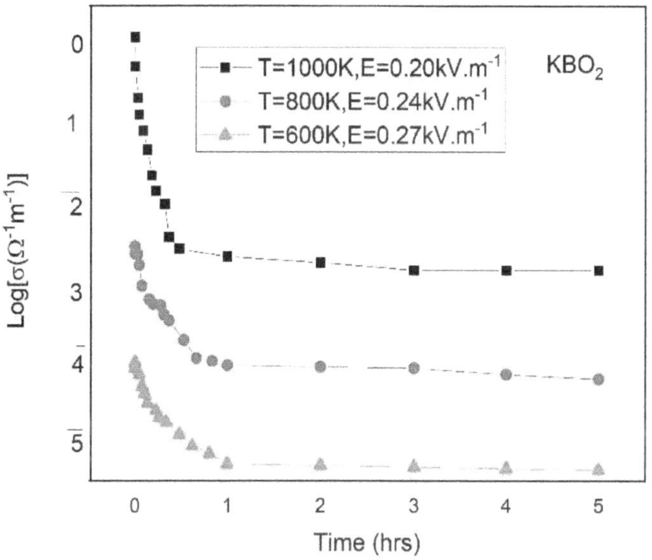

Fig. 2. The plots of logarithmic conductivity with time.

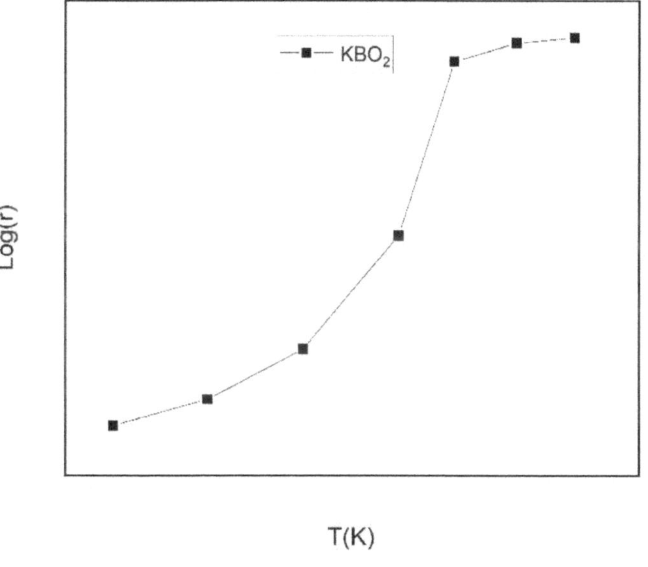

Fig. 3. The plots of the logarithmic ratio of thermal to ionic conductivities with respect to temperature.

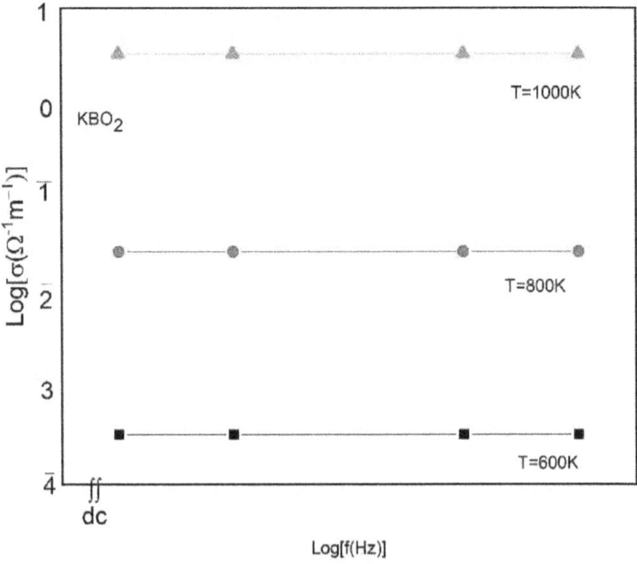

Fig. 4. The plot of logarithmic of electrical conductivity with logarithmic of frequency.

Ionic Conductivity

The curve of Log $\sigma_i T$ Vs T^{-1} for the studied solid is given in Fig-1. These graphs demonstrate that at higher temperatures, there have been essentially no variations among the σ and σ_i values, but that at lower temperatures, there is a little difference.

In various temperature ranges, Log $\sigma_i T$ curves are typically linear and may be separated into 3 regions:(1) linear region below a certain temp. T_1. (2) Non-linear regions for temperature $T_1<T<T_2$. (3) Flat and linear regions $T>T_2$. Temperature T_1, T_2, and T_3 are the three different temperatures for the solid. The equations may be used to express the fluctuations of σ and S in these linear ranges.[239]

---

[239] 5. K. SINGH and V.K. DESHPANDE, *Solid State Ionics 13 (1984) 157.*

$$T \sigma_i = C \exp.\left(\frac{-Ea}{KT}\right) \qquad (4)$$

and

$$S = \frac{\eta}{eT} + H \qquad (5)$$

Where c is a constant that is unaffected by temperature, E_a denotes activation energy, η denoted as the slope of the curve that plots S against T^{-1}, and H is a constant value. Table 3 presents the results of all of these measurements as their respective values.

In the third temp. region, σ_i values are very high (1.09 $\Omega^{-1}m^{-1}$), and the energy of the activation not being large (0.40 eV) (Table 3). Therefore, this is the superionic phase region of the given solid. σ values of the solid increase with temperature and reach a value of 1.09 $\Omega^{-1}m^{-1}$ at 930K. Above 930K, hence is a bending of the Log σ_iT Vs T^{-1} plots. Therefore, the real superionic phase of these materials could be employed for application purposes from 930K to 1120K for KBO_2. The electronic conductivity in this given range is insignificantly small and thus both the σ and S must grow completely because of ions.

Table 1: Total conductivity (σ_T), Ionic conductivity (σ_i) Electronic conductivity (σ_e), and ratio of ionic to electronic conductivity (r) at various temperatures for KBO_2.

T(K)	$\sigma_T(\Omega^{-1}m^{-1})$	$\sigma_e (\Omega^{-1}m^{-1})$	$\sigma_i(\Omega^{-1}m^{-1})$	r	Log r	% σ_i
1000	1.09	1.50×10^{-3}	1.0885	7.26×10^2	2.86	99.86
960	0.79	1.15×10^{-3}	0.7885	6.86×10^2	2.84	99.81
900	1.10×10^{-2}	9.00×10^{-5}	1.0910×10^{-2}	1.21×10^2	2.84	99.81
800	3.00×10^{-3}	6.10×10^{-5}	2.9390×10^{-3}	4.82×10^1	1.68	97.97
700	8.20×10^{-4}	2.57×10^{-5}	7.9430×10^{-4}	3.09×10^1	1.49	96.87
600	9.80×10^{-5}	4.02×10^{-6}	9.3980×10^{-5}	2.34×10^1	1.37	95.90
500	8.70×10^{-6}	4.15×10^{-7}	8.2850×10^{-6}	2.00×10^1	1.30	95.23

Table 2: Electrical conductivity at few fix temperatures.

Compound	Electrical conductivity σ ($\Omega^{-1}m^{-1}$) at					
	500K	600K	700K	800K	900K	1000K
KBO_2	8.70×10^{-6}	9.80×10^{-5}	8.20×10^{-4}	3.00×10^{-3}	1.10×10^{-2}	1.09

Table 3: Summarized result of electrical conductivity (σ) of KBO_2 compound.

Compound	Higher region Temperature $(T>T_2)K$		$T_2(K)$	Lower region Temperature $(T<T_1)K$		$T_1(K)$	T_c
	$E_a(eV)$	$\sigma_0(\Omega^{-1}m^{-1}K)$		E_a (eV)	$\sigma_0(\Omega^{-1}m^{-1}K)$		
KBO_2	0.40	2.16 X 10^5	960	0.72	8.13 X 10^4	900	930

Table 4: Summarized findings of the thermoelectric power (S), and changes along the temperature of the KBO_2 compound.

Compound	Higher Temperature Region $(T>T_2)$			Lower Temperature Region $T<T_1$					
				$T_1>T>T_2{}^l$		$T<T_1{}^l$			
	$\eta(eV)$	H(mv K^{-1})	$T_2(K)$	$\eta(eV)$	H(mv K^{-1})	$\eta(eV)$	H(mv K^{-1})	$T_1(K)$	$T_2(K)$
KBO_2	-0.36	-0.30	950	0.0	-0.90	0.07	-0.44	910	930

Thus, the slope of S Vs T^{-1} plot in this region provides the transportation of heat $(Q\cong\eta)$ for the ions of mobile and the log" σ T Vs T^{-1} plot slope, its activation energy $(E_a=h_m)$. It has been observed in Table 5 that h_m is found slightly larger than Q. This suggests that the extended lattice gas model is appropriate for all solids.[240] This model takes the merit of all other models. In this model Q and h_m are related by the equation

$$h_m = Q + h'_m \tag{6}$$

and

---

[240] H.B. Lal, K. Gaur and A.N. Thakur, J. Mat. Sci. lett. 10 (1991),1113-1115.

$$h'_m = \frac{q^2}{4\pi^2 a \varepsilon_0}\left(\frac{1}{K_\infty} - \frac{1}{K_0}\right) \tag{7}$$

where

$$h'_m = \frac{E_B}{2}$$

E_B denotes the polar ion binding energy, q signifies the mobile ion charge, a is its average separation, the permittivity constantε_0, K_0&K_∞ are the static and optical dielectric constants, correspondingly, and an is the average distance between them. The h'_m experimental values are also been presented in Table 5. The span of the superionic phase, melting point (T_M), transition temperature (T_C), thermoelectric power (S) & Electrical conductivity (σ) at 1000K of the KBO_2 compound is given in Table 6.

Table 5: Mobile ion enthalpy (h_m), temperature-dependent constants (C_2), mobile ion heat (Q), and constant (H) in the superionic phase of the KBO_2 compound.

Compound	$h_m=E_a$(eV)	$C_2=\sigma_0$($\Omega^{-1}m^{-1}K$)	$Q=\eta$ (eV)	H(mvK^{-1})	$H_m'=(h_m-Q)$ eV
KBO_2	0.40	2.16 X 10^5	0.36	-0.30	0.04

Table 6: Span of Superionic phase (δT), Melting point (T_M), Transition temperature (T_C), thermoelectric conductivity (σ)and Electrical conductivity (σ) and thermoelectric power (S) at 1000K of KBO_2 compound.

Compound	δT(K)	T_C (K)	T_M(K)	σ at 1000K $\Omega^{-1}m^{-1}$	S at 1000 K mvK^{-1}
KBO_2	190	930	1120	1.09	-0.68

The ionic and electronic contribution to total electrical conductivities has been obtained through the time-dependent studies of DC electrical conductivity of the studied material. Ionic contribution to overall electrical conductivity has been shown to rise with temperature, although it stays below a critical temperature at less than 99%. However, at the critical temperature, its contribution abruptly rises and surpasses 99.8%. This demonstrates unequivocally that the solid under investigation has 2 phases, one below and one above the critical temp. Consequently, the critical temp. might also be referred to as the temp. of the phase transition (T_P). With a 1–5% electronic contribution, ionic conduction dominates the phase below the transition temp. ($T < T_P$). Thus, this phase, which we refer to as the typical ionic phase, has mixed conduction. The electrical conduction of the phase which is above T_P is virtually entirely ionic, with practically little electronic input. We can call it the superionic phase. Thus, the time-dependent study of σ_{dc} itself shows that the studied solids have two phases. They have a phase in which the entire contribution to electrical transport is due to ions. What are these mobile ions? To resolve this question, by looking at our data of thermoelectric power (S). Due to the fact that the thermoelectric power is always negative across the whole temp. a range that was tested, the mobile carriers have a positive charge. 2 kinds of +ve charged ions are there in KBO_2 compound namely K^+ and B^+ ions. B^{3+} ions are not likely to be moveable due to their higher +ve charge whereas A^+ ions have been anticipated to have maximum mobility due to their low +ve charge and size is small. Such ions often move across the environment through hopping. On the other hand, because of the high activation energy that is necessary, the intrinsic hopping conduction of such ions through one lattice site to another is an extremely unlikely occurrence (-5eV or more). Because electrical conductivity is high, it may be concluded that only one kind of charge carrier is accountable. The thermoelectric effect indicates a positive charge carrier nature. As a result, it seems that there are several Frankel defects present in the examined materials' normal ionic phase and that more may be produced at higher temperatures. The thermal development of a significant number of Frankel defects is less likely to occur at lower temperatures, or in the typical ionic phase, since their formation requires more energy. As a result, below the temperature of the phase transition, their number largely stays constant. In a case like this the σT variations along the T that is presented below.[241]

$$\sigma T = C_1 \exp.\left(\frac{-h_f}{kT}\right) \qquad (8)$$

where C_1 represents constants that are unaffected by temperature and h_f represents the enthalpy required for the mobile defects migration. Because of this, the slope that appears in linear plots of Log σT Vs T^{-1} below the temperature at which the phase transition appears, E_a, is in fact the enthalpy for the mobile defects migration (h_f). The results of this evaluation may be seen in Table 3 and $E_a = h_f$ are presented for each of the three solids in the series that were under investigation. These are on the order of 0.8 eV, which is a value that is fairly acceptable for the migration enthalpy of Frankel defects.

There are a few different models that can be used to describe the superionic phase. The structural disorder model, the free ion model, the ionic polaron model, the lattice gas model, the extended lattice model, and others like them all play an important role in the literature to describe how the electrical transport mechanism works. They hypothesize that there is a connection between the heat of transport, denoted by Q, and the enthalpy involved in the mobile ions movement (h_m). After these given parameters have been discovered, one is able to make a prediction regarding the appropriateness of a specific model for the conduction of electrical current.This demands for homogenous thermoelectric power (S_{hom}) measurement, which in this situation translates to the measurement of S utilizing respective electrodes made of alkali metals. The observed thermoelectric voltage for other electrodes, however, includes a contribution due to the electrode-electrolyte interface's contact potential's temperature dependency. Because of the temp. variation between the two phases during the S measurement is just -10 K, it is possible that this

---

[241] 7.J. Mair, Solid State Ionics, 86-88 (1996) 55.

contribution is not a very significant one. Therefore, we can deduce that $S = S_{hom}$. If just one kind of ion is mobile, then the expression that describes the variation of S can be written as follows.

$$S = S_{hom} = \frac{Q}{eT} + H \qquad (9)$$

and

$$T\,\sigma = C_2 \exp.\left(\frac{-h_m}{KT}\right) \qquad (10)$$

Where Q represents the mobile ions' heat & H represents a constant, C_2 represents a temp-dependent constant, and h_m represents the mobile ion activation enthalpy. We are able to determine the values of H, Q, h_m, and C_2 due to the linear nature of the plots of S and Log σT Vs T^{-1} Table 7 has these data in their respective columns. As can be seen from the chart, h_m is discovered to be slightly more than Q. This indicates that the extended lattice gas model can be successfully applied to all solids. This model is superior to every other model in every respect. [242]

Electronic conductivity

The log $\sigma_e T$- T^{-1} charts (Fig-1) for the material is quite similar to the log σT-T^{-1} plots. At the same temperature at which one finds a surge, one also observes a jump σ in the electronic conductivity that is various orders of magnitude larger. We have referred to this as the phase transition temperature. It would appear that a structural change takes place in this given solid when they are subjected to the temperature that causes the phase transition. Below the given temp, the Log $\sigma_e T$- T^{-1} plot is linear, and it may be modeled utilizing the equation.[243]

$$\sigma_e T = exp.\left(\frac{-W}{kT}\right) \qquad (11)$$

---

[242] 8. K.M. Mishra, A.K. Lal, F.Z. Haque, *Solid State Ionics,167 (2004) 137-146.*
[243] 9.S. Tripathi, K.M. Mishra, S.N. Tiwari, *Journal of scientific and Technical Research 1, (2011) 70-74.*

W is the activation energy for electronic conduction, and σ_0 is a constant. Table- 7 provides values for σ_0, W, and the phase transition temperature. This table shows that the values of W are high, but not high enough to be related to the solid's energy band gap. The electrons hopping trapped at the center defects seem to be the cause of electronic conduction.

Table 7: consequences of the electronic component's contribution to the electrical conductivity of the KBO_2 compound.

Compound	W(eV)	σ_0 $(\Omega^{-1}m^{-1} K)$	T_P
KBO_2	1.35	4.24 X 10^6	930 ± 5

Conclusion

The studied material is a superionic solid and shows the transition at a certain temperature, termed phase transition temperature T_p. Below T_p, this behaves as a normal ionic solid, and above it as a superionic solid and remains so up to its melting point. In the normal ionic phase, the electrical conduction is predominantly ionic but has also an appreciable (5%) electronic contribution for the studied solid. In the normal ionic phase, electrical conduction occurs mainly due to Frankel defects. In the superionic phase, the electrical conduction is almost ionic with a negligibly small (10^{-2} %) electronic contribution. The occurrence of phase transition has been clearly observed in the form of an anomaly in the σ and S studies.

12. Japanese Encephalitis Virus (JEV): A Review

- *Rakesh Kumar Tiwari*

Department of Physics, Deen Dayal Upadhyaya Gorakhpur University, Gorakhpur

Introduction

The Japanese Encephalitis Virus (JEV) is a mosquito-borne flavivirus that poses a significant threat to human health, particularly in South and Southeast Asia. JEV is maintained in a zoonotic cycle between mosquitos and animals, primarily pigs and birds. Humans are considered dead-end hosts, meaning they can become infected but do not transmit the virus further. It can lead to Japanese Encephalitis (JE), a severe neurological disease characterized by inflammation of the brain. The virus has a high mortality rate, and survivors often experience long-term neurological complications. JEV has a plus sense single-stranded RNA genome approximately 11kb in length, which is capped at the 5' end but lacks modification of the 3' terminus by polyadenylation. The genome is translated and processed by host and viral proteases to produce three structural proteins, capsid C protein, prM and E, and seven non-structural proteins, NS1, NS2A, NS2B, NS3, NS4A, NS4B and NS5[244].

Among the non-structural protein NS1 plays a dominant role in RNAreplication, immune modulation and invasion, allowing viruses

---

[244] *Sumiyoshi et al., 1987.*

to hijack host cell mechanisms[245]. NS2A is a membrane-associated hydrophobic protein, that functions for RNA replication and cleaves the NS1-NS2A junction after translation. It functions as a component of viral replicated complex, viral assembly, and secretion. Along with the NS3, NS2B remains a hetero dimer that initiates the heterodimeric complex's anchoring into the endoplasmic rectulum membrane[246]. NS3 enzymes are involved in viral replication and viral assembly[247]. NS4A acts as an interferon antagonist, which is a hydrophobic protein. NS5 is the largest and contains MTase activities in the N-terminus and RNA-dependent RNA polymerase (RdRp) activities in the C-terminus[248]. NS5 is a multifunctional protein that includes terminal RNA transferae, RNA helicase, and RdRp. NS5 like NS3 is a multi-enzymatic protein with guanyl transferase/methyltransferase that is required for 5' capping. It also collaborates with other viral replication factors such as viral RNA, the host, and viral co-factors to amplify the viral genome[249]. Currently, there are four types of JE vaccines are available for humans in different regions of the world.

1. Mouse brain-derived killed inactivated.
2. Cell culture-derived live-attenuated.
3. Cell culture-derived killed-inactivated.
4. Genetically engineered live-attenuated[250] chimeric-vaccines.

Since 1990 a significant progress has been made in the JE prevention and vaccination programs. Among them, the most prominent vaccines are SA14-14-2 and 821564XY (Indian Kolar strain). Live attenuated Japanese encephalitis vaccine (JE-LV) is made up of attenuated SA 14-14-2 strain virus and produced from primary culture of hamster kidney cells[251]. The vaccine was developed by CDIBP (Chengdu

---

[245] *Vonderstein et al., 2018.*

[246] *Esposito et al., 2015.*

[247] *Edeling et al., 2014.*

[248] *Arenas et al. 2020.*

[249] *Martin and Santos, 2020.*

[250] *Beasley DW. Lewthwait P. et al. Current use and development of vaccines of Japanese Encephalitis. Expert Opin Biol Ther 2008; 8: 95-106.*

[251] *Yu, Y. Phenotypic and genotypic characteristics of Japanese encephalitis attenuated live vaccine virus SA14-14-2 and their stabilities. Vaccine 2010, 28, 3615-3641.*

Institute of Biological Product), China in 1988. Although it is an effective vaccine, it has symptoms of various side effects, including fever, drowsiness, irritability, nasopharyngitis, gastroenteritis, conjunctivitis and rhinitis in the clinical trials[252]. JENVAC is a Vero cell adopted inactivated vaccine developed from the Indian Kolar strain (821564 XY) manufactured by the Indian pharma company, Bharat Biotech International Ltd, Hydrabad, India, and licensed in 2014[253]. The vaccines has minimal records of adverse effects such as headache, vomiting, pain at the site of injection and body ache.

Despite various studies conducted by academicians and scientists have improved our comprehension of the virus and throw a light how it interacts with the host cell, JE, still poses a serious threat to public health and potential to spread globally. A coordinated effort has been required to control and management of JE, ranging from mosquito control to the development of specific antiviral drugs and effective vaccines. In the light of the above context, we develop our research in this direction and found some more detailed results.

It has a single-stranded RNA genome, a positive-sense with approximately 11kb in length, and capped at 5' end but lack modification of the 3' terminal by polyadenylation. NS3 is a multifunctional protein consisted with 619 amino acid residues. The one-third of NS3, N-terminal had a serine proteaseactivities and participate in the processing together with a co-factor protein NS2B. The two-third domain of NS3, C-terminal had a catalytic domain for helicase, nucleotide 5' -triphosphate (NTPase), as well as 5' terminal RNA triphosphate activity. The anzymatic activities of the helicase and ATPase had been confirmed in the NS3 proteins derived from several members of the family Flaviviridae, including viruses from genus

---

[252] *Kwon, H.J.; Lee, S.Y.; Kim, K.H.; Kim, D.S.; Chao, H.S.; Jo, D.S.; Kang, J.H. The Immunogenicity and Safety of the Live-attenuated SA 14-14-2 Japanese Encephalitis Vaccine Given with a Two-dose Primary Schedule in Children. J. Korean, Med. Sci, 2015, 30, 612-616.*

[253] *Singh, A.; Mitra, M.; Sampath, G.; Venugopal, P.; Rao, J.V.; Krishnamurti, B.; Gupta, M.K.; Krishna, S.S.; Sudhakar, B.; Rao, N.B. et al. A Japanese Encephalitis Vaccine From India Induces Durable and Cross-protective Immunity Against Temporally and Spatially Wide-range Global Field Strains. J. Infect. Dis. 2015, 212, 715-725.*

Flavivirus, such as JEV, DEN, YFV and from the genus Hipacivirus, such as hepatitis C virus (HCV)[254,255,256,257]. A precise biological function of the helicase/NTPase domain was unclear, one possible explanation was that the domain may resolve a double stranded RNA intermediates formed during trancription or replication of the genome RNA. The DEN mutants impaired in NTPase and helicase activities[258], suggesting that flaviviral helicase/NTPase was essential for the development of antiviral drugs.

The NS5 is a non-structural protein of JEV, a polyprotein with 900 residues comprises N-terminal S-adenosyl-L-methionine (SAM) dependent methyl transferase (MTase) domain and C-terminal RNA-dependent RNA polymerase (RdRp) region. The MTase domain fold the multiple helices flanking around a conserved 7-stranded β-sheets. The conformation of JEV MTase domain exhibit highest similarity among all other structures such as Murray Valley Encephalitis virus (MVEV), West Neil Virus (WNV). The functions of NS5 are crucial as it harbors both MTase domain bearing 5' cap structure and RdRp for all RNA viruses which are responsible for inter-regulations and co-operativity and hence, hypothesized as a prosperous site for the drug activity[259]. SAMe (S-Adenosyl-Methionine) a potential drug is required for the synthesis of norepinephrine, dopamine, and

[254] *Cui, T., Sugrue, R.J., Xu, Q., Lee, A.K., Chan, Y.C., Fu, J., 1998. Recombinant dengue virus type 1 NS3 protein exhibits specific viral RNA binding and NTPase activity regulated by the NS5 protein. Virology 246, 409-417.*
[255] *Kuo, M.D., Chin, C., Hsu, S.L., Shiao, J.Y., Wang, T.M., Lin, J.H., 1996. Characterization of NTPase activity of Japanese encephalitis virus NS3 protein. J. Gen. Virol. 73, 3108-3116.*
[256] *Li, J., Tang, H., Mullen, T.M., Westberg, C., Reddy, T.R., Rose, D.W., Wong-Staal, F., 1999b. A role of RNA helicase A in post-transcriptional regulation of HIV type 1. Proc. Natl. Acad. Sci. U. S. A. 96, 709-714.*
[257] *Warrener, P., Tamura, J.K., Collett, M.S., 1993. RNA-stimulated NTPase activity associated with yellow fever virus NS3 protein expressed in bacteria. J. Virol. 67, 989-996.*
[258] *Wengler, G., Wengler, G., 1991. The carboxy-terminal part of the NS3 protein of the West Nile flavivirus can be isolated as a soluble protein after proteolytic cleavage and represents an RNA-stimulated NTPase. Virology 184, 707-715.*
[259] *Kofler, R. M., Hoenninger, V. M., Thurner, C. and Mandl, C. W. (2006). Functional analysis of tick born encephalitis virus cyclization Elements Indicates major differences between mosquito-borne and tick-borne flaviviruses. J. Virol. 80 (8), 4099-4113.*

serotonin. SAMe facilitates glutathione usage, which improves the body's antioxidant defense. S-Adenosyl-3-thiopropylamine (SAT) is indicated as a potential inhibitor based on the S-Adenosyl homocysteine SAH scaffold[260].

Methodology

The initial coordinates of NS3 and NS5 protein were obtained from the RCSB protein data bank[261,262] (PDB ID: 2Z83 & 4K6M). Ligands (drugs) were prepared by adding the missing hydrogens atoms using the LEAP module of the Amber20 package[263]. The initial co-ordinates of ligand ATP for NS3 as reported in the crystal structure, SAM, SAT and SFN were taken from the Pub Chem, a drug liberary. The parameters of the ligands (ATP, SAM, SAT and SFN) were generated using antechamber module of Amber20 for GAFF parameters. The partial atomic charges and missing parameters of ligands were obtained from the RESP[264] charge fitting method of a quantum mechanical (QM) optimized geometry using HF/6-31g(d,p) level of theory. The optimized ligands, were docked in the active sites (reported in the crystal structure) of NS3 protein of JEV using AutoDock Vina/Dock6[265] which uses the Lamarckian genetic algorithm (GA) in combination with grid-based energy estimation

[260] *J. Sekut., D. E. McCloskey, H. J. Thomas, J. A. Secrist, A. E. Pegg, S. E. Ealick, Binding and inhibition of human spermidine synthase by decar- boxylated S-adenosylhomocysteine, Protein Sci. 20 (11) (2011) 1836–1844.*
[261] *Tetsuo, Y., Hideaki, Unno., Yoshio Mori., Hideki Tani., et al. Crystal structure of the catalytic domain of Japanese encephalitis virus NS3 helicase/nucleoside triphosphatase at a resolution of 1.8 Å. 2007. Virology 273 (2008) 426-436.*
[262] *Y. Wang, S. H. Bryant, T. Cheng, J. Wang, A. Gindulyte, B. A. Shoemaker, P. A. Thiessen, S. He, J. Zhang, PubChem BioAssay: 2017 update, Nucleic Acids Res. 45 (D1) (2017) D955–D963.*
[263] *Salomon-Ferrer, R., Case, D.A., Walker, R.C. An Overview of the Amber Biomolecular Simulation Package. Wiley Interdiscip. Riv. Comput. Mol. Sci. (2013), 3 (2), 198-210.*
[264] *Bayly, C.I., Cieplak, P., Cornell, W.D., Kollman, P.A. A Well-Behaved Electrostatic Potential Based Method Using Charge Restraints for Deriving Atomic Charges: The RESP Model. J. Phys. Chem. (1993) 97(40), 10269-10280.*
[265] *Trott, O., Olson, A.J., AutoDock Vina: Improving the Speed pf Accuracy of Docking with a Ne Scoring Function, Efficient Optimization and Multithreading. J. Comput. Chem. (2009), https://doi.org/10.1002/jcc.21334.*

incorporated in PyRx[266]. This algorithm is optimized for site-based targeted docking. In order to improve the docking scores, these selected ligands were re-optimized by using density functional theory (DFT) at the B3LYP/6-31G(d,p) level. The atomic parameters of protein molecule and the ligands were created by Amber ff14SB force field. After proper parameterizations of the protein and ligands, the systems were solvated in a truncated octahedral box with a TIP3P[267] water model, dimensions extending up to 10 Å from the protein surface. Again, the resultant charge of the prepared complex (protein-ligand complex) was neutralized with counter ions depending upon the total charge of the system[268]. The selected systems were proceeded for further molecular dynamic (MD) simulations and binding free energy calculations on the basis of best docking scores.

MM-PBSA/GBSA calculations were initiated after examining the production dynamics of 100 ns. The interactions were studied for the most suitable trajectories for each of the system. It is a classical method to calculate binding free energy of protein-ligand complex. The MM region was described using the Amber ff14SB force field. The energy was further corrected using B3LYP-D3[269] functional. For the structural analysis of each system, the MD trajectories were analyzed using the CPPTRAJ, a module of Amber20 package and visual molecular dynamics (VMD)[270]. The 2D plots representing the intrinsic dynamical stabilize in terms of root-mean-square deviation (RMSD), root-mean-square fluctuation (RMSF), the radius of gyration (R_g),

[266] Dallakyan, S., Olson, A. J. Small-molecule library screening by docking with PyRx, in: J. Hempel, J. E., Williams, C. H., Hong (Eds.), C. C. Chemical Biology, Sprnger New York, New York, NY, 2015, pp. 243-250.
[267] Jorgensen, W. L., Chandrasekhar, J., Madura, J. D., Impey, R. W., Klein, M. L., Comparison of Simple Potential Functions for Simulating Liquid Water. J. Chem. Phys. (1983), 79 (2), 926-935.
[268] Ibragimova, G. T., Wade, R. C. Importance of Explicit Salt Ions for Protein Stability in Molecular Dynamics Simulation. Biophys. J. (1998), 74 (6), 2906-2911.
[269] Grimme, S. Semiempirical GGA-type Density Functional Construct with a Long-Range Dispersion. J. Comput. Chem. (2006), 1787-1799.
[270] Humphrey, W., Dalke, A., Schulten, K., VMD: visual molecular dynamics, J. Mol. Graph. 14 (1) (1996) 33-38.

principal component analysis (PCA), and H-Bond distance of the complexes were generated with XM-GRACE program.

Results and Discussion

Binding of the NS3 protein of JEV with the inhibitors S-Adenosyl derivatives

NS3 was a multifunctional protein consisting of 619 amino acid residues. The overall structure of the JEV helicase/NTPase domain ranging the amino acid from residue 171 to 619 was obtained based on the data collected at 1.8 Å resolution. One-third of NS3, N-terminal had a serine protease activities and two-third domain of NS3, C-terminal had a catalytic domain for helicase, nucleotide 5'-triphosphate (NTPase), as well as 5'-terminal RNA triphosphate activity. The crystal structure of the non-structural protein of (JEV) NS3 with PDB ID: 2Z83[1] at 1.8 Å resolution was derived from the RCSB (Protein Data Bank). The missing hydrogen and residues such as Ser246, Ala247, Val248, Gln249, Arg250, Glu251, His252, Gln253, Arg275, Glu413, Met414 and Gly415 were added by using x-Leap of Amber20 package. Based on the crystal structure of the NS3 protein of JEV, the ATP molecule was localized with the cleft between domain-1 and domain-2 and the positively charged residues, Lys200, Arg461, and Arg464 are present on the active sites of motifs I, II, and VI. Lys200 protrudes into the active pocket, recognizing the β- or γ-phosphate of ATP and forming a salt bridge with Asp285 and Glu286 for the stabilization of the active sites of the structure. Arg461 and Arg464 in motif VI form an arginine finger that works as sensors recognizing the γ- and α-phosphate of ATP, and are critical for conformational switching upon ATP hydrolysis. A snapshot showing the active pocket in the binding cleft is shown in Figure 1.

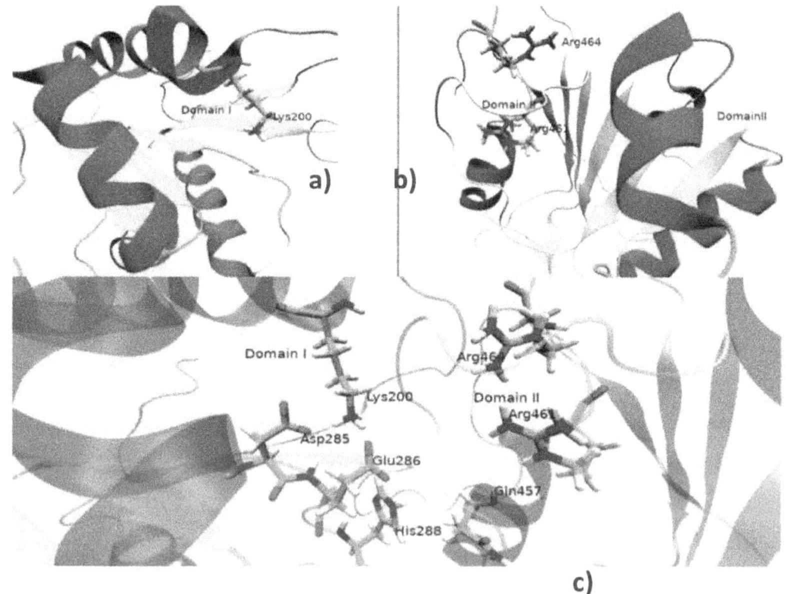

*Figure 1. A snapshot representing two active site domains of NS3 protease **a)** and **b)** shown separately with the complete active site region in **c)***

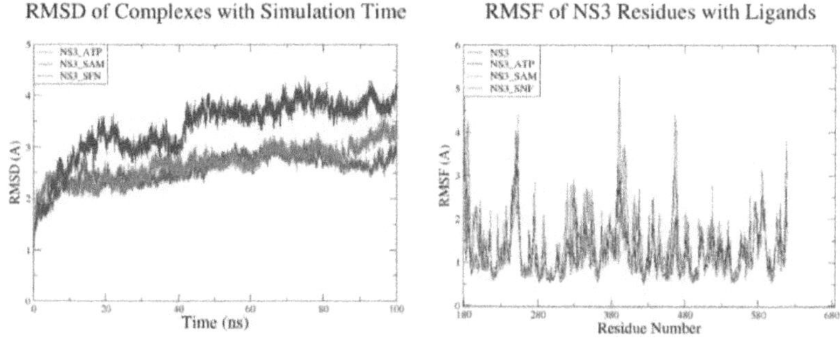

Figure 2. (left) Plots of RMSD as a function of simulation time for NS3-ATP (violet), NS3-SAM (magenta) and NS3-SFN (blue) complexes; (right) Plots of RMSF as a function of residue number for NS3 (blue), NS3-ATP (red), NS3-SAM (magenta) and NS3-SFN (green) complexes.

Three best-docked scored candidates (ligands) from the prepared drug library were docked at the same active site region at which the crystal structure of NS3 was determined with a resolution of 1.8 Å. During the docking, the best-chosen three ligands were reported and proceeded for MD simulations of 100 ns whose docking score with the ligands ATP, SAMe and SFN was -5.2, -6.5, and –7.8 respectively, with their role in the enzymatic activity. RMSD and RMSF are shown in Figure 2. The radius of gyration (R_g) describes the level of compaction of protein in terms of mass-weighted root-mean-square distance for a collection of atoms from their common center of mass. Therefore, R_g provides the evolution of the overall dimension of a protein during a dynamic simulation shown in Figure 3. Proteins control their functions by changing their shape and hence molecular configuration. The collective movements of atoms in the protein determine the overall conformational change. The relative conformational dynamics and atomic fluctuations of the functionally relevant substructures in the ligand-bound forms were studied using principal component analysis (PCA). A cross-correlation matrix was produced by removing the translational and rotational movements and monitoring the relative backbone atomic fluctuations. The generated eigenvalues represented the energetic contribution from the corresponding principal components (PCs), while the eigenvectors represented the directions of motion.

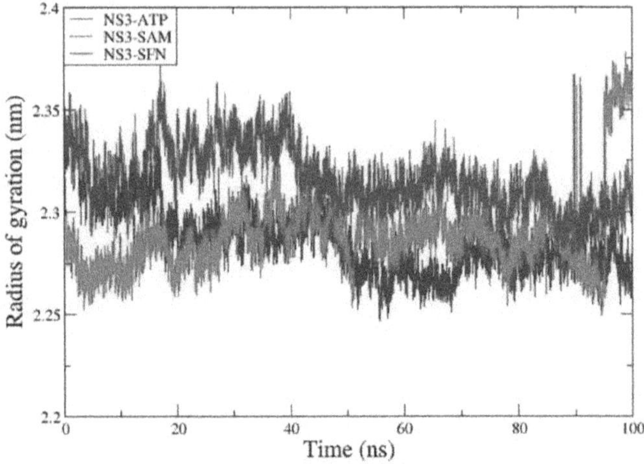

Figure 3. Plot of the radius of gyration (R_g) of the NS3-ATP complex (blue), NS3-SAM complex (red) and NS3-SFN complex (violet).

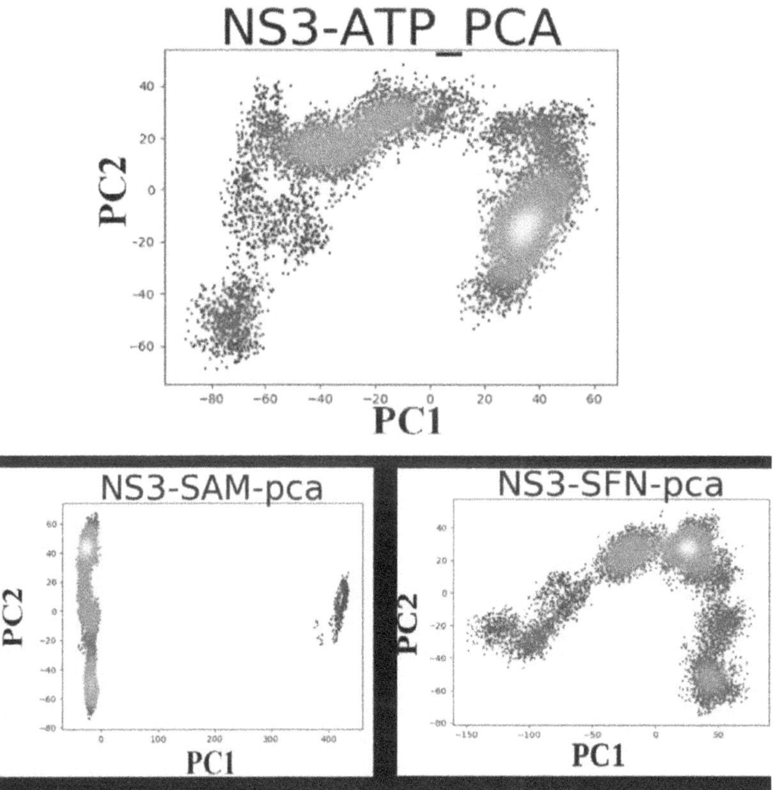

Figure 4. 2D projection plot of the first two principal eigenvectors of (upper) NS3-ATP complex, (lower left) NS3-ATP complex and (lower right) NS3-SFN complexes (nm).

The principal component analysis observes the conformational motion relevant to protein functions. The 2D projection of trajectories with the trace value of covariant matrix is shown in Figure 4 provides the degree of conformational changes due to decreased collective motion of atoms. The distance between specific residues at the active site region with the ligands was plotted using the CPPTRAJ module of Amber20, with the specificity in terms of hydrogen bonding (Hbond) shown in Figure 5.

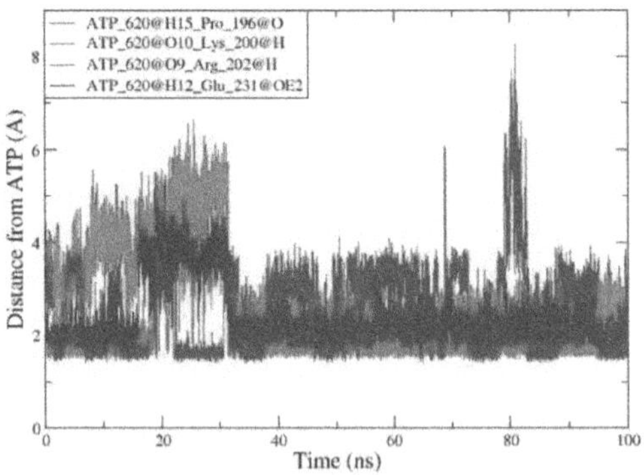

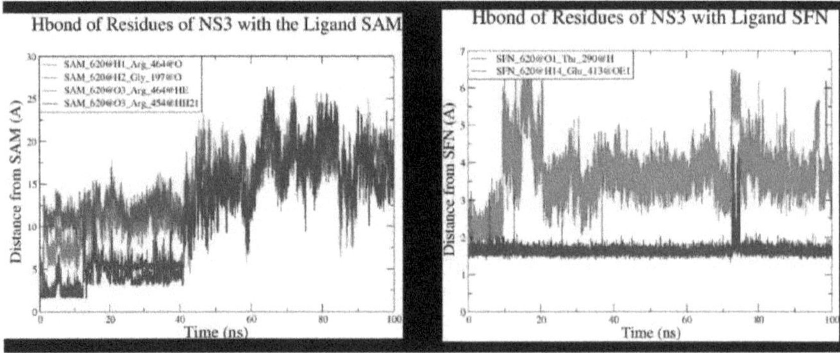

Figure 5. Distance of ATP, SAM, and SFN from the active site residues of NS3 protease made Hbond during MD simulations upper), lower left) and lower right), respectively.

In Figure 5 (upper), the distance of hydrogen bonding was demonstrated with the amino acid residues Pro196, Lys200, Arg202, and Glu231 with the simulation of 100 (ns). From the simulation time 0-35 ns, when Lys200 and Glu231 broke the hydrogen bond drastically, the Pro196 and Arg202 stabilized the H-Bond with some fluctuations. However, beyond 35 ns of simulation time, the Lys200 and Glu231 maintained their H-Bond, continuously, while H-Bond fluctuation between Pro196 and Arg202 remained in such a way that, the spike and fluctuations of Arg202 were balanced by Pro196 such that it always maintained stability. Figure 5 (lower left) represents the distance of the H-Bond with the ligand SAM. The simulation profile for H-Bond consists of two regions. Region-1 simulation time 0-40 ns, produces the H-Bond profile with the amino acid residues Arg464, Gly197, and Arg454. O3 of SAM has two sites of H-Bond with Arg464 (HE) and Arg454 with HH21. In Domain-2, the O and HE sites of Arg464 produce two strong H-bonds with the SAM at the sites H1 and O3 of SAM. This shows the importance of amino acid residue Arg464 as it has emerged as a dominant active site residue of Domain-2. On the other hand, O of Arg464 and Gly197 produce loosely bound H-Bond with hydrogen H1 and H2 respectively of SAM. Beyond the region of simulation time 40 ns, fluctuation of distance between donor and acceptor atoms for all the three amino acid residues are higher value. Which clearly indicate the presence of a loose H-Bond, but close inspection of snapshots of MD simulation shows that they coordinated in such a way that if one bond is broken the atoms of the other two residues play complementary and supplementary ways to undertake the H-Bond to maintain the overall stability of the complex. Therefore, these results support the findings obtained from RMSD and RMSF results discussed above.

Figure 5 (lower right) represents the distance of the H-Bond with the ligand SFN in the NS3-SFN complex with respect to the simulation time of 100 ns MD. Fluctuations of distances between OE1 of Glu413 of the amino acid residue produce a strong H-Bond with the H14 of the ligand SFN and the bonding was stable throughout the simulation time despite some peaks observing their instability but it quickly disappeared within 10 ns simulation time. The H of Thr290 again formed a H-Bond with the O1 of SFN. The pattern of H-Bond was again very strong, but there are some higher fluctuations observed, ranging the simulation between 10-20 ns and 72-74 ns, approximately. But this deformation is temporary and never detached from making the strong H-bonding, reason is already explained in the above paragraph.

MM-PBSA/GBSA analysis

The energy components of complexes NS3-ATP, NS3-SAM, and NS3-SFN such as van der Waals, electrostatic, Generalized Born, SASA, gas, and solvation energy were calculated using the MM-PBSA/GBSA method. The non-polar and hydrophobic interactions are the most important interactions calculated during MM-GBSA analysis in the ligand-protein interactions as they provide stability in the complex. The docking study satisfactorily predicts the active sites of the receptor. The conformation of active sites agrees well with the corresponding experimental study[271]. The analysis indicates that the van der Waals component of energy plays a leading role over two other, electrostatic and internal energy components. The electrostatic component of the binding energy of ATP is the lowest among the ligands. The study predicts that the active pocket of the receptor is made by the 24 important amino-acid residues such as Pro196, Gly197, Ser198, Gly199, Lys200, Thr201, Arg202, Glu231, Ala235, Hie288, Phe289, Thr290 and Asp291, within the Domain-1 and Asp410, Ile411, Glu413, Lys431, Ile450, Thr451, Ser454, Asn417, Arg464, Asn465 and Hie488 within the Domain 2.

The ΔG_{bind} values computed with MM-GBSA of NS3-ATP, NS3-SAM, and NS3-SFN complexes were -34.84, -22.26, and -36.54 kcal/mol respectively. In the different components of energy contribution of ΔG_{bind}, the solvation energy was an important positive contributor, of energies 83.58, 86.96, and 61.11 kcal/mol for all the three complexes respectively, which opposes the binding and reduces the absolute values of the total binding energy. The remaining van der Waals (ΔE_{vdw}), electrostatic (ΔE_{elec}) and solvation accessible surface area (SASA) energies were negative, favorably contributing to the binding in all three complexes. The low ΔE_{vdw} (-32.92 kcal/mol) and high ΔE_{elec} (-85.49 kcal/mol) led to low ΔG_{bind} (-34.84 kcal/mol) providing a considerable binding between NS3 and ATP, but again low value of ΔE_{vdw} (-49.38 kcal/mol) and ΔE_{elec} (-48.27 kcal/mol) provide a

---

[271] Kumari, R., Kumar, R., Lynn, g_mmpbsa -a GROMACS tool for high-throughput MM-PBSA calculation, J. Chem. Inf. Model. 54 (7) (2014) 1951-1962.

relatively high value of ΔG_{bind} (-36.54 kcal/mol) and hence, a strongest binding between NS3 and SFN among all the three complexes.

Binding free energy

The estimation of absolute conformational entropy is important because it allows a detailed understanding of the thermodynamical driving forces at the molecular level. This method calculates the thermodynamic conformational entropy of a bio-molecule during molecular dynamic simulations.

ATP Binding free energy

The per residue decomposition energy of the complex NS3-ATP showed that the residues Arg464 (-11.36), Arg202 (-9.83), Lys200 (-8.94), Glu231 (-8.41), Thr201 (-7.14) and Asn465 (-5.38) (energy in decreasing order in kcal/mol) largely contributed in the side-chain energy. However, the other residues of the complex Pro196 (-3.63) and Gly199 (-3.51) had also contributed significantly and provided the stability of the complex. Here, van der Waals component energy with the decreasing order of sequence of Arg464 (-3.96), Asn465 (-2.44), Arg202 (-2.38), Lys200 (-1.56), and Thr201 (-1.41) with the electrostatic component of energy Arg464 (-0.40), Asn465 (-0.84), Arg202 (-7.13) and Lys200 (-4.96) and Thr201 (-4.04). Therefore, Arg202, Lys200 and Thr201 produce the negative effect of stability of the complex under considerations. Now, the contribution of polar-solvation energy of Arg464 (-4.18), Gly199 (-2.05), Ser198 (-1.55) and Lys200 (-1.45) were important as the affecting positively the stability of the complex. The non-polar solvation energy of Arg464 (-2.81), Arg202 (-1.92) and Asn465 (-1.62) were also significant for the stability of the complex. Here, Arg464, Arg202, Lys200, Glu231 and Asn465, were hydrophilic polar residue, while Thr201 was neutral and polar.

ATP Hydrogen bonds

The NS3-ATP complex forms four hydrogen bonds with the three hydrophilic residues Lys200, Arg202, and Glu131 and one hydrophobic residue Pro196. The hydrogen bond distances of Lys200, Arg202, Pro196, and Glu231 during MD simulation are (shown in Figure 6). The H of Lys200 residue forms a hydrogen bond with the O10 of the ATP, where Lys200 acts as a proton donor and ATP as a proton acceptor. Similarly, the O9 atom of ATP forms a hydrogen bond with the H atom of Arg202 where Arg202 acts as a proton donor while ATP as a proton receptor. Again, H15 of ATP forms a hydrogen bond with the O atom of Pro196 of receptor residue, with ATP as a proton donor and Pro196 as a proton receptor, and H12 of ATP forms a hydrogen bond with OE2 of Glu231, where ATP acts a proton donor and Glu231 as a proton acceptor.

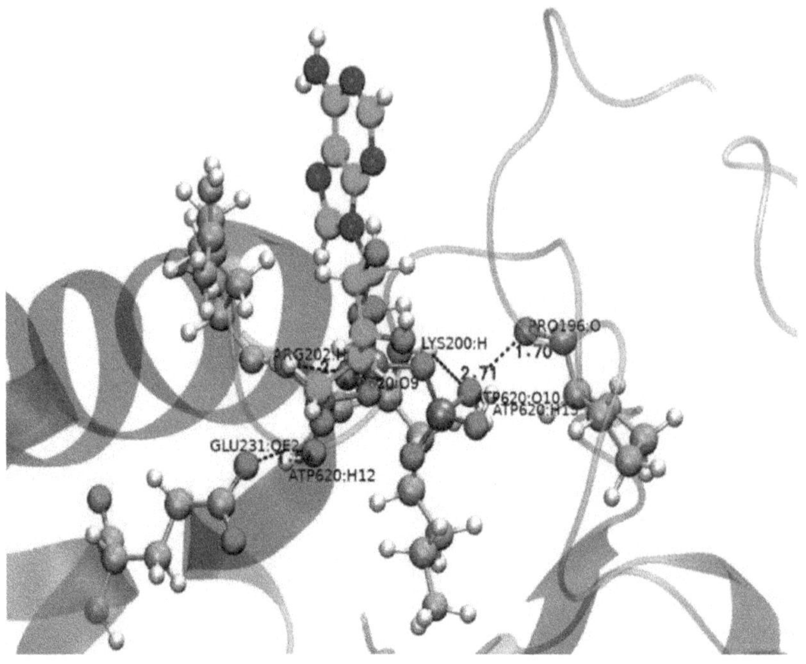

Figure 6. Snapshot showing the distance of active site residues Pro196, Lys200, Arg202, Glu231 (cyan), of NS3 making a hydrogen bond with the ligand ATP (green).

SAM Binding free energy

The adenosyl derivative SAM acts as an inhibitor, during the MD made their interactions with the active site residues and reside into the cleft between the domain 1 and domain 2 (active pocket) of the NS3 receptor almost all the time of simulations. The decomposition energy of NS3-SAM complex with the decreasing order of Arg464 (-13.61), Glu231 (-9.06), Asn417 (-6.37), Arg202 (-5.10), Glu231 (-2.59), Thr201 (-2.34), Gly199 (-2.01), Ala235 (-1.81) and Lys200 (-0.55) largely contributed in the side chain composition (energy in kcal/mol). Out of these residues Arg464, Glu231, Asn417, Arg202, Glu234, Thr201 and Lys200 are hydrophilic, while Gly199 and Ala235 are hydrophobic in nature. The electrostatic component of energy of Arg464 (-25.37), Glu231 (-15.44), Asn417 (-7.75) and Glu235 (-4.84) are significant with respect to the van der Waals component of energy of Arg202 (-2.75), Glu231 (-1.94), Glu234 (-1.19), Thr201 (-0.86) and Ala235 (-0.81). The high electrostatic component of energy of Arg464, Glu231, Glu234, and Asn417 is counter-balanced by the polar-solvation energy having the values, 13.01, 9.83, 4.24, and 2.24 kcal/mol. The non-polar solvation energy of Arg202 (-1.79), Glu231 (-1.50), Arg464 (-.99), Glu234 (-0.8), and Gly199 (-0.72) are significant for their role in the stability of the complex. Out of the above Arg202, Glu231, Glu234, Ala235, Thr201, and Gly199 are the most stable residues of the receptor, while Arg464, Asn417, and Lys200 are the most reactive residues of the receptor.

SAM Hydrogen bonds

The NS3-SAM complex forms four hydrogen bonds with the two different residues of the NS3 receptor namely Arg464 (two hydrogen bonds with different binding sites) and Gly197. The O3 of SAM made two hydrogen bonds with Arg464 with the two protonated sites at HE and HH21 and O of Arg464 with H1 of SAM, representing the importance of the residue for the active capability. Further, the residue Arg464 having the capability as a proton donor and proton receptor both but proton donor capability predominated over the proton receptor capability. The O of Gly197 made hydrogen bond with the H2 of SAM with SAM as a proton donor. The O of Gly197 made a hydrogen bond with the H2 of SAM with SAM as a proton donor (shown in Figure 7).

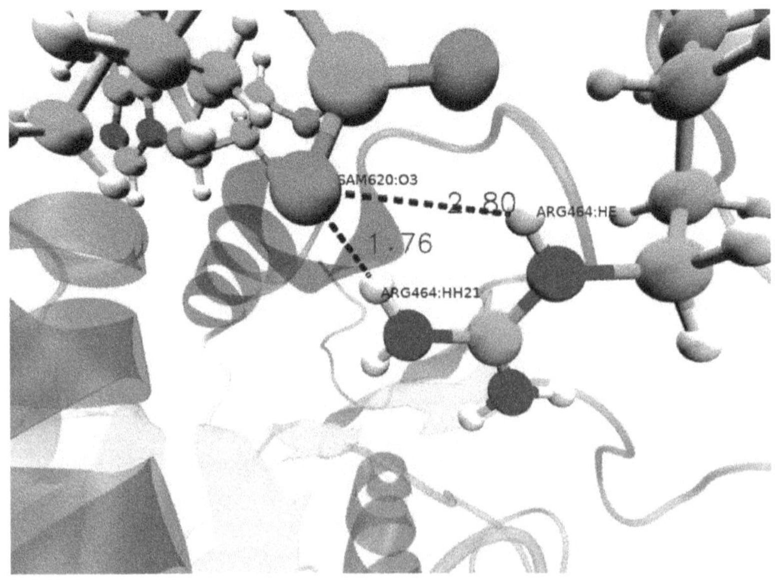

Figure 7. Snapshot showing the distance of the active site residues Arg464 (cyan) of NS3 making the hydrogen bond with the ligand SAM (green).

SFN Binding free energy

The SFN (sinfungine) another member of the adenosyl derivative resided in the close vicinity of the active site of the NS3 receptor within the same craft and made their interaction throughout the whole MD simulation period. The free energy of the complex NS3-SFN in the decreasing order of their energy Lys431 (-12.34), Glu413 (-11.56), Thr290 (-5.79), Phe289 (-5.48), Ile411 (-4.35), Asp291 (-3.91), Ile450 (-2.79), Ser454 (-2.39), taking part for the significant contribution for the side-chain interactions. Inspite of this, there are other residues of receptor NS3 such as Hie288, Thr451, Asp410 and Hie488 made their role in the stability of the complex. Here, Lys431, Glu413, Thr290, Asp291 and Ser454 are hydrophilic and polar in nature, while, Phe289, Ile411 and Ile450 are hydrophobic and non-polar in nature. The electrostatic component of energy of Glu413 (-16.50) was highest producing their instability. The other residues Lys431 (-7.09), Ser454 (-1.25), Asp410 (-1.48), Phe289 (-1.37) and Ile411 (1.31) having significant electrostatic energy contributor. The van der Waals component energy of Ile411 (-2.97), Lys431 (-2.41), Thr290 (-2.65), Phe289 (-2.20), Asp291 (-1.93), Asp410 (-1.32) and Ser454 (-1.32) produce their role in stability against the electrostatic interactions. The non-polar solvation free energy in the decreasing order term Ile411 (-2.25), Lys431 (-2.09), Phe289 (-1.82), Thr290 (-1.69), Asp291 (-1.40) and Glu413 (-1.02) would support the stability of the complex. Comparing these residues of the different components of energy, it has been concluded that the relatively high value of van der Waals and non-polar solvation energy of Hie288, Phe289, Thr290, Asp291, Ile411, Lys431, Ile450, Thr451 and Ser454 produce their role in the stability of the complex for whole simulation time.

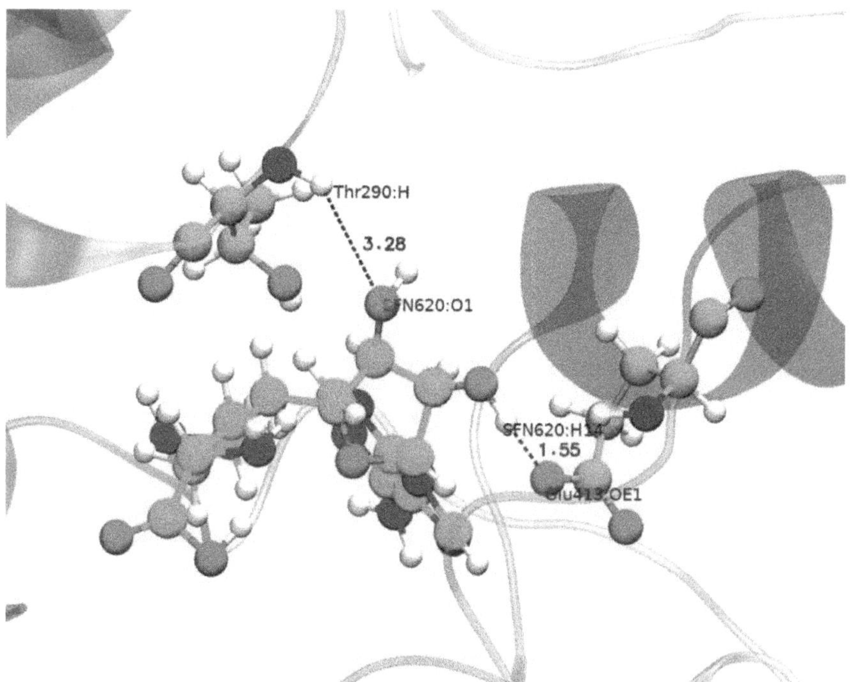

Figure 8. Snapshot showing the active site residues Thr290 and Glu413 of NS3 making the hydrogen bond with the ligand SFN (green).

SFN Hydrogen bonds

There were two strong hydrogen bonds formed between two residues of the receptor NS3 with the ligand SFN in the complex NS3-SFN. The H of Thr290 made hydrogen bonds with the O1 of SFN so that Thr290 acts as a proton donor and O1 of SFN acts as a proton acceptor. Similarly, OE1 of residue Glu413 made a hydrogen bond with the H14 of SFN, meaning thereby, SFN acts as a proton donor, while Glu413 as a proton acceptor. Out of these two hydrogen bonds, the interactions of other residues Phe289, Asp291, Ile411, Lys431, Ile450, and Ser454 with the ligand SFN provide the stability of the complex and it acts as an inhibitor in the normal replication process (shown in Figure 8).

Conclusion

During the docking and MD simulation of NS3 with the ligands ATP, SAM and SFN, the active site residues identified as Pro196, Gly199, Lys200, Thr201, Arg202, Glu231, Glu234, and Ala235 corresponding to the domain-1 (motif I) and Ile411, Glu413, Asn413, Arg464, Asn465, Ile450 and Ser454 from the domain-2 (motif VI). In the above active pocket residues Gly199, Lys200 and Thr201 in the domain-1 and Gln457, Arg461 and Arg464 shown in the crystal structure exactly matched with our findings with the exception that Gln457 and Arg461 having low or insignificant binding energy and reside behind the residue Arg464. In our findings Lys200 protrudes into the active pocket, recognizes the phosphate of ATP, other residues taking part in the interactions were Gly199, Thr201, Arg202 and Glu231 in which Gly199 a non-polar and neutral (a hydrophobic residue) acts to stabilize the complex, while Thr201, Arg202 and Glu231 were hydrophilic residues. When the protein docked with an inhibitor SAM two other more residues Glu234 and Ala235 with a significant energy, in which Glu234 was hydrophilic and Ala235 a hydrophobic again stabilize the complex. In the other domain (motif II &VI), in which Arg464 form an argenine finger, work as a sensor recognizing the phosphate of ATP, and plays a greater role for conformational switching upon ATP hydrolysis. In our findings, the other significantly interacting residues with ATP was Asn465 a hydrophilic residue acts to stabilize the complex. When NS3 was docked with the SAM and SFN there were other residues with a significant energy contribution came into account such as Asn417, another hydrophilic residue along with Asp410, Ile411, Glu413, Lys431, Ile450, Thr451 and Ser454, in which Asp410 , Glu413, Lys431, Thr451 and Ser454 were hydrophilic residues, where as Ile411 and Ile450 were hydrophobic in nature. Out of the above residues, the SFN interacted significantly in Domain-1 with residues Hie288, Phe289, Thr290 and Asp291, in which Hie288, Thr290 and Asp291 were hydrophilic and Phe289 was hydrophobic in nature. The hydrogen bonding with the ligand and residues produce their compact interactions, made their role in the prohibition of viral replicating protein driven by Domain-1 (motif I) to Domain-2 (motif II & VI) and made a path-breaking exercise for the drug industry for the further research and development. The author is thankful to Mr. Vinayak Pandey for his contribution in preparing the chapter and Ms. Aditi Tiwari for processing and cleaning the PDB files of the NS5 protein and charge derivation of the ligands.